RECOVERING FROM GENOCIDAL TRAUMA

An Information and Practice Guide
for Working with Holocaust Survivors

Recovering from Genocidal Trauma is a comprehensive guide on how best to understand Holocaust survivors, respond to their unique needs, and develop specialized services to meet those needs. It is informed by Myra Giberovitch's twenty-five years as a professional social worker, researcher, educator, and community layperson, and as a daughter of Auschwitz survivors. She uses auto-ethnography in an accessible style to record experiences and explain the socio-cultural context illustrated by her family's pre-war, wartime, and post-war journey.

Giberovitch employs a strengths-based approach that stresses listening to and learning from Holocaust survivors. She draws upon current research and practice literature from social work, sociology, medicine, neuroscience, and gerontology in the development and application of innovative service models and programs, practical techniques, and individual and group interventions to empower survivors as they recover from tragedy and adversity. She discusses the limitations of viewing survivors from primarily a pathological perspective and provides a balanced approach through discussion of adaptation and achievements, vulnerabilities related to war experiences, and the challenges of ageing.

Topics include mass atrocity crimes and international human-rights legislation, survivor contributions to society, the therapeutic relationship, psychological and environmental factors that mitigate trauma and aid psycho-social adjustment, interaction between trauma and ageing, group services, intergenerational programs, environmental triggers, vicarious trauma and self-care, and recommendations for a national resource centre for mass atrocity survivors. Supplemented with detailed case examples, appendices, and references, the book is a valuable resource for anyone who studies survivors of mass atrocity or who interacts, lives, or works with them.

MYRA GIBEROVITCH is an adjunct teaching professor and field placement supervisor in the School of Social Work at McGill University as well as the founder of Services for Holocaust Survivors at the Cummings Centre in Montreal. Visit the author online at www.myragiberovitch.com.

MYRA GIBEROVITCH
with Raymond Barry

Recovering from Genocidal Trauma

An Information and Practice Guide
for Working with Holocaust Survivors

UNIVERSITY OF TORONTO PRESS
Toronto Buffalo London

University of Toronto Press
Toronto Buffalo London
www.utppublishing.com
Printed in Canada

ISBN 978-1-4426-4632-2 (cloth)
ISBN 978-1-4426-1610-3 (paper)

Printed on acid-free, 100% post-consumer recycled paper with vegetable-based inks.

Library and Archives Canada Cataloguing in Publication

Giberovitch, Myra, 1947–, author
Recovering from genocidal trauma: an information and practice guide for working with holocaust
survivors / Myra Giberovitch.

Includes bibliographical references and index.
ISBN 978-1-4426-4632-2 (bound). – ISBN 978-1-4426-1610-3 (pbk.)

1. Holocaust survivors – Psychology. 2. Holocaust survivors – Mental health. 3. Genocide survivors –
Psychology. 4. Genocide survivors – Mental health 5. Psychic trauma – Treatment. 6. Holocaust
survivors – Counseling of – Quebec (Province) – Montréal. 7. Holocaust survivors – Services for –
Québec (Province) – Montréal. I. Title.

RC451.H62G52 2014   616.85'210089924   C2013-906382-X

Parts of chapter 2 and 4 are adapted from my article 'The contributions of Holocaust survivors to
Montreal Jewish communal life,' *Canadian Ethnic Studies* 26(1) (1994), and reprinted with the permission of that journal.

Parts of chapter 7 are adapted from my article 'A proposal for a service network for Holocaust
survivors,' *Journal of Jewish Communal Service*, 75(4) (1999), and reprinted with the permission of that
journal.

Parts of chapter 9 and 11 are adapted from my article 'A drop-in centre for Holocaust survivors:
Inspiring hope, meaning and purpose,' *Journal of Jewish Communal Service*, 81(3/4) (2006), and
reprinted with the permission of that journal's publisher, the Jewish Communal Service Association
(www.jcsana.org).

Parts of chapter 14 are reprinted from 'Caring for aging Holocaust survivors: A practice manual,'
with permission from Baycrest Geriatric Health Care System; and 'Painful memories: Understanding
the special needs of aging Holocaust survivors,' with permission from Menorah Park Center for
Senior Living.

**Canada Council
for the Arts**

**Conseil des Arts
du Canada**

ONTARIO ARTS COUNCIL
CONSEIL DES ARTS DE L'ONTARIO
50 YEARS OF ONTARIO GOVERNMENT SUPPORT OF THE ARTS
50 ANS DE SOUTIEN DU GOUVERNEMENT DE L'ONTARIO AUX ARTS

University of Toronto Press acknowledges the financial assistance to its publishing program of the
Canada Council for the Arts and the Ontario Arts Council.

University of Toronto Press acknowledges the financial support of the Government of Canada
through the Canada Book Fund for its publishing activities.

I dedicate this book to members of the Drop-in Centre for Holocaust Survivors at the Cummings Jewish Centre for Seniors and to Holocaust survivors around the world who overcame the most severe forms of persecution and went on to become productive members of society. Your survival is an example of the human spirit's ability to adapt, rebuild, and recover from mass atrocity crimes. You inspire and give hope to all survivors of traumatic life events.

Contents

Acknowledgments

Many people have inspired me over the years, helped shape my work, and assisted with this book. Some have had a significant influence on me and I want to acknowledge them here.

I extend my deepest appreciation and respect to the late Dr John Sigal, a pioneer in research with Holocaust survivors, who directed me to the McGill University School of Social Work in the early 1980s. For many years he continued to guide me, provided professional support such as recommending pertinent literature, and promoted me as a presenter at conferences.

I gratefully acknowledge my mentors in the literature, some of whom I have come to know personally. They have contributed knowledge to the field and enhanced and enriched my understanding of Holocaust survivors. My mentors include: Yael Danieli, Paula David, Eva Fogelman, Roberta Greene, Aaron Hass, Judith Hassan, William Helmreich, Judith Herman, Robert Krell, Maria Rosenbloom, and Bessel van der Kolk.

My teachers at the McGill University School of Social Work provided me with an academic environment where I formulated my ideas and developed the foundation for my work with Holocaust survivors. In 1986 I wrote a paper analysing a task-oriented group of Holocaust survivors that I organized while at Jewish Family Services. When Professor Estelle Hopmeyer read my paper, she suggested that I submit an abstract of it to the upcoming international group-work symposium at the Boston University School of Social Work. She worked with me to prepare my presentation at an academic conference, the first of many to come. I am also grateful to my masters thesis adviser, Professor Jim Torczyner, for his friendship and stimulating discussions about survivors' adjustments in the post-war period and their enriching impact on

Jewish communal life. Since 1991, I have been affiliated with McGill's School of Social Work as a guest lecturer on trauma and aging, a sessional lecturer in gerontology, a thesis adviser, a supervisor of social-work interns, and, most recently, an adjunct professor.

I am fortunate to have friends and colleagues at McGill University who continually support my ongoing work with Holocaust survivors. My dear friend Professor Shari Brotman, with whom I shared an office when I became a social worker, continues to offer insight, support, and inspiration. Professor Myriam Denov, the author of *Child Soldiers*, encouraged me to submit this manuscript for publication, directed me to publishers, and provided helpful comments on my proposal. Professor Tamara Sussman gave me encouragement and support during the publication process.

Many colleagues have supported my efforts to explore innovative approaches to service delivery for Holocaust survivors. I gratefully acknowledge Helena Sonin, former coordinator of the Community Services to the Elderly Unit at Jewish Family Services, and the late David August, senior caseworker, for opening doors which allowed me to organize the first mutual-aid group in 1986 for survivors at a social-service agency in Montreal. I am also indebted to Dr Harry Grauer, former director of the Psychogeriatric Clinic at the Jewish General Hospital, for helping to organize and then supervising support and discussion groups.

I wish to acknowledge Herb Finkelberg, executive director of the Cummings Jewish Centre for Seniors (CJCS), Robert Kleinman, executive director of the Jewish Community Foundation of Montreal, and Brigitte Amor, formerly of the Planning Department at Federation CJA for supporting my vision and providing resources to create the Drop-in Centre for Holocaust Survivors at CJCS. This program evolved into Services for Holocaust Survivors and Their Families, the first community-sponsored social-service program dedicated to serving Holocaust survivors in Quebec and the rest of Canada.

I also want to acknowledge Harriet Tobman and Rebecca Levy, former and present directors of the Social Services Department at CJCS and the entire social-services staff, including my fellow supervisors Karen Figler, Michelle Greenberg, Tanya Nemiroff, Debbie Ungar, and Noga Yudelevich. I am privileged to work with a wonderful team of dedicated colleagues and volunteers at CJCS who maintain a supportive environment for Holocaust survivors. I am especially indebted to my present and former staff – Vikki Brewster, Igor Epshtein, Kathy Viragh, Mara Schneiderman, Stephanie Geller, Sharon Gulko, and Lorri Frankel – for their expertise and contributions.

My thanks to Professor Frank Chalk, director of the Montreal Institute for Genocide and Human Rights Studies (MIGS) at Concordia University, for reviewing chapter 1 – Mass Atrocity Crimes – and a list of these crimes in appendix A. He also directed me to pertinent literature on this subject.

I am indebted as well to the following individuals who commented on my original book proposal and reviewed parts of this manuscript: Vikki Brewster, Professor Myriam Denov, Igor Epshtein, Karen Figler, Dr Roland Grad, Mara Schneiderman, Olga Sher, Dr John Sigal, Barbara Steiman, Harriet Tobman, Debbie Ungar, Kathy Viragh, and Noga Yudelevich.

I am grateful to Doug Richmond and Eric Carlson, my former and present acquisitions editors at University of Toronto Press, for their guidance and advice in supporting this project. Eric's strong support and his appreciation of the sensitivities surrounding this topic have made the book a reality. Thanks also to Anne Laughlin, managing editor at the University of Toronto Press, for overseeing the final publication process, and Curtis Fahey for his meticulous copy editing. I am thankful, too, to the anonymous reviewers for their constructive suggestions that improved the scholarship of my original manuscript.

I thank my children, Andrea, Joel, and Rhonda, as well as Andrea's husband, Richard, and Joel's wife, Emilie, for their love, support, and encouragement throughout the years. They light up my life, as do my grandchildren, Zackary, Kacey, Abby, Noah, and Ella, who show *bubby* (grandmother) how to be a child again and play. I have a special love and appreciation for my parents, Moishe and Fela Grachnik, who survived the Holocaust and shared their knowledge about our family's pre-war, wartime, and post-war lives. My brothers, Allan and Issie, along with my father and late mother, have provided ongoing encouragement and support throughout my life.

My heartfelt respect and appreciation goes to the hundreds of survivors with whom I worked over the years, especially to the members of the Drop-in Centre for Holocaust Survivors at CJCS, who taught me so much about human suffering and recovery. Their ability to overcome extreme obstacles and ordeals and rebuild their lives are inspirational achievements which continue as valuable lessons for humanity.

Although I have referred to them by pseudonyms to protect their confidentiality (Mrs G., Mr K., and so on), each has shared their personal journey and contributed to the spirit of this book.

Finally, my deepest gratitude goes to Raymond Barry, my partner in life, for his steadfast support and encouragement. He became sensitized to survivors' concerns and needs through his volunteer work at CJCS. Over the course of a year, he photographed the Drop-in members and helped organize an exhibit for the launch of our memoir book *Preserving Our Memories*. He continues to photograph important events at the Drop-in Centre. He spent many hours restructuring and editing my original manuscript. His sharp intellect, constructive comments, and technical expertise transformed it from a professional manual to a book of general interest for a broader audience.

RECOVERING FROM GENOCIDAL TRAUMA

An Information and Practice Guide
for Working with Holocaust Survivors

Introduction

Recovering from Genocidal Trauma is about understanding and working with survivors of mass atrocity crimes. In the late 1980s I started the first community-based social service for Holocaust survivors in Canada. Over the course of the next twenty years, as I endeavoured to address the needs of hundreds of Holocaust survivors and their families in the Montreal Jewish community, this book took shape. It is the culmination of my life's work, which is devoted to promoting a fuller comprehension of Holocaust survivors and initiating programs and services that are sensitive and responsive to their unique requirements. My colleagues refer to me as 'a walking manual' on the subject of the survivor community. *Recovering from Genocidal Trauma* is written in response to their requests to 'write it down.'

The material in this book is based on my experiences, readings, and observations in my professional role as a front-line social-work practitioner, clinical supervisor, community organizer, researcher, therapist, educator, consultant, and volunteer – and in my personal life as a daughter of Holocaust survivors. I include excerpts from my publications and presentations at national and international conferences, content from courses taught in universities, colleges, and high schools, and handouts from workshops given in social-service centres, community organizations, hospitals, long-term care facilities, religious institutions, and documentation projects. It also incorporates information from, and references to, current literature and research.

While the Holocaust targeted several groups of people, it was primarily a genocide directed at the Jewish people in Europe. It remains one of the largest examples of a state-sponsored genocide, and is one of the most researched and documented. Today, Holocaust survivors are among the oldest living survivor populations of genocide and war. Lessons learned from working with Holocaust survivors as they recovered from and transcended victimization can benefit survivors of other mass atrocities around the world.

WHY THIS BOOK IS NEEDED

Today, specialized services are needed even more than ever because Holocaust survivors, who were in their late teens and early twenties at the end of the war, are now in their eighties. Until recently, they lived independently and rarely sought assistance. Time, however, is taking its toll. Ageing and associated challenges, including the loss of loved ones, may remind survivors of wartime experiences, triggering feelings of grief, vulnerability, fear, dependency, and helplessness. Illness or personal crises bring survivors into the system involuntarily where they may become dependent on health-care and social-service providers. Some come into hospitals and social-service agencies because of illness, loss of autonomy, dementia, caregiving responsibilities, or a need to relocate to an institution or residence. Others require help completing forms for new restitution and compensation programs. Still others, with limited financial resources, are inquiring about assistance programs like those funded by the Conference on Jewish Material Claims against Germany (Claims Conference). Communities around the world are dealing for the first time with large numbers of survivors.

This increase of Holocaust survivors looking for assistance creates challenges for communities and their health-care and social-service agencies. I notice that many service providers lack knowledge about survivors' history, psycho-social functioning, demographics, and diversity, as well as about the impact of ageing on traumatic memory and specialized survivor-assistance resources. I find, in my research, many books and articles about the Holocaust, the theory and pathology of severe trauma, the psycho-social effects of such experiences, and clinical treatment of associated symptoms, but not much information about survivors' adaptation and resilience or about recovery programs. Consequently, I believe there is a need for a book – a practice guide for communities and health-care professionals – that provides information, sets out creative service models, programs, and practical techniques, and suggests empowering interventions for recovery and growth from tragedy and adversity.

Recovering from Genocidal Trauma fills this information gap and promotes a better understanding of Holocaust survivors and their unique needs. I believe the interventions and service models described within can be replicated and adapted for trauma victims of other mass atrocities. Unfortunately, genocide and war did not end with the Holocaust. Mass murders took place in Rwanda and Bosnia in the 1990s and continue in Darfur and other parts of the world. Those of us who work with Holocaust survivors have learned important ways of responding to individuals traumatized and displaced by war. I believe it is important that we share our knowledge with other communities.

With this in mind, *Recovering from Genocidal Trauma* attempts to:

- provide information and a context for understanding survivors of genocide and war trauma based on the experiences of Holocaust survivors;
- describe programs, services, and interventions (including my case examples and personal interactions) that assist and empower survivors to recover from genocide and war trauma;
- help survivors and their families understand the impact of genocide and war trauma and how it affects family dynamics;
- increase public awareness of the unique issues and challenges faced by ageing survivors;
- change perceptions and attitudes that view survivors as traumatized victims suffering from psychological, physical, and social maladaptation;
- acknowledge and validate survivors' strengths, adaptive coping behaviours, and achievements; and
- assist survivor populations of other mass atrocity crimes by sharing information about how Holocaust survivors were affected and journeyed towards recovery.

PRACTICE PHILOSOPHY

As service providers, it is essential to have a theoretical framework for practice to guide our work with individuals and groups. In this book, accordingly, I describe a strengths-based philosophy, which is the foundation for my practice. Listening to survivors and learning from them provides valuable insights that influence my approach when responding to their needs. Strengths-based practice is person-centred and includes concepts like resilience, empowerment, healing, recovery, transformation, and human capabilities (Saleebey, 2006). It asserts that human beings are resilient and continue to learn, grow, and change throughout their lives, despite trauma and hardships (Kisthardt, 2006; Greene, 2010). Conventional perceptions of Holocaust survivors, as reflected in the mental-health literature, focus on pathology and deficits. Such perceptions often lead to assumptions that survivors are permanently scarred and cannot recover. A strengths perspective requires a shift in thinking. I view survivors, not as debilitated victims, but as competent, adaptive, resourceful, and resilient individuals who cope as best they can with their Holocaust experiences and present-day challenges. This does not mean I turn a blind eye to their suffering, or have a 'Pollyanna' naivety (Saleebey, 1996). I recognize that many survivors suffer from post-traumatic symptoms such as anxiety, depression, recurring traumatic memories, and a variety of other medical conditions. To deny that these symptoms exist is to deny the atrocities perpetrated against them. However, to focus exclusively on these pathological aspects causes generalizations which do not acknowledge survivors' adaptive coping abilities and resilience. Simply stated, every individual has strengths – positive attributes, knowledge, and skills – that coexist with their weaknesses and vulnerabilities. Research studies confirm these observations (Helmreich, 1992; Kahana, Harel, & Kahana, 2005; Shmotkin et al., 2011; Shrira et al. 2011; Sigal & Weinfeld, 1989).

Survivors continuously demonstrate the human ability to overcome the most severe forms of dehumanization and degradation. Their survival serves as an example of the human being's ability to adapt, persevere, rebuild, and move on to become a productive member of society. Their achievements provide hope for all survivors of severe traumatic life events. Consequently, in this book, I provide a balanced perception of Holocaust survivors by discussing their adaptive nature as well as their pains, struggles, and present-day challenges – some of which are caused by their past.

I began to develop my strengths-based perception early in life because I am the daughter of Holocaust survivors: both of my parents were interned in the Łódź Ghetto in Poland and were imprisoned in the Auschwitz death camp. I was born in a displaced persons (DP) camp in Germany at the end of the Second World War and grew up in Israel and Montreal. Consequently, I have an 'insider's view' of this community. My parents, like many, married in the DP camps and struggled to rebuild their lives in spite of deep scars and painful memories. They created new surrogate families; learned new languages, trades, and professions; recreated their destroyed communities in new environments; and involved themselves in organizational activities (for example, my parents were actively involved with the Lodzer [Farband] and Ladies Auxiliary of Montreal, a mutual-aid organization). Their achievements and contributions to society were very much in my mind when I chaired regional and national Holocaust Remembrance Committees at the Canadian Jewish Congress. From 1984 to 1998 I was chairperson of the Holocaust Remembrance Committee, Quebec Region; chairperson of the Montreal Jewish Community's Holocaust Commemoration Service; and co-chair, with Nate Leipciger, of the National Holocaust Remembrance Committee.

My master's research study (Giberovitch, 1988) at McGill University identified the contributions that Holocaust survivors made to Montreal Jewish communal life and further enhanced my understanding of strengths-based practice. However, it was not until I worked in a clinical setting at a government social-service agency that I came to understand the powerful effect a strengths-based approach has on empowering survivors. I encouraged individuals to recognize their accomplishments and contributions by helping them to organize a commemoration program for agency staff. This group effort was the first time that survivors, who were beneficiaries of services, performed a service for the agency by arranging a memorable and meaningful event. Consequently, my colleagues began to see them as capable, empowered, and articulate individuals as well.

METHODOLOGICAL APPROACH

I use auto-ethnography, a qualitative research method, to record my personal and professional experiences. This autobiographical genre uses first-person narratives, draws on and recounts personal details and emotional experiences, and recognizes the interactive relationship between the worker and the population served (Ellis, 2004). It is a form of self-narrative writing that places the personal experiences of the self / author / researcher within a broader sociocultural context (Chang, 2008). This approach attempts to establish a cultural understanding of others through the experiences, observations, and perceptions of the writer. 'The writing style is intensely personal, often passionate and confessional' (Wolcott, 2008:211). Doty (2010) identifies the benefits of auto-ethnographic academic writing. She claims it makes scholarly writing more accessible to a wider audience and more interesting to read. It also connects readers with the people being discussed and encourages them to care about the subject matter.

My view of the survivor community is shaped by the ethnographic concept of reflexivity: a process of inward awareness and reflection outward to the sociocultural and historical origins that influence my thoughts, values, and practice (White, 2001; Hammersley & Atkinson, 2007). I am also immersed in this cultural community, which is another core concept of ethnography (Scott-Jones, 2010). As an insider of the survivors' community, I understand the social world and issues that affect their lives. I also speak Yiddish, the language of many survivors. Gradually, upon reflection, I came to realize that my strengths perspective developed through experiences in two areas: my membership in the community; and my professional observations and practice. Both areas contribute to my view of survivors as capable individuals rather than fragile victims.

In keeping with this approach, I include my parents' life histories and autobiographical information that helped to shape my personal and professional development. Integrating personal stories provides an understanding of the social, cultural, and historical context of survivors' lives in the pre-war, wartime, and post-war years. I note the significant events and experiences in my career that led to the development of specialized services in the community. Chronicling successes and failures along my journey of self-discovery may encourage other service providers to apply this knowledge. In addition, I interject personal observations and opinions in an attempt to illustrate how I apply theoretical knowledge and clinical skills in my approach. By presenting case illustrations from my professional interactions, I hope to engage the reader with the subject matter. Clinical challenges and how they were resolved are also discussed.

INTENDED AUDIENCE

I approach this material from a less formal perspective in an attempt to reach as diverse an audience as possible. References are included for the academic and health-care communities, and for those who want to read more about these subjects. This book can be used as a supplementary undergraduate- and graduate-level university text for the disciplines mentioned below. I have attempted, however, to write in a language suitable for all audiences.

Recovering from Genocidal Trauma is written with five categories of readers in mind:

- health-care and social-service providers such as social workers, doctors, psychologists, nurses, physiotherapists, occupational therapists, dieticians, recreational therapists, and home-care workers who work with survivors and their families;
- survivors of mass atrocity, especially Holocaust survivors, their families, and communities;
- university and college professors, teachers, students, and anyone involved in related academic disciplines such as social work, sociology, genocide studies, education, medicine, and law;
- government agencies, community agencies, and policy makers; and
- anyone working or interacting with survivor populations, such as chaplains, filmmakers, volunteers, interviewers, writers, colleagues, and friends.

BOOK STRUCTURE

Recovering from Genocidal Trauma is divided into five parts. Part I begins with a discussion of international human-rights legislation which helps survivors of mass atrocities achieve social justice. A brief description of mass atrocity crimes during the past century is also included in appendix A. I provide a framework for understanding and working with Holocaust survivors as well as the historical context of their lives before, during, and after the Holocaust. I use survivors from Poland as an example that reflects the ordeals of thousands of people. This section concludes with a discussion about the value of having a strengths-based perspective when interacting with survivors. The shift in attitude and perception is important because it changes the approaches used in working with survivors.

Part II begins with a theoretical overview of trauma and its consequences, both the vulnerabilities and the health-enhancing factors. This section also considers the practice implications of recent developments in neuroscience research. It continues with an examination of the psychological and environmental factors that helped to mitigate the negative consequences of trauma and aided Holocaust survivors in their psycho-social adjustment. The section concludes with comments on the issues and challenges unique to Holocaust survivors.

Part III begins with a discussion of empowerment philosophy and an approach to creating a specialized service for survivors. It goes on to describe specific empowerment programs and services I developed or adapted while working with the Montreal survivor community. These service models can be adapted to other survivor populations.

Part IV presents professional interventions and responses to survivors encountering common issues, triggers, and emotional reactions. It also discusses eclectic therapeutic modalities, including interventions ranging from complementary and alternative medicine (CAM) to techniques to help survivors achieve peace of mind. This discussion is intended for health-care professionals and other service providers. However, the format, easy to understand and use, can be useful for anyone working or interacting with survivor populations. The section concludes with reflections on the professional issues and self-care techniques that help prevent vicarious trauma – the cumulative emotional impact of working with survivors of traumatic events.

In Part V I summarize major milestones that Holocaust survivors accomplished on their journey towards recovery that are applicable to other survivor populations. These milestones include acknowledging that a mass atrocity crime has taken place, mobilizing resources, and developing recovery and healing processes. I also share my thoughts about creating a national resource to assist survivors of mass atrocities.

PART I

Survivors of Mass Atrocity

1 Mass Atrocity Crimes

Crimes against humanity and genocidal killings are threats to global security and have remained all-too prevalent.

– F. Chalk et al. (2010)

GENOCIDES, CRIMES AGAINST HUMANITY, AND WAR CRIMES

Human beings have committed mass atrocities (genocide, war crimes, crimes against humanity, and ethnic cleansing) against each other throughout history. Since the Second World War, it is estimated that over 170 million people have been killed in more than 250 armed conflicts (Shelton, 2004).

The twentieth century has been dubbed the Century of Genocide (Levene, 2000). Professor Raphael Lemkin coined the word 'genocide' in 1944, combining the Greek *genos* – referring to a race or tribe – with the Latin *cide* – meaning murder. Lemkin believed that the extermination of 'the Armenians during World War I, and of the Jews during World War II, called for the formulation of a legal concept that would accurately describe the deliberate killing of entire human groups' (Makino, 2001:55). He was a 'driving force' behind the 1948 United Nations (UN) Convention on the Punishment and Prevention of the Crime of Genocide (Jacobs, 2002). This Genocide Convention, as it is commonly referred to, establishes genocide as an international crime. The member states of the United Nations, which ratified this treaty, were obligated to take action by preventing its occurrence and punishing offenders. Article 2 of this Convention defines genocide as:

... any of the following acts committed with intent to destroy, in whole or in part, a national ethnic, racial or religious group, as such:
a. Killing members of the group;
b. Causing serious bodily or mental harm to members of the group;
c. Deliberately inflicting on the group conditions of life calculated to bring about its physical destruction in whole or in part;
d. Imposing measures intended to prevent births within the group;
e. Forcibly transferring children of the group to another group.

The UN Genocide Convention became part of international law in January 1951 after more than twenty countries ratified it. However, during the ensuing years, there was limited international action to enforce the convention; millions of people continued to be murdered in state-sponsored atrocities. Things did not begin to change until 1993, when the UN Security Council established the International Criminal Tribunal for the former Yugoslavia (ICTY) at The Hague. This was the first international criminal tribunal since Nuremberg, and the first mandated to prosecute genocide crimes. In 1994 the mandate was expanded to include the International Criminal Tribunal for Rwanda (ICTR), located in Arusha, Tanzania. Four years later, the ICTR handed down its first conviction for genocide, finding Jean-Paul Akayesu of Rwanda guilty as charged.

Unfortunately, the criteria for determining genocide proved to be too narrow for the international legal system to prosecute most perpetrators of human atrocities. Only five mass atrocities were declared to be genocides by the UN during the twentieth century even though mass atrocities have occurred virtually non-stop over that period (see list in appendix A). Consequently, in 1998, the International Criminal Court (ICC) was established with an expanded mandate to prosecute 'genocide, crimes against humanity, and war crimes' (http://www.ushmm.org/genocide/take_action/genocide). The ICC's statute (Article 7 of the Rome Statute of the ICC) provides the most authoritative listing of acts that constitute a 'crime against humanity.' Falling into that category are the following acts, when committed knowingly as part of a widespread or systematic attack directed against any civilian population:

a. Murder;
b. Extermination;
c. Enslavement;
d. Deportation or forcible transfer of population;

e. Imprisonment or other severe deprivation of physical liberty in violation of fundamental rules of international law;
f. Torture; rape, sexual slavery, enforced prostitution, forced pregnancy, enforced sterilization, or any other form of sexual violence of comparable gravity;
g. Persecution against any identifiable group or collectivity on political, racial, national, ethnic, cultural, religious, gender … or other grounds that are universally recognized as impermissible under international law, in connection with any act referred to in this paragraph or any crime within the jurisdiction of the Court;
h. Enforced disappearance of persons;
i. The crime of apartheid;
j. Other inhumane acts of a similar character intentionally causing great suffering, or serious injury to body, or to mental or physical health. (http://untreaty.un.org/cod/icc/statute/romefra.htm)

The Rome Statute of the ICC also affirms that crimes against humanity can be perpetrated in times of peace as well as war. There is no legal requirement for the attack on a civilian population to be linked with armed conflict, whether international or non-international in character.

Article 8 of the Rome Statute defines war crimes that are also under the ICCs jurisdiction. These include violations committed during international armed conflicts and civil wars as defined by international law, such as the ill treatment of civilian populations within occupied territories; atrocities against individuals; attacks against, and destruction and appropriation of, private property; and the torture and execution of prisoners. A detailed definition of war crimes can be found on the website of the Aegis Trust (http://www.aegistrust.org), the leading British non-governmental organization (NGO) founded in 2000 to prevent genocide.

The Aegis Trust points out the shortcomings of the United Nations definition of genocide, namely a narrow focus that excludes groups defined by their politics, culture, or sexual orientation. However, Zimmerer (2006) points out that there is broad agreement on two points: (1) 'the primary aim of genocide is to eradicate an entire group of people' (380); and (2) genocide is a 'crime perpetuated by a state or state-like actor' (380).

The debate over the scope and meaning of the term 'genocide' continues, and some scholars have come up with alternative definitions and new terms. In correspondence with Professor Frank Chalk, director of the Montreal Institute for Genocide and Human Rights Studies at Concordia University, I learned that some scholars use the term 'mass atrocity crimes' when referring to genocide, crimes against humanity including ethnic cleansing, and war crimes. The scope of genocide scholarship is expanding.

ACKNOWLEDGING ATROCITIES AND INTERVENING TO STOP THEM

Holocaust survivors describe how their suffering and pain in post-war years were exacerbated when the communities where they settled greeted them with ignorance, indifference, and denial. Survivors taught me the importance of acknowledging and validating their experiences as victims of mass atrocity crimes. Although this book focuses on my work with Holocaust survivors, I wish to acknowledge the mass atrocities committed against other populations during the past hundred years. At the time of this writing, mass atrocities are occurring in countries across the Middle East and North Africa in what is called the 'Arab Spring.' Since December 2010 thousands of protesters and ordinary citizens have been murdered and tortured in a series of pro-democracy demonstrations and movements against authoritarian regimes. Genocide Watch states that the Syrian regime of President Bashar al-Assad is 'committing intentional crimes against humanity' and warns that its 'massacres could turn genocidal' (http://migs.concordia.ca/documents/Stanton GenocideandMassAtrocitiesAlert.pdf).

A partial listing of mass atrocities committed during the past hundred years is found in appendix A. This is not a comprehensive list because I am not an expert in genocide studies and research; nor does the list imply any 'hierarchy of suffering.' However, I found this list eye-opening because it shows the frequency of mass atrocities in our time. Some of these crimes are listed on the website of the McGill Centre for Human Rights and Legal Pluralism (http://efchr.mcgill.ca/Genocide_en.php?menu=3), while up-to-date reports on current mass atrocities are listed on the website of the Montreal Institute for Genocide and Human Rights Studies (http://migs.concordia.ca). In *Mobilizing the Will to Intervene*, Chalk et al. (2010) point out the international community's inability to effectively stop mass atrocity crimes. They also present a roadmap for intervention and prevention.

By acknowledging these mass atrocities, we validate the experience and suffering of the victims. All too often, scholarly arguments over which atrocities qualify as genocide, discussions of alternative definitions of genocide, or strategies focused on prevention in the future lose sight of the very survivors against whom crimes have been committed. We cannot forget the long-term devastating effects these crimes have on their victims – they need help today. More attention needs to be focused on helping existing populations recover from trauma by consulting directly with survivors and implementing recovery programs that respect their cultures, traditions, values, and beliefs.

2 Understanding the Historical Context

Looking back, I don't know myself how we survived and where we took our strength from.

— P. Trepman (1957)

It is important to understand a survivor population before working closely with it. This includes knowing about the mass atrocity that the survivors lived through and what their lives were like before, during, and after. Survivors' experiences pre- and post-atrocity shape their perceptions in significant ways.

This book documents my work with Holocaust survivors living in the Montreal area. The majority of these survivors were born in Poland (Torczyner & Brotman, 1994). Other countries of origin include Romania, Hungary, the former Soviet Union, Czechoslovakia, Germany, France, Belgium, the Netherlands, Norway, Denmark, Austria, Italy, and Yugoslavia. Each country has its own traditions, cultural distinctiveness, and religious and social practices. It is beyond the scope of this book, however, to explore the different historical contexts in all these countries. Consequently, only the historical context of Polish Jews is described here for illustrative purposes. For a condensed description of Jewish communities in other countries before the Holocaust, readers should consult Lucy Dawidowicz's 1975 book *The War against the Jews: 1933–1945*.

Because I am the daughter of parents who were born and raised in Łódź, I have an affinity for the city that is filled with mixed emotions. On the one hand, it is my parent's *heim* (home) where they grew up in large families and shared a core of *yiddishkeit* (Jewishness). It is also where they were subjected to degradation and suffering.

Many years ago I was asked whether I intend to visit Łódź to trace my family's roots – a journey many families make together. I surprised myself when I responded: 'I hope to return to Łódź someday.' The word 'return' implied that I had physically lived in Łódź at some point. In reality, I had not. On reflection, I came to understand that I used the word 'return' because I lived there vicariously through my parents' memories. My parents' pre-Holocaust lives were destroyed in 1940 when the Łódź Ghetto was created. Afterwards, their families and communities existed only in their memories. Realizing that I knew very little about my parent's pre-Holocaust lives, I decided to explore my roots. I interviewed my parents about the neighbourhoods in which they lived, their family and social relationships, livelihoods, educational backgrounds, religious practices, political involvement, and customs. In so doing, I started to comprehend the continuity of life between my parents' past and my present life. In the discussion below I integrate my parents' oral recollections into my historical research to make this context real. My father, Moishe Grachnik, and my mother, Fela Zylberstajn, lived on the same street before the war and knew each other casually. I use their story as an example of one family's journey through the Holocaust.

Understanding historical, religious, and socio-cultural factors is important for several reasons. Holocaust survivors' lives are intricately interwoven with their pre-Holocaust experiences within communities that are now extinct. Their values, belief systems, religious traditions, and ideas about family and community – which they brought with them to their new environments – are based on their life in the Old World. Transplanting their Old World values enabled them to establish continuity with their ancestors, a fact that is especially evident among Orthodox Jews. In addition, Holocaust survivors encountered other crises and upheavals, especially during the post-liberation period, which significantly affect their lives.

LIFE BEFORE THE HOLOCAUST: COMMUNITY LIFE IN POLAND

Approximately 3.3 million Jews lived in pre-war Poland, constituting nearly 10 per cent of the total Polish population (Dawidowicz, 1975). They lived in small towns and *shtetls* (villages), as well as larger urban centres. More than three-quarters of Polish Jews lived in cities and towns, with the remainder in rural villages (Mendelsohn, 1983). In 1931 approximately 750,000 Jews – 25 per cent of the total Jewish population – lived in one of Poland's five largest cities: Warsaw, Łódź, Vilna, Cracow, and Lwow (Dobroszycki & Kirshenblatt-Gimlett, 1977).

In their landmark anthropological study, Zborowski and Herzog (1962) discuss two central characteristics of *shtetl life*: a strong sense of identification with the Jewish community, and a 'core of continuity' with traditions of the past. *Shtetl* inhabitants venerated the family, the Sabbath, the cemetery, the synagogue, and the school or other learning centre. Among the important values inculcated from one generation to the next were obedience to the Torah, including observances of customs, rituals, and dietary laws; pursuit of learning; the performance of *mitsvas* (good deeds), including the giving of *tsdakah* (charity); obligations to extended family and the entire Jewish community; and reverence for the dead. At the core of *shtetl* culture was a *yiddishkeit*, or Jewishness, 'in which religion, values, social structure, individual behavior are inextricably blended. It means the way of life is lived among "us," and "us" means the *shtetl* ... We are "the" Jews, our way of life is "the" Jewishness, and the word for it is *yiddishkayt*' (Zborowski & Herzog, 1962:428).

A vibrant Jewish cultural life, both religious and secular, also existed in the large urban areas of Poland. Some Jews migrated to the large cities during industrialization in the late 1800s. Dobroszycki and Kirshenblatt-Gimlett (1977) describe Jewish cultural life in the cities and towns: 'Each town had its literary circles, drama groups, local library, sports clubs, educational facilities, and political and social organizations' (155).

The richness and depth of the Jewish culture in Eastern Europe created a strong desire in survivors to maintain their traditions of communal involvement after they immigrated to Montreal.

Family Life and Customs of the Jewish Working Class in Łódź

History of the Jews in Łódź

Poland was primarily an agricultural country until the mid-1800s, and its Jews served as middlemen between farmers who grew produce and consumers abroad (Baskerville, 1909). This changed in 1863 when Poland began intensive development of its industrial resources. During this period of industrialization, factories replaced farms and manual labour was replaced with machinery imported from England and

Germany. The Jews' role as middlemen – the traditional area of Jewish economic activity – also disappeared. Consequently, middlemen and farmers were forced to find another way to make a living. Many Jews, searching for employment, migrated to cities such as Łódź where they entered the industrial sector as entrepreneurs, workers, and managers (Dobroszycki & Kirshenblatt-Gimlett, 1977). Łódź was one of the five largest cities in Poland during the early 1900s.

Industrialization in Poland, especially during the second half of the nineteenth century, turned Łódź into a large industrial city that became known as the 'Manchester of Poland.' In two generations it grew from a village to the second-largest city in the country. At the end of the eighteenth century, the Jewish population there numbered eleven; on the eve of the Second World War, it was over 200,000 (Lestchinsky, 1946).

Jews settled in the Jewish ghetto – established in 1825 – within the old part of the city. It quickly became congested, and so many Jews were forced to settle in Vilki, the German sector, where, legally, they were forbidden to live. This caused a public outcry from the German population and all approaches between the ghetto and the city were blocked, which, in turn, caused shortages of food, wood, and merchandise. The bordering town of Balut was purchased from the Polish nobility to deal with the chaos in the overpopulated ghetto. Rosenfarb (1985) writes that houses were erected in a hurry and situated chaotically with no sanitary facilities, paved streets, or building lights.

Urbanization created desperate conditions for Jewish families (Meltzer, 1976). Sickness, malnutrition, and overcrowding were rampant. Nevertheless, by the beginning of the twentieth century, Jews had organized workers' circles to improve conditions on the job. The Bund became a powerful economic and political force. Between the end of the eighteenth century and 1929, the last year before the Great Depression, per-capita real income for Jews went up by 350 per cent (Marcus, 1983). However, there was a wide disparity of wealth in this urban Jewish society. During the years immediately preceding the Holocaust, compared to Jewish people living in urban settings in the Western world, the average Jew in Poland was poor.

Neighbourhoods and Homes

Just before the Second World War, about 100,000 people lived in Balut, the working-class suburb where the Łódź Ghetto was located. Both my parents were born in Balut.

Homes in Balut were apartment buildings, some large and built of brick and others smaller wood-frame structures, grouped around a common courtyard. The average apartment consisted of two rooms, a kitchen and a bedroom shared by all members of the family. This created congested living quarters for larger families. For example, in Fela's home, seven people shared one bedroom. Apartments had no running water and hygienic facilities were rudimentary. Water was brought up from a well in the courtyard. Outhouses were located in this same courtyard. Fela's father, Itzhak, was a coal dealer. He ran his business out of the home and stored his coal and wood in the courtyard shed.

Apartments were often working quarters as well as dwelling places. It was common for wage earners in Balut to work out of their homes. For example, Moishe's father, Eliyahu, was a shoemaker or *halupnik* (home worker). His workshop was located in the attic of their apartment building. Hena, his mother, and older sister, Mala, operated a restaurant out of their kitchen. Other people – potential customers – were attracted by the home-cooked meals.

Economic Survival in Łódź

There was hope for social reform in Poland when Marshal Jósef Piłsudski seized power in a military coup in May 1926. Hope soon faded, however, as the new government nationalized industries. Thirty-five per cent of Jewish businesses closed in 1930 (Krantiz-Sanders, 1984). This significantly affected the economic conditions of the *halupniks* in Balut who depended on those businesses to supply them 'with raw materials and dispose of their finished products' (Glicksman, 1966). The worldwide depression during the late 1920s and 1930s further impoverished the Jewish community.

The new government's control of the economy was also accompanied by discriminatory regulations and restrictive practices. For example, Jews were taxed excessively. Although the Jews of Łódź comprised only 2 per cent of the taxpayers, they paid 44 per cent of the total taxes (Lestchinsky, 1947).

The rise of Nazism in Germany, and 'Poland's accelerating fascist course following Marshal Pilsudski's death in 1935, brought near disaster to the Jewish community' (Dawidowicz, 1975). In 1934, 30 per cent of the Jews in Łódź were without food; by 1937, 41 per cent of Łódź's Jews had applied for state assistance for clothing and *matzoth* (unleavened bread eaten at Passover). The state did not provide assistance to the Jewish poor. Unlike other Poles, Jews 'were deprived of social insurance, public work, or other state assistance' (Marcus, 1983:231). Owing to these dire circumstances, especially in Balut, children helped the family financially. Moishe, then in his teens, gave 99 per cent of the salary that he earned as a tailor to his parents and kept only a small allowance for himself.

Women and children also played an important role in the family's economic survival. To cut down on hiring employees in family businesses, women and small children helped out. Fela's mother, Mirla, helped my grandfather sell coal. When she became unable to do so, the children assisted him when the school day ended. The entire family functioned as an economic unit.

Religious Observances

The years between the two world wars were characterized by erosion of religious traditions on account of acculturation and secularization, especially evident among the younger generation (Heller, 1977). During this period, only about one-third of the total adult population in Poland was Orthodox. Adherence to Orthodoxy was stronger in the *shtetl* and among older people.

In Balut, according to my parents, there were varying degrees of Orthodoxy. In general, the community observed the Sabbath, the Jewish holy day that begins Friday night at sunset and ends on Saturday night after sunset. It also practised observance of *Kashruth*, such as the eating of ritually slaughtered meat and the separation of milk and meat products. There was only one large synagogue in Balut. Most Jewish people attended religious services in *shtibls* – the home of a rabbi where one room was reserved as a chapel.

All Jewish businesses closed at the onset of the Sabbath. Barbershops were full of older men waiting for their weekly shaves on the Sabbath eve (males of the younger generation shaved more often). Bakers were then busy too because people dropped off pots of *cholent* (mixture of meat, potatoes, and beans) to put into their ovens overnight for a fee. The *cholent* was eaten for lunch on the Sabbath.

The Sabbath was a special celebration for most Jewish families in Balut. Fela's parents and siblings dressed in their holiday clothes for the Friday evening meal. Special meals were prepared in both my parents' homes. Meat, considered a luxury, was reserved for the Sabbath meal.

Educational Background

The Republic of Poland replaced the Polish Kingdom in 1918 after a treaty with the Allied powers was signed. For the country's minorities, this treaty supposedly guaranteed their civil and political equality with other Poles, safeguarded their rights as citizens, and extended to them the right to establish their own educational, religious, charitable, and social institutions (Dawidowicz, 1975). From the beginning, however, these guarantees were not implemented. For example, the Minorities Treaty declared that Jewish schools, controlled by Jewish authorities, would be funded by the state. In fact, the state not only refused to subsidize these schools but even hampered their operation. Graduates of Yiddish- or Hebrew-language high schools were not allowed to enter Polish universities (Mendelsohn, 1983). At the same time, the majority of Jewish students were forced to attend Jewish high schools because Polish high schools discriminated against Jews (Mendelsohn, 1983).

The majority of Jewish children in Balut attended public elementary schools where Polish was the language of instruction. Children started school at age seven and attendance was compulsory until age fourteen. Because private Jewish schools charged tuition, most school-age Jewish children were forced to attend the free Polish state schools. About 60 per cent of all Jewish pupils studied in the state schools (Mendelsohn, 1983).

Fela attended a state school. Her school day lasted from 8 a.m. until 3 p.m. The grade levels were segregated by gender and consisted of approximately thirty students per classroom. Moishe, on the other hand, attended a private Jewish school where Yiddish was the language of instruction. Only one hour per day was spent on Polish-language instruction. Private schools, under the control of the Bund, were divided between three movements: Orthodox, Zionist, and Yiddishist (Marcus, 1983).

Most Balut children did not attend secondary schools after graduation from elementary school because of economic hardships during this time. Some children, especially boys, went to vocational schools that taught various trades. My father attended a Polish trade school in the evenings for three and a half years to train as a tailor. During the day he worked for a tailor and received wages.

Languages Spoken

Yiddish was spoken in the home. Polish was reserved for the outside world.

Social Relationships and Political Involvement

For the older generation, social life revolved around the family. They maintained close relationships with extended family members and were friendly with neighbours. Fela recalled that Saturday evenings, and sometimes whole weekends when they did not have to work or study, were spent with her parents' circle of friends. Both my parents described other activities such as trips to dance halls, ice skating, and parlour games like dominoes and cards. In the words of my mother, 'although the life of Balut was poor, it was full and enriched.'

The younger generation was involved in youth movements. Moishe belonged to the Poalei Zion (PZL), which supported Jewish work in Palestine. This organization was a small political party that, in 1935, claimed 5,000 registered adult members and another 3,500 members in its Jugend (youth) branch. In addition, Moishe played soccer for Maccabeah Lodz. Fela belonged to Hashomer Hatzair, a Zionist organization. Most of these activities took place on the weekend.

Contact with Gentiles

Most people in Balut were Jews, who, in this self-contained ghetto, created the religious, cultural, educational, and political networks that governed their lives. Yet, although limited, contact with the non-Jewish world did exist. For example, the superintendent of most courtyards was not Jewish. In addition, some Poles worked for Jews. My maternal grandfather hired Poles to help out with the coal business, especially during the winter months. Fela remembered friendly relations with her Gentile neighbours.

Moshe's experiences, on the other hand, were different. In his Polish trade school, Jews sat on one side of the room and Gentiles on the other. Fistfights took place during recess breaks because Poles called Jewish boys obscene names.

Family Relationships

Jewish society in Łódź was patriarchal. Although the father was feared, he was also loved and respected. Families were large and close relationships with extended family members were maintained. Grandparents were also an integral part of the family unit. When a celebration took place, strangers were rarely invited because there was no room to accommodate them.

The mother attended to household functions, especially child care. However, since many fathers worked from home, they also had close contact with their children's day-to-day activities. Fela remembered a loving relationship between her parents and her siblings. Weekends and evenings were devoted to family activities. After Friday night dinner, her father read newspaper stories to them, focusing on those he regarded as the most interesting or, occasionally, humorous. At other times, the family sat around the stove cracking and eating sunflower seeds. In my mother's family, although each parent had separate responsibilities, both parents shared in nurturing and disciplining the children. Children were brought up to honour and respect their parents.

Intergenerational Conflict

Some working-class families were being torn apart as the younger generation acculturated to norms of the majority population. Forces such as Polonization (assimilation into Polish society) and secularization caused many young people to break from the traditions that had governed their lives, particularly religious ones (Heller, 1977). The public-school system was the primary catalyst in the Polonization process where Polish-ness was both exalted and celebrated. Many children also belonged to political organizations that did not adhere to religious traditions. This confused children who were raised in traditional Jewish homes.

These factors, which contributed to acculturation of the young people, imposed Polish standards of modernity and produced new values and norms that distanced children from their parents. My parents both described how some of their male neighbours, who had an ultra-Orthodox background, rejected their traditional values outside the home. As soon as they left their houses, they removed their *kipot* (skull caps) and traditional garb.

Family Life-Cycle Customs

BIRTH
Midwives delivered babies in the family home. During delivery, children were sent out of the house and could not return until the new sibling was born. Mothers usually returned to their official duties a few days after delivery.

On the eighth day after birth, a baby boy was circumcised by a *mohel* (one who performs circumcisions). The *mohel* usually visited the baby a day or two before the ceremony to confirm that he was well enough for the *bris* (circumcision). In Fela's home, a *zukhar* (special celebration) was held on the Friday evening before the *bris*. Participants recited prayers, drank wine, and ate special foods such as chickpeas. The official term *shalom zukhar* means 'peace unto the male child.' It is derived from a verse in the Talmud that states: 'If a boy is born, peace comes to the world' (Bermant, 1974). Usually no ceremony took place when a girl was born.

The newborn child and mother were believed to be susceptible to evil spirits. *Cheder* (elementary school-age boys) were brought into the home each day to chant protective prayers.

Marriages in my parents' immediate environment were not arranged by *shadchanim* (matchmakers) although it was customary in other Orthodox communities. Romantic love determined a marital union. On the Sabbath before the wedding, the bridegroom was called to the Torah for a reading. Before he proceeded with the readings, women in the synagogue threw candies, nuts, figs, and raisins at him. A rabbi performed the marriage outdoors, under a *chupah* (canopy). A celebration followed the official wedding ceremony, usually in the home of the bride or bridegroom's parents. Furniture was removed from rooms to accommodate a crowd. The celebration was festive and all the food was homemade. After the meal, while everyone was still sitting at their tables, guests announced or pledged their wedding gifts to the newlyweds. The young couple usually lived with either of their parents until they were able to afford a home of their own.

DEATH

When someone died at home, a doctor was called to certify the death. Once this was done, the deceased was placed on the floor with arms beside the body and feet pointing towards the door. The body was covered with a sheet and two lit candles placed at the head. It remained in the home until the funeral. The body was never left alone during this time. Either close relatives or members of the *Chevra Kadisha* (honorary burial society) constantly prayed by the body as a sign of respect. Mirrors in the home were covered to discourage personal vanity.

A death was announced immediately after a person died by placing printed notices on poles and walls throughout the neighbourhood.

Burial followed as quickly as practical. The *Chevra Kadisha* picked up the body and brought it in a black carriage to a small house on the cemetery grounds for burial preparation; family and members of the community followed the hearse on foot to the cemetery. The body was dressed in a shroud after purification and a brief service was held. The body was not put in a coffin. Instead, it was placed on wood slats in a hole in the ground and covered with earth. After the funeral, the immediate family sat *shiva* – a seven-day mourning period.

Before the Holocaust, there was a deep reverence for the deceased. In fact, not only were the dead considered part of the living family and community, they were believed to still influence the living spiritually. Gravesites of cherished ones were visited before holidays, especially Rosh Hashanah (Jewish New Year) and Yom Kippur (Day of Atonement), during crises, and before joyous occasions such as weddings. Fela remembered visiting the graves of her grandparents when a family member was ill to seek their advice; during a crisis when the protection, provided by the deceased, was needed; before a wedding to invite the soul of the dead to attend; and to say farewell before a family member embarked on a journey.

LIFE DURING THE HOLOCAUST: HISTORICAL OVERVIEW

'The Holocaust' refers to the planned, systematic destruction of approximately six million Jews – approximately two-thirds of European Jewry – by the German state and its collaborators over a twelve-year period between 1933 and 1945. This destruction of European Jewry was unique for several reasons (Berenbaum, 1999).

First, never before had a state sponsored the systematic bureaucratic extermination of an entire group of people in the interests of 'national salvation.' Governmental policies were enacted to purge an entire 'inferior race' from society – in this case, all people with Jewish blood flowing through their veins. Jews were killed regardless of their economic circumstances, political views, or religious beliefs. Nazi Germany's murder of Jews took precedence over its war effort (Berenbaum, 1999). All segments of German society participated in this industry-of-murder: ordinary civilians, bureaucrats, doctors, lawyers, the military, educators, and so on.

Second, the process for exterminating the Jews of Europe was unprecedented. Jews were systematically killed using new instruments of destruction in specially built extermination camps. They were murdered in massive gas chambers using the powerful insecticide Zyklon-B that produces a lethal gas when exposed to heated air. Auschwitz was distinguished for its assembly-line techniques in disposing of the corpses. After the gassings were completed, squads of inmates – known as the *Sonderkommando* – shaved hair off the corpses and extracted any gold teeth. Then they moved the corpses to crematoria for disposal.

Finally, the Holocaust was the largest known genocide on record. The Jewish community, especially in Eastern Europe, was destroyed. In addition, Nazi racism targeted other groups that were deemed to be racially inferior. These included approximately 220,000 Roma Gypsies; at least 200,000 mentally and physically disabled patients – mainly Germans living in institutional settings; between two and three million Soviet prisoners of war; Polish intelligentsia and civilians; homosexuals; political opponents, including communists, socialists, and trade unionists; and religious dissidents such as Jehovah's Witnesses (United States Holocaust Memorial Museum, 2012).

Adolph Hitler's ascent to power became possible owing to social, political, and economic circumstances that arose during the inter-war years, a period of deep anger among Germans over the humiliating and punitive Versailles Peace Treaty, imposed after the conclusion of the First World War in 1918. Furthermore, the economic situation progressed through periods of inflation, relative stability, and finally the Great Depression, which started in 1929. By 1932, there was a severe economic recession in Germany, with six million people unemployed. In his bid for power, Hitler promised to solve these problems.

Hitler's war against the Jews consisted of three distinct stages (Rabinowitz, 1979). The National Socialist (Nazi) Party's accession to power in 1933 began the first stage of 'The Final Solution of the Jewish Question' – the code name used by the German bureaucracy for destruction of the Jews. This stage, consisting of mounting persecution, lasted until the onset of the Second World War, in 1939. In a series of government-sponsored boycotts and virulent anti-Jewish legislation, Jews were deprived of their livelihood, ousted from civil-service positions, blocked from attending public schools, and disenfranchised. In 1938 they were subjected to massive violence in a pogrom commonly referred to as *Kristallnacht* (night of broken glass), during which synagogues and Jewish institutions, businesses, and homes were destroyed. In addition, nearly one hundred Jews were killed and another 30,000 Jewish men were arrested and interned in concentration camps at Dachau, Buchenwald, and Sachsenhausen (Dawidowicz, 1975). There then followed a policy of forced emigration and confiscation of Jewish property and assets. Of the 500,000 Jews who lived in Germany in 1933, 300,000 had fled by 1939 (Dawidowicz, 1975).

The second phase of the destruction of European Jewry began with the Nazi conquest of Poland on 1 September 1939 and lasted until the German invasion of the Soviet Union in 1941. During this period, marked by incidences of wanton violence and murder, Jews were turned into the outcasts of society and interned in ghettos where they were isolated from the rest of the population. Thousands died daily from overwork as slave labour for German war industries, as well as from extreme overcrowding, constant hunger and starvation, substandard sanitary conditions, and diseases.

The third and last phase of the 'Final Solution' began in 1941, after Germany invaded the Soviet Union, and lasted until the end of the war in May 1945. This period targeted Jews from all countries in Nazi-occupied Europe and focused on mass executions, liquidation of the ghettos, and deportations to death camps. Millions of Jews were killed in the death camps at Auschwitz, Chelmno, Treblinka, Majdanek, and so on. While some people died in the gas chambers, others died from starvation, slave labour, medical experiments, infectious diseases, beatings, and torture. During the Holocaust, the approximately 5.9 million Jewish people who were killed represented roughly two-thirds of an estimated pre-war European Jewish population of 8.9 million (Dawidowicz, 1975).

Nazi Germany surrendered to the Allied forces on 7 May 1945. Only a small number of Jews remained alive to be liberated. According to an article published by the United States Holocaust Memorial Council from the International Liberators Conference (Liberation of the Nazi concentration camps, 1981), 'of the more than four million Jews in Eastern and Western Europe who were deported to concentration camps, only two percent remained alive to be liberated by the Allied forces' (4).

At the onset of the war in 1939, three-quarters of the Jews in Europe were concentrated in Eastern Europe. By the end of the war, of the approximately 3.3 million Jews who lived in Poland before the outbreak of the war, three million had been killed (Dawidowicz, 1975). This destruction marked the demise of a thousand-year-old Eastern European Jewish civilization, encompassing Jewish homes, synagogues, communal and educational institutions, and a way of life.

My Parents – Fela and Moishe's Holocaust Experience

The Germans annexed the city of Łódź and renamed it Litzmannstadt after their army invaded Poland on 1 September 1939. In February 1940 they began to systematically enclose Jews within a ghetto in the Balut district where both Fela and Moishe lived. Within two months the ghetto was sealed off and 160,000 Jews were confined there. The Łódź Ghetto was the first major ghetto in which Jews were enclosed (Dawidowicz, 1975). Chaim Rumkowski, the head of the Jewish Council (*Judenrat*), believed that he could ensure survival of the ghetto's inhabitants by producing goods for the German war effort with the more than one hundred sweatshops and factories then in operation. Fela worked in a straw factory where she made straw outer boots for German soldiers.

In her memoirs (Grachnik, 1996), Fela describes a mass shooting that took place on 'Bloody Thursday,' 16 March 1940. One hundred Jewish people were ordered out of their homes and shot. The first deportations began in December 1941. Additional deportations followed. Fela's parents, Mirla and Itzhak, younger sister Pesa, and two younger brothers, Aron and Shloimele, were deported to the Chelmno death camp. She never saw her family again; they were asphyxiated by carbon-monoxide gas from the trucks that transported them. Alter Ber, Fela's older brother, was sent to a forced-labour camp in 1940 and never returned. Fela remained in the ghetto and continued to work under deteriorating conditions. Another family moved into her family's apartment. She missed her family and cried herself to sleep every night dreaming about being reunited with them.

The Germans began liquidating the ghetto during the summer of 1944. In efforts to avoid panic, the ghetto administration told remaining inhabitants that the community was being transferred to another location and families would remain together. People were encouraged to pack their possessions and join the transports. Most inhabitants had high hopes and a strong will to survive, so they complied. Fela was shipped by cattle car to the Auschwitz death camp that August. She describes her transport and arrival at Auschwitz:

> Not only were we packed into these cattle cars, but we were treated worse than animals. There was no food, no water, and no facilities to relieve ourselves. Pots were used as toilets. With no fresh air, the smell was terrible. Occasionally someone fainted. There were also a number of deaths. After

countless days, we finally arrived at Auschwitz. When the wagon doors opened, we heard a loud yelling: *Alles raus* (everybody out). We crawled out exhausted, leaving the dead and our possessions behind.

As we got to the gate of Auschwitz, there was another traumatizing scene, the selection. Men were separated from women. Children were torn away from their mothers. The frail and elderly were immediately selected for the gas chambers. At the gate there was this S.S. man who we later learned was Dr. Mengele. He was the master of life and death. He pointed his thumb which direction to go: left or right – life or death. After I was selected to live, I was taken with many other women to a shower. Our hair was shaved and we were given rags to wear which barely covered our bodies. We had no underwear. When we got out of the shower, we were numb and speechless. There were no tears. No one cried. We were absolutely frozen. We didn't recognize each other. We were then taken to barracks where conditions were horrific. We slept on the cold ground, awakened during the night and forced to stand outdoors for long hours in thin clothing during the cold weather. We were also starved slowly. For example, one small bowl of soup fed five women. The air was filled with the smell of burning flesh. We were often beaten on our heads. After spending two weeks in Auschwitz, there was another selection. I passed the selection. (Grachnik, 1996:5–7)

Soon after, Fela was transported to a slave-labour camp in Bad Kudova, a satellite of the Gross Rosen camp in Czechoslovakia. She was selected to work in the kitchen. Within a few weeks she became ill and suffered frequent gallstone attacks. She was placed in a separate room – a makeshift hospital – that was periodically emptied by sending sick inmates to the gas chambers. Fortunately, Fela had some good friends who took care of her, especially Mala, whom she knew from the ghetto. Mala kept Fela's condition a secret and covered for her at work. Miraculously, both Mala and Fela survived. In early May 1945 the German guards took all the inmates on a long march to Prague. Everyone was locked in a school and the guards disappeared. The next day the Russian army liberated them.

Moishe worked in a sewing sweatshop when the ghetto was initially created. In 1941 he was taken from the ghetto for a limited period and shipped to Germany where he worked as a slave labourer building a railroad. When he was returned to the ghetto, Moishe unloaded food from wagons and trucks that came into the ghetto. Occasionally he was able to hide some food that he brought home to his family.

The ghetto soon became overcrowded because the German Nazis were cramming Jews into it from surrounding areas and other countries. Conditions were deplorable. Food was severely rationed and infectious diseases broke out. Hundreds died daily of starvation, sickness, exhaustion, and hypothermia during the winters. Rachel Leah, Moishe's sister, along with her husband and baby all died of typhus during 1941.

When the ghetto was being liquidated, Moishe was also shipped by cattle car to the Auschwitz death camp, in August 1944. Heniek and Hena, his brother and mother, hid in a cellar to avoid deportation. A fellow Jew turned them in. They were also deported to Auschwitz where his mother was immediately sent to the gas chambers.

When he got off the train at Auschwitz, Moishe refused to turn over a sack of potatoes he had brought with him. An inmate, who knew Moishe from his soccer days in Łódź, told him to part with it or he would end up in the crematoria to which he pointed. Moishe gave up his potatoes but refused to believe that Jews were being burned to death. He quickly learned the truth. Fortunately, Moishe and his father passed Dr Mengele's selection and were considered fit for slave labour. They were sent to satellite camps of the Dachau concentration camp in Germany. At Kaufering Lager 4 he worked day and night shifts loading bags of cement on trains for the construction company Holtzman. His already weakened condition deteriorated quickly owing to regular beatings, harsh conditions, and malnutrition. He developed typhus and was quarantined. He and his father were then forced on a death march first to Allach and then Tyrol, Germany. The American army liberated them during the march.

LIFE AFTER THE HOLOCAUST

The Post-War Years

Liberation, the Search for Families, and a Quest to Rebuild Shattered Lives

The Holocaust officially ended in May 1945 with the Allied victory. Concentration camps were liberated as the Allied forces came across them. Survivors returned to their countries of origin to search for families and friends. Many realized their worst fears when they found themselves to be the sole surviving members of once large nuclear and extended families. For the most part, Jews from Western Europe were reabsorbed into their native countries and their land and material possessions returned to them. The situation was different in Poland, however, where anti-Semitism existed before the war and continued to exist afterwards.

Many Polish survivors did not want to reconstruct their lives in Poland. Most of the extermination camps were constructed on Polish soil. Poland represented a vast graveyard where their families were annihilated in mass murders, and their homes and religious, educational, and communal institutions had been destroyed. Those who tried to return to Poland to search for family members, and reclaim property and possessions, were met with hostility and violence. 'Between November 1944 and December 1945, 351 Jews suffered fatal attacks and by the summer of 1947 the numbers had exceeded 1,500' (Mankowitz, 2002:18). In 1946 a brutal massacre took place in the Polish city of Kielce where forty-seven Jews were killed and another fifty wounded. This incident created a strong impetus for a Jewish exodus from Poland (Mankowitz, 2002).

Displaced Persons Camps

At the end of the war, Germany and Austria were divided into four Allied occupation zones: British, French, American, and Russian. Ironically, Germany became a haven for Jews. Surviving Jews, who had nowhere else to go, migrated into the American and British zones. Of a total of 300,000 Jewish displaced persons in Germany and Italy, the majority settled in the American zone (Lavsky, 2002). By 1947, sixty DP camps existed. The most significant were Bergen-Belsen in the British zone and Landsberg, Feldafing, and Foehrenwald in the American zone (Lavsky, 2002).

Not until the 1980s did research begin to focus on the post-war experiences of Holocaust survivors in the DP camps of Europe (Geller, 2005; Konigseder & Wetzel, 2001; Lavsky, 2002; Mankowitz, 2002; Marcus & Peck, 1982). In spite of the difficulties endured, survivors demonstrated remarkable resilience in rebuilding their lives and reconstituting their religious, cultural, educational, and social institutions. They became known as the *She'erith Hapleitah*, the surviving remnant (Mankowitz, 2002).

As survivors waited in the DP camps to immigrate to new countries, they vacillated between periods of hope and despair when they encountered new challenges. Countries around the world, including Canada and the United States, established stringent immigration quotas that effectively barred entry (Abella & Troper, 1982; Wyman, 1984). Many DP camps were located on, or near, former concentration-camp sites. The British closed the gates to Palestine, which was a preferred destination for many. In addition, living conditions were dire in the DP camps. Inhabitants lived in substandard wooden barracks without privacy and endured sanitation problems, food rations, overcrowded conditions, and insufficient clothing (Marcus & Peck, 1982).

In spite of these obstacles, however, the camps were characterized by an 'affirmation of life' and guiding principles that included the slogan 'to start anew, to take hold of life and work for the future' (Mankowitz, 2002:288). The following account, by the late Holocaust survivor Paul Trepman (1957), graphically describes post-liberation life in the Bergen-Belsen DP camp:

> Looking back, I don't know myself how we survived and where we took our strength from. The fact is that a new people had arisen on the graves of the martyrs and we found untapped sources of spiritual and physical strength to carry through an incredibly difficult task. Teachers created excellent schools from nothing; editors published papers. God knows how, but they were good, readable papers. Some actors amongst us even created a theatre. The ordinary day-to-day duties and chores connected with the complex life of a newly created Jewish community were executed. (134)

The Partisan hymn *Zog nit keyn mol as du geyst dem lestn veg* (never say that you have reached your journey's end) became a rallying cry for the survivor community. The last sentence particularly underscored their existence: *mir zainen do* (Yiddish for we are here).

Survivors immediately began reconstructing their shattered lives in the DP camps. Reconstruction – literally out of the ashes and often with the help of Jewish and international relief organizations – took many forms. Survivors reconstructed families by marrying other survivors, usually someone with a link to their past. For example, many formed intimate relationships with individuals who originated from their former cities and towns. These survivors gave birth to a new generation. 'The marriage and birthrate in the DP camps, was remarkably, one of the highest per capita in the world' (Mankowitz, 2002:133). Cultural activities flourished. Newspapers were published. A network of schools sprung up offering both elementary and vocational education. A 'people's university' provided cultural and leisure activities (Marcus & Peck, 1982). Youth movements flourished, providing educational and cultural activities that prepared people for eventual emigration to Palestine. Camp committees were formed that linked with the Central Committee for Liberated Jews in Munich (Marcus & Peck, 1982). Religious institutions, sports clubs, political parties, theatre groups, choirs, and orchestras proliferated (Federber-Salz, 1980).

Birth in a DP Camp

After liberation, Fela and Mala returned to Łódź to search for surviving family members. Fela discovered that she was the only survivor of an extended family of eighty. Her friend Mala was more fortunate. She found her father, Eliyahu, and two brothers, Heniek and Moishe. The remaining family, including Fela, moved into one house. Eventually Fela and Moishe began a relationship. However, living in Łódź was difficult because anti-Semitism was rampant. Everyone realized they had no future there and, like thousands of others, made their way to the DP camps. The family migrated to Schwandorf, a DP camp in Bavaria, Germany – part of the American zone. There, in February 1946, Fela and Moishe married in a simple ceremony attended by family and friends. I was born the following year and named after my maternal grandmother, Mirele, and paternal grandmother, Hena. My mother wrote about my birth in her 1996 memoirs: 'Mirele Hena meant the world to us. I suddenly realized that there was a purpose to survive the horrible tragedies that we went through. Our newborn daughter filled our lives with joy and hope to build a good life for her' (11).

I was the first child born in my parents' circle of friends. Fortunately, I have baby pictures taken during this period, something very rare. In all of them, I am dressed impeccably in dresses made by a dressmaker whom my parents met in the DP camp. In some pictures I am holding a doll, and in others I stand in a rattan pram (baby carriage). My parents often described the satisfaction they, and their friends, derived from seeing numerous baby carriages in the camp.

Resettlement: Restrictive Immigration Policies

Abella and Troper (1982) provide a devastating indictment of Canada's immigration policy towards European Jews who were seeking refuge from Nazi persecution. They make clear that the Canadian government had no intention of helping threatened European Jews and indeed deliberately enacted policies that prevented any possibility of rescue.

Before the Second World War many factors contributed to ensuring that only a handful of Jewish refugees found sanctuary in Canada. Foremost was the unyielding opposition of certain key officials, the most outspoken being Frederick Charles Blair, director of the Immigration Branch of the Department of Mines and Resources. Blair reflected the anti-immigration spirit of the times. Since 1928, Canada had restricted the flow of Eastern European immigrants, of whom substantial numbers were known to be Jewish. It was no secret in Canada that British and American immigrants were preferred. Other factors that restricted European Jews from immigrating to Canada before the war included the Depression, which left one-third of Canadians jobless and Canada reluctant to admit job-hungry immigrants; general apathy in English Canada towards immigration; Quebec's outright hostility towards immigrants because it was vehemently opposed to admitting Jewish refugees; Prime Minister Mackenzie King's fear that any move to allow the entry of Jewish refugees would cost him political support and votes; anti-Semitism, particularly in Quebec, where it was fuelled by anti-Semitic politicians; and lack of endorsement from the Catholic Church.

Even when the scope of the Holocaust became plain at war's end, Canada was not about to open its doors. The government, still believing that public opinion in Canada did not favour absorbing large numbers of Jewish refugees, did not want to face a backlash once the displaced survivors arrived. A poll in October 1946 confirmed this perception: 49 per cent of those polled felt that Jews were undesirable immigrants (Abella & Troper, 1982).

By 1948, there was an extraordinary turnaround in government policy. But the new attitude towards immigration had nothing to do with compassion. In the words of Abella and Troper (1982), it was the result of 'national economic self-interest' (239). C.D. Howe, the powerful minister of reconstruction and supply, became an outspoken advocate for increased immigration, including that of displaced persons. Howe saw immigration, even of Jews, as 'the simplest, cheapest, and quickest way to find labor, skilled and unskilled' (Abella & Troper, 1982:242).

People in the European DP camps gained entry into Canada through a series of special programs such as those allowing the entry of war orphans (approximately 1,000 Jewish war orphans were admitted under this program) and others permitting the immigration of needle-trade workers, furriers, milliners, domestics, dressmakers, and first-degree relatives. Around 65,000 refugees had entered Canada by March 1948. Of this number, however, only 15 per cent were Jewish (Abella & Troper, 1982).

The DP camps gradually shut down once the United States and Canada eased immigration restrictions and the state of Israel was created in 1948. Most camps were closed by 1951, but some remained open as late as 1957. Some displaced persons made their way to various countries around the world, particularly the United States and Canada. The majority of Holocaust survivors, my family included, made their way to Israel.

In 1947 Heniek reached Palestine by way of Aliya Bet, a movement that transported illegal immigrants from the DP camps. At the time, Palestine was ruled by the British government, which continued its pre-war policy of limiting Jewish immigration. When the state of Israel was established in 1948, my paternal grandfather made his way there with Balcha, whom he had married in Schwandorf. He wanted to be reunited with Heniek. In 1949 my parents, together with Mala and her husband, Abram, immigrated to Israel where we shared a house in Jaffa. Economic conditions were difficult and food was rationed. There were mountains of sand with no roads. Transportation was limited. The nearest bus stop was over a kilometre away by foot. My father found a job building roads. Yet, in spite of these difficulties, they adjusted to their new environment. My brother Issie was born. My parents made new friends and enrolled me in kindergarten. In 1952 Mala and Abram immigrated to Montreal, which was a blow for my parents who missed them terribly. They began to explore ways to reunite with them. In 1953 a friend of my mother from Łódź sponsored us for immigration. We arrived in Halifax on 11 October by ship. We stayed with Mala and Abram for two months until my parents found an apartment.

OBSTACLES TO RESETTLEMENT AND INTEGRATION

In their study of twenty-five survivor families on several Israeli *kibbutzim*, Klein and Reinharz (1972) identified a supportive communal environment as an important variable influencing the post-war adaptation of survivors. Through the embodiment of a collective spirit, survivors were able to rebuild their pre-war communities and family networks, as well as have the opportunity to mourn their losses through the creation of rituals.

The reception that survivors who immigrated to other parts of the world received, however, was in sharp contrast to the Israeli *kibbutz* experience. As survivors set about rebuilding their lives in their new environments, they were plagued with the numerous difficulties and ordeals that most new immigrants face when they are uprooted from a familiar culture and relocated into a much different one. They had to make many economic, educational, social, psychological, and emotional adjustments.

Along with the normal stresses of the immigration process and immigrant adjustment, survivors had to deal with the multiple traumas they endured during and after the war when they searched for families and friends only to discover that most had been murdered and their communities destroyed. On top of this, there were three major obstacles to integration in their new environments: negative attitudes on the part of Jews who had not lived through the Holocaust, 'the conspiracy of silence,' and 'the concentration-camp survivor syndrome.'

Negative Attitudes

The literature is replete with examples of negative and often hostile attitudes displayed towards survivors in their new environments. Other things being equal, most survivors would have been well equipped to deal with the stress caused by the immigration process and subsequent adjustment in a new land because they had developed important coping skills during the Holocaust. However, the challenges they faced were compounded when members of communities where they settled greeted them with silence, denial, avoidance, and suspicion (Danieli, 1981a; Giberovitch, 1988). Several survivors describe their post-war reception by the established community as a 'second Holocaust.' The experience was a difficult one for them to accept. For example, some Canadian Jews referred to the new arrivals as *greeners* (greenhorns), a label that accorded them inferior social status. Mrs G. explained that native-born Canadians did not consider survivors to be emotionally and intellectually equal to them. Some natives were even ashamed to be seen in the company of a survivor. Mrs G., a survivor, rationalized their behaviour as follows: 'Maybe our roots were not up to par; maybe the suffering was still in our faces and in our eyes. Maybe they were going around with the guilt they could not work out with themselves when they left us over there. They didn't put up a big fuss' (Giberovitch, 1988:52).

Furthermore, survivors were regarded as somewhat of an oddity (Giberovitch, 1988). Mr K. remembered: 'We were survivors and, you know, everyone looked at survivors like being people from another planet' (52). Many Canadians expected survivors to resemble the emaciated bodies whose pictures they had seen in newspapers immediately after the war. In the words of one surprised Canadian woman to her husband: 'They look just like us.'

Suspicions about survivors were rampant (Giberovitch, 1988). For example, Mrs W.'s landlady accused her of bringing gold and diamonds over from Germany. Others believed that survivors must have committed unethical acts to survive, while still others suspected that they carried diseases. Most people did not, and could not, comprehend the survivors' horrific experiences. Consequently, survivors were told to forget their past and move on. According to Mrs W., a survivor, the insulting behaviour of native-born Montrealers was very painful and created a chasm between survivors and the rest of the community which continues today.

Possible Explanations for Negative Attitudes towards Survivors

Different theories attempt to explain the ambivalent feelings towards survivors in the post-war years. Des Pres (1976) believes that acknowledging survivor experiences, the embodiment of 'hell-on-earth,' could cause psychic imbalance. As a result, people responded to survivors with suspicion, rejection, distance, and denial. In addition, the survivor was made to feel guilty for undermining 'the validity of existing norms' (45). Des Pres's analysis is congruent with the concept of 'death taint' put forth by Lifton (1968) in his studies of survivors of Hiroshima and of Nazi persecution. This idea relates to the 'notion of psychological contagion,' wherein people turn away from the survivor because she or he 'threatens various mechanisms of denial of death as well as related issues about death symbolism' (187).

Holocaust trauma also conjured up guilt in non-survivors, which may have created taboos about the subject. Terry (1984) points out that discomfort felt by a person listening to a survivor's story may be 'partly explained by the activation of guilt for having remained passive and silent' (143). This type of guilt was disclosed to me in a conversation I had with the late David Rome, chief archivist for many years at Canadian Jewish Congress. He said, 'How does one look a victim in the eye knowing what they experienced and how I lived during those years?'

Srebrnik (1982) posits that native Quebec Jews were unfriendly towards survivors because they feared that anti-Semitic forces operating in the province would create a backlash against all Jews. For example, he cites the Société Saint-Jean-Baptiste, which was supported by many Montreal city councilors. It assembled a petition in 1944, with 100,000 signatures, requesting the government to ban entry of Jewish immigrants. Moreover, the 1944 provincial elections fuelled anti-Jewish sentiments when Union Nationale leader Mauricé Duplessis spoke 'of an international Zionist conspiracy to settle 100,000 Jews in Quebec after the war' (Srebrnik, 1982:14). In addition, the province 'had an ultra-nationalist, semi-fascist party, the Bloc Populaire, which managed to win some seats' (Srebrnik, 1982:14).

The Conspiracy of Silence about the Holocaust

Along with the negative attitudes that host communities displayed towards survivors, the latter also had to deal with a pervasive silence about, and denial of, the horrors they experienced in the Holocaust. This is referred to as the 'conspiracy of silence.' Danieli (1981a) describes how societal taboos about the Holocaust impeded survivors' integration:

> Their war accounts were too horrifying for most people to listen to or to believe. They were, therefore, easy to ignore, avoid, and / or deny. Bystander's guilt led many to react to survivors as if they were pointing an accusing finger at them. Survivors were also confronted with negative reactions, expressed in such comments as 'That is the past; let bygones by [sic] bygones,' in the myth of their having contributed to their victimization by 'going like sheep to the slaughter,' and by suspicion that they had performed immoral acts to survive. Such reactions led most survivors, in their interactions with non-survivors, to become silent about the Holocaust.
>
> The resulting 'conspiracy of silence' proved detrimental to the intrapsychic well-being of survivors and to their familial and socio-cultural integration. Not only did this conspiracy intensify the survivors' sense of isolation and mistrust of society but it also formed yet another obstacle to mourning. The silence imposed by others proved particularly painful to those who had survived the war determined to bear witness. (7)

To this day, survivors recount stories about the responses of their relatives and established community when they came to Canada.

Survivors consistently say that few people wanted to hear about their Holocaust experiences. This contradicts some of the literature, which states that survivors in the post-war period were unable or unwilling to talk about what had happened to them in the war. That may be true for some who wanted to forget and concentrate on rebuilding their lives, but many others were determined to remember and remind. There are many anecdotes that illustrate this phenomenon. For example, some people reacted with remarkable ignorance about survivors' experiences. The following excerpt summarizes an incident related to me by a leader in the survivor community:

> Mr. K. was asked to relate his experiences of having worked as a slave laborer to a communal leader active in labor unions. When he explained to him that in addition to 11 to 12 hour working days, approximately four hours per day were spent marching to and from work, the communal leader asked him why a union had not been organized to demand better working conditions. Realizing that this person knew nothing about the history of the Holocaust, Mr. K. pledged never to discuss his experiences again with a non-survivor. (Giberovitch, 1988:52)

Survivors responded creatively to their rejection by turning to each other for support and action. Some banded together to establish mutual-aid societies or *landsmanschaften* (organizations of people who originated from the same European geographic area). The members became each other's surrogate families. My parents became members of the Lodzer (Farband) Society, where they found a supportive environment that did not exist in the general community. They were able to talk about their past and comfort each other as they mourned their losses. These organizations are discussed in more detail in chapter 4.

Some survivors lobbied communal institutions to establish Holocaust-related committees. Both the National and Regional Holocaust Remembrance Committees of the Canadian Jewish Congress were the direct result of such lobbying efforts. Other survivors rebuilt their religious institutions. Unfortunately, in their interactions with the non-survivor community, the conspiracy of silence about the Holocaust continued.

There are other theories that attempt to explain the conspiracy of silence as well. Hamburg (1980) states that scholars and the general public avoided the painful topic of the Holocaust in the hope that such a catastrophe could not happen again. Eitinger (1980) interprets this silence as an attempt to forget horrible and painful events: 'As is the case with every unpleasant experience, war and victims are something the community wants to forget; a veil of oblivion is drawn over everything painful and unpleasant' (159).

The Concentration-Camp Survivor Syndrome

Two key events brought an end to the 'conspiracy of silence' about the Holocaust in the 1950s and early 1960s: the West German Federal Indemnification Law – known as *Wiedergutmachung* or BEG – which means, 'to make whole' (Claims Conference, 2001:2), and the 1961 Adolf Eichmann trial in Jerusalem. The reparation payments created by the Indemnification Law provided compensation for survivors to redress injustices suffered. The Claims Conference, however, does not use the term *Wiedergutmachung* because 'it strongly believes that, however meaningful the amounts paid by the German government, there can be no "making whole" for the immeasurable losses suffered by the Jews in the *Shoah*' (Hebrew word meaning the Holocaust) (Claims Conference, 2001:2). The Eichmann trial was reported in newspapers around the world and was internationally televised. Eichmann headed the Bureau for Jewish Affairs at the Reich Security Headquarters in Germany during the war. His trial renewed interest in the Holocaust around the world.

Unfortunately, the German legislation increased the pathologization of survivors. Post-Traumatic Stress Disorder (PTSD) was not a recognized and an acknowledged syndrome in the 1950s. The psychiatric and psychoanalytic literature, for the most part, focused on cases of survivors who applied for help to private mental-health professionals to relieve stress and anxiety and / or to the German government for restitution payments. To apply for restitution, survivors were required to submit to both medical and psychiatric examinations so that a causal relationship could be established between their present-day health problems and their years of persecution. This was an important development because, until this time, the German medical community believed that psychological disturbances resulted from survivors' 'infantile neurosis' and not their traumatic life experiences (Hass, 1990:16).

As these studies continued, the term 'concentration-camp syndrome' was coined in the early 1960s by psychiatrist Dr W.G. Niederland to describe the long-term impact of persecution on survivors. Symptoms of the syndrome include chronic anxiety and depression; sleep disturbances; cognition and memory disturbances; survivor guilt; withdrawal from social life; physical disabilities; and psychosomatic symptoms (Krystal & Niederland, 1968).

This labelling was necessary to identify and legitimize the massive trauma that the Holocaust inflicted on its victims, and it paved the way for restitution payments from the German government. Unfortunately, it also had a negative effect by stereotyping and stigmatizing thousands of people. Epstein (1979) captures the devastating effects of such labelling on the lives of survivors when she states that 'it ... made their condition appear to be an insidious disease contracted in equal measure by every Jew who had survived the Holocaust ... The term set Holocaust survivors apart from other "normal" people' (202).

3 Identifying a Holocaust Survivor

I will not minimize another person's suffering because I feel that I have suffered more.

— Auschwitz survivor

Holocaust survivors may be encountered anywhere. They may be spouses, parents, grandparents, or friends. They may be business owners, employees, colleagues, patients, clients, or customers. They may be easily identified and open to self-disclosure, or may have kept their past a secret. Whatever the situation, personal, casual, or professional, knowing who survivors are and understanding them will enhance relationships and improve interactions with them. So who is a Holocaust survivor?

DEFINITION OF A HOLOCAUST SURVIVOR

Defining and identifying Holocaust survivors is not straightforward and may, at times, be a contentious issue (American Gathering The Jewish Week, 1983:14). Various definitions exist, ranging from a broad, metaphorical one which argues that, in a sense, all Jews are survivors because the 'Final Solution' was meant to destroy all world Jewry, to a more stringent one which considers only those who survived the ghettos, concentration camps, and death camps to be 'true' survivors. Others define a Holocaust survivor as a person who was physically present in Nazi-occupied territories in Europe. This latter definition excludes several categories of people: the approximately 300,000 Polish Jews who sought refuge in Russia in order to escape the Nazi onslaught and suffered tremendous hardships (Dawidowicz, 1975); some war refugees who, despite worldwide indifference to their plight, managed to find a safe haven in countries such as the United States, Palestine, Britain, Argentina, Brazil, China, Bolivia, Chile, and Canada (Abella & Troper, 1982); and German and Austrian Jews who emigrated between 1933 and 1939, before the implementation of the 'Final Solution.' Regarding this last category, it is important to keep in mind that when Hitler came to power in 1933, he enacted the Nuremberg Laws – virulent, anti-Jewish legislation. Between 1933 and 1934 Germany had already built fifty concentration camps. The largest were Dachau in Munich, Buchenwald near Weimar, and Sachsenhausen near Berlin.

The literature cautions us to view survivors as individuals and to understand that there is no typical survivor (Kahana, Harel, & Kahana, 1988; Rosenbloom, 1983; Sigal & Weinfeld, 1989). Survivors come from diverse European countries and speak different languages. They differ in their religious, cultural, and political beliefs as well as in their educational and socio-economic backgrounds. The environments in which they survived the Holocaust are also diverse, as is the manner in which they coped within them. They coped, and are still coping, in different ways with the extreme stress caused by their experiences. Furthermore, they are adjusting to the ageing process in different ways.

In my work with survivors I learned the importance of accepting survivors' definition of survivorship. Survivors who escaped to Russia and endured severe hardships are a case in point. Many are disappointed they are not recognized as 'real survivors' within the survivor community, where a 'hierarchy of suffering' exists. When I chaired the Montreal Jewish community's Holocaust Commemoration Service, some committee members tried to exclude Russian survivors from lighting a memorial candle. Also, in the early days of the Drop-in Centre (discussed in more detail in chapter 11), several of the concentration-camp survivors tried to prevent Russian survivors from attending. One woman was so angry that she hit a Russian survivor with her purse. The Russian survivor left the program and never returned.

It took a significant effort, over time, to change perceptions. We employed a number of strategies. For example, in large group discussions, Russian survivors described the hardships they endured in environments such as Siberia, the Ural Mountains, and Tashkent. They usually prefaced their remarks with: 'There is no comparison and we did not go through the same hardships as the ghetto and concentration camp survivors, but we too suffered.' Their families and friends were also murdered and they lost material possessions. The process evolved into having members break up into small groups, each with a Russian survivor describing and answering questions about their experiences. This exercise prompted an Auschwitz survivor to say: 'All of our suffering matters. I will not minimize another person's suffering because I feel that I have suffered more.' I also taught anger-management techniques as another strategy. Eventually the Russian survivors were accepted as 'real survivors' and are included today as candle lighters in the Drop-in Centre's Holocaust Commemoration Service. Their acceptance is no longer a divisive or contentious issue and the Russian survivors feel that their experiences and losses have been validated. As a result of these strategies, the definition of a Holocaust survivor adopted by Drop-in Centre members is:

1. A person who survived in Nazi-occupied Europe during the Holocaust in any of the following ways:
   a. was confined to a ghetto, incarcerated in a concentration and / or a death camp, or forced to provide slave labour in a work camp;
   b. hid in such places as an attic, a safe house, underground bunker, a forest, a haystack, a grave, etc.
   c. posed as a Christian with a false identity; or
   d. fought with the underground Partisan resistance movement.
2. A person who fled to Russia when Germany invaded Poland.
3. A war refugee who fled to a safe haven.
4. German and Austrian Jews who fled to other countries between 1933 and 1939, including children and teenagers whose parents made the decision for them. (E.g., between 1938 and 1940, rescue efforts known as Kindertransport – children's transport – brought thousands of refugee Jewish children to Great Britain from Nazi Germany.)

This definition of a Holocaust survivor is consistent with the widely accepted definition used in academic circles (Hollander-Goldfein et al., 2012). The Transcending Trauma Project (TTP) defines Holocaust survivors as follows: 'Jewish individuals who lived in Europe and were in danger after 1933 with the rise of Hitler because they resided in countries controlled by Nazi Germany. Even those individuals who emigrated from Europe prior to the start of World War II were considered survivors by this definition' (Hollander-Goldfein et al., 2012:12).

Negotiated Definitions of a Holocaust Survivor

Different definitions of a Holocaust survivor are used to determine eligibility for compensation and restitution payments. The criteria vary by program and evolve over time. Since 1952 the Claims Conference has been the primary negotiator of compensation programs for Holocaust survivors around the world, resulting in a number of funds and services in seventy-five countries (Claims Conference, 2010).

The Claims Conference maintains a detailed description of each Holocaust victim's persecution history. What follows below are the general environmental criteria used in 2012 to determine overall eligibility for compensation programs and social-service assistance funds. Specific eligibility criteria for each compensation program can be found on the Claims Conference's website (www.claimscon.org). Additional criteria, such as financial status, may be required for some of the programs and funds.

A Nazi victim is considered to be any Jewish person who lived in Germany, Austria, or any of the countries occupied by the Nazis or their Axis allies or who emigrated from any of the countries below after the following dates and before liberation (Never Again, Summer / Fall 2012):

- Germany after January 1933;
- Austria after July 1936;
- Czechoslovakia after September 1938;
- Poland after September 1939;
- Algeria between September 1940 and March 1943;
- Denmark and Norway after April 1940;
- Belgium, Netherlands, Luxembourg, and France after May 1940;
- Morocco between July 1940 and November 1942;
- Libya after February 1941;
- Bulgaria, Romania, Hungary, Yugoslavia, and Greece after April 1941;
- Tunisia between November 1942 and July 1943;
- Italy after August / September 1943;
- Albania after September 1943; and
- areas of the former Soviet Union after June 1941.

IDENTIFYING A HOLOCAUST SURVIVOR

Some survivors are reluctant to disclose their identities. The following clues may be helpful in identifying a Holocaust survivor (adapted from a handout compiled by Ann Hartman, 1997).

A Numbered Tattoo or Scar on Their Forearm

The German Nazis kept detailed statistics and tracked internees by tattooing numbers on their forearms. Not all survivors have these tattooed numbers because some concentration camps did not tattoo their prisoners, and many individuals survived outside these camps. In addition, some survivors removed their tattoos with laser treatments that left a scar in this area. However, with growing interest in the Holocaust in recent years, some survivors regret having removed their tattoos, which serve as a reminder of the atrocities committed.

Age and/or Year of Birth

There are two subgroups of survivors: the child survivors who were sixteen years of age or younger in 1945, and the adult survivors. As of 2012, adult survivors are in their mid-eighties and above and child survivors are in their late-sixties to early eighties.

Country of Origin or Year of Immigration

Individuals who emigrated from Eastern and Western Europe in the late 1930s, 1940s, or 1950s are probably Holocaust survivors. The last displaced persons' camps were closed in the late 1950s. Many survivors immigrated to Israel after it was established in 1948 and then made their way to other countries during the 1950s. Many Hungarian survivors emigrated after the Hungarian revolution of 1956. Russian survivors began to emigrate in the 1990s after the collapse of the Soviet Union in the late 1980s.

Individual Speaks with an Accent

Some survivors did not assimilate to their new communities and are more comfortable speaking their mother tongues, such as Yiddish, Hungarian, Romanian, or Russian.

4 Changing Perceptions of Holocaust Survivors

The majority of survivors have normalized their lives, achieved prosperity – even happiness – obviously an extraordinary achievement for survivors.
– V. Rakoff cited in A. Russell (1980)

CONVENTIONAL PERCEPTION OF SURVIVORS

In my educational workshops for health professionals, students, and volunteers, I sometimes begin by asking participants to describe a Holocaust survivor in one or a few words. Common responses include: traumatized, depressed, angry, scarred, tragic, hysterical, neurotic, guilty, silent, nightmares, cynical, haunted, inner turmoil, paranoid, mentally and emotionally crippled, hoarders, mistrustful, ambitious, fragile, lost souls, resilient, grieving, sense of loss, helplessness, have unfinished business, clever, unable to speak about their experiences, fatalistic, aggressive, wounded, weak, defiant, hard-working, intense, strong character, clever, resourceful, strong will to survive, thankful, hopeful, and family-oriented. Usually the descriptions lean heavily towards perceiving survivors as impaired and traumatized individuals.

Labelling of Holocaust Survivors

Where does this negative perception of Holocaust survivors come from? It is well documented that mass migrations of Jewish immigrants from Lithuania, Poland, and Russia in the late nineteenth and early twentieth centuries – following persecution and pogroms – enhanced the Montreal Jewish community. Consequently, one might expect that the large group of immigrating Holocaust survivors, most originating from the cradle of Jewish civilization in Eastern Europe (Rosenberg, 1957), would also adapt and make contributions to their new home. So why are Holocaust survivors perceived differently? While there may be many explanations, two predominant ones come to mind.

The first involves the emergence of extensive mass media in the twentieth century. An intrinsic characteristic of news media is a focus on gruesome events, and nothing, of course, could be more gruesome than the Holocaust. Conventional Holocaust photographs, therefore, depicted corpses in mass graves, nude people awaiting execution, and emaciated survivors behind barbed-wire fences. Although these photographs provided important evidence about the depths of depravity to which a large segment of humankind sank, they also had a negative impact by searing into our minds images of a victimized group of people bereft of human identity. Their widespread distribution helped to shape our perceptions of survivors.

Clinical-research literature also promoted negative perceptions, especially the psychodynamic case studies of the 1960s, 1970s, and 1980s. These studies focused on the Holocaust survivor as a traumatized victim suffering from psychological, physical, and social maladaptation, with little appreciation of the extent to which survivors had succeeded in adapting to their new environments and their new lives. This bias contributed to a perception of survivors as emotionally and mentally crippled individuals unable to function normally. For example, the 'concentration-camp survivor syndrome' label that emerged during the 1960s stereotyped and unnecessarily stigmatized thousands of survivors (discussed in chapter 2).

Several anecdotes from my own practice illustrate this labelling and stigmatization. In one situation, I referred an isolated Holocaust survivor to low-cost housing within the Jewish community. She had lost her entire family during the war but was able to marry and create a new family. After her husband and son died, however, she found herself living alone, isolated and alienated from the Jewish milieu. Upon receiving the acceptance letter for housing, she refused to accept the apartment because she had subsequently learned about a series of robberies there. One official called to berate me for taking on the cause of a Holocaust survivor 'who was paranoid.' This official refused to acknowledge that lax security precautions in the housing development contributed to the woman's sudden change-of-heart. He preferred to blame the 'paranoid' survivor.

In another case, the son of survivor parents wanted to marry the daughter of native-born Montrealers. Upon learning about their prospective son-in-law's background, the girl's parents attempted to put a halt to the relationship, claiming that their daughter would experience a 'pack of problems' if the marriage went ahead.

Labelling survivors as different from other people has negative consequences for the survivor community. It represents a social judgment that is first generalized, and then internalized within a survivor's self-concept. This can also be transmitted to second- and third-generation offspring. In his discussion of labelling theory, McPherson (1983) notes the implications of labelling as a social judgment: 'Primary labeling occurs when significant others perceive an individual's behavior to differ in quality or type from normative standards. As a result of this perception, an individual is labelled as "delinquent," "unstable," "eccentric," "senile," or "charismatic." That is, the labeling is a social judgment' (134–5). Secondary labelling occurs when the labelling process is persistent and becomes 'internalized within the individual's self concept' (135). In short, the individual accepts society's negative image of herself or himself. The most direct result is a gradual loss of self-respect and self-esteem. The following incident illustrates this point.

* * *

Over the years I have given numerous community talks about Holocaust survivors and their contributions to Canadian society. Many survivors, saying that they felt validated by my words, requested copies of my presentations to share with their families. One person, a former Jewish teacher, stands out in my mind. With tears in her eyes, she shared the self-doubt she had lived with for many years. Although she was an educator in the Jewish community, she felt stigmatized as a Holocaust survivor. After reading the clinical literature, she doubted her own capabilities as a parent, especially since research studies suggested that trauma could be transmitted to subsequent generations. She appreciated my public acknowledgment of survivor capabilities, accomplishments, and contributions to society.

* * *

Conventional perceptions of survivors, which focus on pathology and associated attitudes, also have direct implications for practice because our perceptions determine how we, as health-care and other service providers, work with them. If providers believe that survivors suffered permanent, irreparable damage, then recovery becomes an unrealistic goal. Conversely, when strengths and coping capabilities in the face of traumatic experiences are acknowledged, providers are able to empower survivors and help them recognize and appreciate their abilities and accomplishments. As Roberta Greene (2002) points out: 'We must remember that survivors were resilient' (16).

Changing the 'dysfunctional victim' perception of survivors must be done consciously. For example, I was interviewed on local television about a survivor who had committed suicide. With little background information, the reporter wanted me to link the suicide to the presupposition that she may have been a 'depressed' survivor. Instead I chose to give dignity to her memory by focusing on her positive attributes and volunteer work in the community.

RECOGNIZING STRENGTHS AND ADAPTIVE COPING ABILITIES

Events that occurred in Europe between the years 1933 and 1945 influence my life today. I first became conscious of my heritage in April 1978 after viewing *Holocaust*, a four-part television mini-series. Shortly thereafter, I joined a consciousness-raising group for adult offspring of Holocaust survivors. This group changed me because, for the first time, I explored the impact of my parents' experiences on my own life, felt the pain of my family losses, and began coming to terms with my roots. I searched for books and articles to learn about the Holocaust and, in November 1979, attended a Second Generation conference in New York City. Subsequently I helped organize the first Canadian Children of Survivors conference, held in Montreal in November 1980.

At the New York conference, the first two panels included prominent international psychiatrists and psychologists who had distinguished themselves in their work with survivors and their offspring. While their presentations provided valuable information about the after-effects of trauma, they focused on survivors' psycho-pathology. After the Montreal conference, mental-health professionals asked many of the participants, including me, to conduct research on the transmission of Holocaust trauma to second- and third-generation offspring. I noticed a common theme emerge that focused on the pathology of survivor families.

As I familiarized myself with the psychological and psychiatric literature on survivors, I began to question the assumption that survivors are permanently damaged victims. My relationships with survivors over the years were not congruent with the clinical-research literature. I grew up among survivors and witnessed their resilience and strength as they rebuilt their lives, finding new homes in strange environments, learning new languages, trades, and professions, starting new families, and creating new organizations.

I started to realize that survivors did not 'just survive.' They gave meaning to their experiences by preserving memories of beloved relatives and friends who had been murdered, and by ensuring that the values and cultural attributes of pre–Second World War Jewish civilization in Eastern and Central Europe continue to flourish in present-day Jewish community life. As they struggled to establish themselves in a world that did not, and could not, comprehend the tragic abyss from which they had emerged, most became useful and productive members of the communities where they had settled.

My recognition of survivor strengths and capabilities led to a qualitative master's research study in 1987, a study that explored and drew attention to a neglected research area: the contributions of Holocaust survivors to Jewish communal life. These contributions were evidenced, in part, through the organizations they formed. During interviews with forty-nine survivors, I learned about the stresses caused by their immigration process and adjustment; the community's 'conspiracy of silence'; the negative reactions that greeted them upon arrival; the importance of establishing *landsmanschaften*, which helped ease their transition into a new society; and the contributions they made in a variety of areas.

Survivors' Contributions to Canadian Society

Holocaust survivors endured one of the most horrific tragedies in world history. Violently uprooted from their European countries of origin, they travelled long distances to find safe havens where they could rebuild their lives. In 1948 the doors into Canada opened slightly for post-war Jewish immigrants. Many survivors entered the country, and the majority settled in Montreal.

Indoctrinated with a strong sense of traditional heritage, culture, and communal involvement, many carried their Old World values, beliefs, and knowledge into their new communities. They sought the companionship of fellow *landsleit* – people originating from the same geographic location in Europe – who would help with their integration.

During their recovery process, survivors also adapted to their strange new environment, as had earlier waves of immigrants, and became useful and productive members of the community. They transmitted their cultural heritage and established continuity with their ancestral world. It stands to reason, however, that Holocaust survivors would be more highly motivated than other immigrants to ensure that their pre-war communities, culture, and traditions would be remembered and preserved. Previous waves of immigrants did not have their Old World communities eradicated. Many still maintained connections to the 'old country' by correspondence and parcels, and sponsored relatives and friends for immigration. These ties were in sharp contrast to the experiences of Holocaust survivors, particularly those from Eastern Europe, whose entire world – family, friends, homes, communal institutions, and towns – had been destroyed. As a result, many survivors see themselves as the only remaining record of their history. With a now intangible past that exists only as painful memories, they are more determined than other immigrants to nourish their Old World values, beliefs, and knowledge and instil them into the community life of their new home.

Consequently, Holocaust survivors played an important role in the cultural and institutional development of the Montreal Jewish community (Giberovitch, 1988; 1994). For example, they rejuvenated Yiddish culture in Montreal, influenced Jewish education, reconstituted religious institutions, and invigorated existing Jewish communal organizations. They also created many new organizations, primarily *landsmanschaften*, where they engaged in various social, cultural, and philanthropic activities. Several Holocaust survivor organizations, particularly the Association of Survivors of Nazi Oppression, the Holocaust Remembrance Committee of the Canadian Jewish Congress, and the German Jewish Heritage Association, assumed the role of moral conscience for the Jewish community. They lobbied on behalf of anti-hate legislation and remained vigilant to issues of anti-Semitism, alleged Nazi war criminals living in Canada, and the Holocaust-denial movement. Several articles in the literature recognize that Holocaust survivors raised the level of moral consciousness in the communities where they settled (Giberovitch, 1988; Helmreich, 1992; Sigal & Weinfeld, 1989). In the 1960s, the Association of Survivors of Nazi Oppression spearheaded a campaign against a resurgence of neo-Nazism in Quebec, which culminated in the incorporation of anti-hate legislation into the Criminal Code in 1970. This legislation makes incitement or acts of violence against any race or ethnic group an offence against society and punishable under law. Survivors were distinctly aware of the inherent dangers of the incitement of hatred against any identifiable group of people, and they were determined to prevent future genocides.

Holocaust survivors also live with a 'holy mission' to memorialize their dead and educate the world about genocide and the inherent dangers of racism. They honour their commitments to bear witness with dignity by institutionalizing Holocaust remembrance and education in numerous ways. For example, they established Holocaust remembrance committees, initiated Holocaust educational activities in schools, organized conferences and commemorative events, helped found Holocaust museums and educational centres across Canada, and continue to write memoirs and books.

'Survival is an achievement' (Lifton, 1988:9). Survivors' determination to heal and live normal lives is remarkable. Despite the trauma they endured and the post-war obstacles they faced, most adjusted well to their new environment and enriched Jewish communal life in Canada, and continue to do so today. They also convey an important message. Many have a heightened sense of social justice and are the first to detect human-rights violations. While some remain vigilant and speak out against injustice, others advocate social policies and human-rights legislation that benefit all of humanity.

The contributions of Raphael Lemkin are presented in appendix B as an example of one survivor's ability to overcome adversity and contribute to society.

SHIFTING TO A STRENGTHS-BASED PERCEPTION

In the last decade, we have seen the emergence of positive psychology (Seligman, 2002) and resilience-based research that examines individuals' adaptive nature and factors that help people cope with the damaging effects of adversity (Ayalon et al., 2007; Greene, 2002, 2010; Greene & Graham, 2009). There is a growing body of literature on posttraumatic growth which documents the positive changes experienced by survivors (Calhoun and Tedeschi, 2006; Lev-Wiesel & Amir, 2003). In this regard, many survivors of adversity are role models and have much to contribute to this new research direction. Recovery models that focus on the biological, psychological, and social processes of self-healing (Mollica, 2006) are becoming more widespread. In the words of Richard Mollica, a Harvard Medical School professor of psychiatry and director of the Harvard Program in Refugee Trauma:

The concept of self-healing demands a shift away from emphasizing illness and damage to appreciating natural healing processes. Modern healers, like their ancient Greek counterparts, must accept that their job is to aid the human organism's intrinsic drive to recover from the physical and mental injuries caused by violent acts. Self-healing emphasizes resiliency and well-being. In fact, it is precisely because of the self-healing response that relatively few people actually develop pathological and chronic disease states, such as severe PTSD, after violent experiences. As medicine has profited from intensive study of the normal process of physical wound healing, so it could similarly profit from a deeper understanding of the normal processes underlying the healing of trauma's invisible wounds. (245)

Strengths-Based Practice Philosophy

In my interactions with survivors I notice that they respond to their traumatic life events in different ways. While some individuals exhibit strength and resilience in overcoming numerous obstacles and ordeals on an ongoing basis, others remain adversely affected, permanently scarred for life. Still others experience periodic physical and psychological upsets but are able to draw on coping resources to lead productive lives. If anything, surviving the Holocaust has taught them valuable skills in coping with adversity. Many of these skills have served them well throughout the years, and especially today during the last phase of their lives.

Recognizing individual strengths is a core value of the social-work profession. Acknowledging capabilities, competency, and potential is particularly crucial to a survivor's sense of self-worth because it counteracts the negative self-image imposed by victimization. Focusing on pathological inadequacies implies that survivors suffered irreparable damage and are incapable of determining their needs and organizing their lives. Consequently, we may infantilize them, not accept their views, and/or make decisions for them. When we treat survivors as responsible and capable adults who are knowledgeable about their own needs, we encourage them to take the lead in problem solving and decision making when formulating an intervention plan. We respect their wishes and their right to self-determination. Following such an approach recognizes the inherent strengths of individuals and draws on these strengths to aid in the survivor's recovery.

Studies Shifting away from Pathology

A shift away from a focus on pathology began in the 1980s when sociologists and psychologists conducted studies in which sample populations were drawn from the general community, rather than exclusively
from clinics where survivors had turned for help. They found that survivor families have coped quite well with the trauma of the Holocaust.
As a result, more research today is focusing on resilience to trauma in
Holocaust survivors.

In a Montreal study that sought to identify the effects of the Holocaust
on the attitudes and behaviours of Jewish survivors compared with
two Jewish control groups, Weinfeld, Sigal, and Eaton (1981) found insig-
nificant differences on 'measures of perceived anti-Semitism, economic
and political satisfaction, social segregation, economic achievement, and
propensity to migrate from Quebec' (1). They caution against the over-
generalization of the survivor-syndrome construct, and 'point to the
need for further research into the remarkable capacities of human beings to overcome the most severe forms of victimization' (1).

In a study conducted by Leon et al. (1981), where fifty-two survivors
were compared with a control group to evaluate their present-day functioning, the authors found that, even though 81 per cent of survivors
still ruminated about their war experiences, these experiences did not
affect their moods. They were psychologically similar to the control
group. In addition, the study questioned the earlier notions of survivor
guilt, the manifestation of emotional blunting, and the extremely mal-
adaptive psychological influence on the lives of survivors' children.

Porter (1981) describes the socio-political adaptation of the survivor
community of Milwaukee, Wisconsin. He concludes that survivors tend
to live in closely knit communities apart from other Jews; carry on the
same customs and traditions of the 'old country'; and donate their energies to their synagogues, Israeli causes, and the lives of their children
and grandchildren.

In his sociological study of the lives of survivors after the war, based
on an analysis of 236 oral-documentation tapes deposited at the Yad
Vashem Institute in Israel, Helmreich (1987) examined survivor friendship patterns, involvement in the Jewish community, and attitudes towards other minorities. He found that survivors tend to associate with
those who share similar experiences; are actively involved in the Jewish
community – particularly in the area of the Holocaust and support for
Israel; and are liberal in their views towards other minorities.

Helmreich (1988), in an exploratory study of the impact of Holocaust survivors on American society, discovered the following: survivors settled in many different American communities; overcame vocational deficiencies and entered a wide variety of occupations and trades where they did quite well; gave more charity to Jewish causes than non-survivors; founded new communities and, in some instances, resuscitated dying ones into which they transplanted and preserved traditional Jewish culture; formed survivor organizations; generously supported the state of Israel; and raised the level of moral consciousness of the communities in which they settled.

Helmreich (1992) lists the personality traits of Holocaust survivors who adapted successfully to life in the United States: flexibility and adaptation; assertiveness in ensuring that their needs are met; tenacity in achieving goals; a sense of optimism; an ability to transcend their experiences and a determination to go on despite adversity; street-smart intelligence; group consciousness: identification with a particular group bound together by a shared identity as survivors; confidence and self-respect for having lived through a terrible time; an ability to find meaning in life; and a willingness to take risks.

Greene (2002), in qualitative interviews using a resilience-based perspective, interviewed thirteen survivors. She documented the coping behaviours they used to survive the Holocaust and identified factors which contributed to their resilience during and after the war. Themes include: using adaptive strategies to survive; participating in civilian resistance (for example, stealing food when necessary); being a problem solver; making everyday choices, thus maintaining an inner locus of control; thinking positively of themselves; making a conscious decision to go on with their lives after the war; appreciating family and community; and providing testimony about their experiences.

Greene and Graham (2009) present preliminary findings on survivors' perceptions of their resilience before, during, and after the Holocaust. In interviews with 133 survivors between the ages of sixty-eight and ninety-three, the researchers found that a supportive pre-war family environment mitigated their Holocaust experiences and contributed to their resilience. They also identified resilient behaviours during the war such as resolving to live, maintaining family ties and friendships, and employing survival skills. Survivors' life patterns after the war were positive. They married, had children, and established new careers.

In *Transcending Trauma: Survival, Resilience, and Clinical Implications in Survivor Families*, Hollander-Goldfein, Isserman, and Goldenberg (2012) document findings from their qualitative-research study of Holocaust survivors and their families in the Transcending Trauma Project. Over a twenty-year period, they interviewed 95 survivors and their families, totalling 275 individuals, about their coping, adaptation, and resilience. Their findings 'reflect a continuum of variability among survivors and their families in terms of how well they coped' (12) with their traumatic experiences. The researchers identified pre-war foundations of strength and coping skills that aided survivors with their post-war healing. They also found that the majority of survivors they interviewed practised some form of Judaism, were connected to the Jewish community, and used faith and ritual practices to anchor their lives. The authors conclude: 'Resilience can be found within everyone ... it is neither a trait nor an outcome, but rather a process of healing – sometimes over many years' (12).

KEEPING A BALANCED PERSPECTIVE

I do not mean to imply that Holocaust survivors have not suffered negative effects caused by their exposure to severe trauma. Recovering from mass atrocity crimes is a life-long process. The long-term physical and psychological consequences have been documented in numerous studies, articles, and books. Some individuals develop PTSD, a psychological condition characterized by recurrent memories, flashbacks, and nightmares of the traumatic event; avoid reminders of traumatic memories and / or display emotional numbing; and are easily startled or physiologically aroused, which results in sleep disturbances, irritability, angry outbursts, and / or impaired concentration (American Psychiatric Association, 2000). The term 'complex traumatic stress disorder' is used to describe the repetitive and prolonged exposure to traumatic events experienced by prisoners of war, survivors of mass atrocity crimes, and victims of torture, terrorism, and repeated rape and prolonged sexual violence (Courtois & Ford, 2009; Herman, 1992). These psychological conditions are discussed in chapter 5.

   It is impossible to live through mass atrocity and come away unscathed, without long-term consequences. Although not everyone develops full-blown PTSD, most survivors experience one or more of the psychological effects described above. To deny that these effects exist is to deny the victim's ordeals. However, to focus primarily on the pathological aspects in describing the survivor population causes generalizations that do not acknowledge adaptive coping abilities. Both can, and do, coexist.

Ayalon (2005) confirms that, while there is an abundance of research on the pathological aspects of the Holocaust, not enough research has been conducted on survivors' resiliency. She recommends a more balanced view by studying both the pathological and resilient aspects of survivors' experiences. The vulnerability and resilience integrative model developed by Shmotkin (Shmotkin et al., 2011), discussed in chapter 5, is an important step in this direction.

My work with Holocaust survivors has taught me that, for the most part, their emotional and physical wounds do not prevent social functioning. Many people were determined to go on after the war. Their experiences produced important coping skills which served them well both during the war and in the post-war period. In the words of survivors I have worked with:

> 'I wanted to show the enemy they could not destroy us in spite of everything they did.'
> 'As the only member of my family to survive, I had a mission to go on with my life in their memory.'
> 'I wanted to live, get married and have children.'
> 'My will power was strong – maybe there is a reason I survived.'
> 'I persevered. I never gave up. I learned that in Auschwitz. I learned to cope with whatever came my way.'
> 'I had a strong character and ambition.'

Some people have told me privately that time has been their healer. They are embarrassed to say this in front of peers because they fear being accused of betraying the memory of their murdered families and friends. The human psyche is programmed for recovery, healing, and growth (Mollica, 2006). There is no reason to believe this does not hold for survivors of mass atrocity.

My observations of and work with Holocaust survivors confirms this repeatedly. Right from the time of liberation, in 1945, their energies were directed at recovery and the recreation of family and communities. When Jewish and international relief organizations entered the DP camps, they were surprised to find people reconstructing their shattered lives so quickly. Many Holocaust survivors wanted to make up for lost time and were highly motivated to rebuild and get on with their lives. In the words of Dr Leo Srole, the social-welfare officer of United Nations Relief and Rehabilitation Administration (UNRRA) in the Landsberg DP camp: 'The displaced Jews have an almost obsessive will to live normally again, to reclaim their full rights as free men. Their energies and talents have been dramatically exhibited in the vigorous communities they have created in the camps, despite scant material resources and highly abnormal environmental conditions ... It deserves the world's admiration' (Mankowitz, 2002:21). While their emaciated bodies were recovering with adequate nutrition and medical care, they created an extraordinary self-help movement, beginning cultural activities and setting up committees, youth groups, schools, religious institutions, political parties, and sports clubs.

However, survivors continued to be plagued with the physical and psychological effects of their traumatic experiences. These manifested themselves as physical illness, intrusive memories, and distressing emotions such as depression, anxiety, fear, anger, and guilt. Their recovery process is recounted in numerous memorial books that survivors wrote after the war. In May 1945, just a few weeks after liberation, the following article appeared in the Buchenwald newsletter *Techiyat Hamertim* – Resurrection: 'We know there are various questions which torment us and burn (within) ... we are also fully aware that a variety of physical and psychological difficulties have become part of us in the course of the hard times (spent) in the camp ... we lost contact with normal life and it is our demanding goal to find it again! ... We seek to reenter our new lives as healthy and normal people' (Mankowitz, 2002:23).

To this day, many survivors suffer from the physical and psychological consequences of the Holocaust and, at the same time, exhibit adaptive coping behaviours. Both the vulnerabilities and coping skills exist side by side. Recently Mrs K. told me that she feels her Holocaust experiences in 'every bone in her body,' suffering as she does from severe arthritis and depression which cause her to spend several days at a time in bed. She has learned to have patience in the midst of her difficulties, trusting that her 'bad days' will pass. The rest of the time she attends to the activities of daily living, including social interactions with family and friends.

In my work I focus on strengthening and leveraging survivors' coping skills and minimizing limitations and handicaps. Practising from a strengths perspective begins with the premise that every individual, group, family, and community has strengths (positive attributes and abilities, knowledge, resources) which are mobilized to achieve their goals and visions (Saleebey, 2006). The programs and case studies in this book exemplify this approach. Colleagues and social-work students tell me that adopting a strengths-based perspective gives them a fresh outlook on how to understand and work with a survivor population.

PART II

Understanding Survivors

5 Impact of Trauma:
Vulnerability and Resilience

By considering physical, psychological, and social functioning of survivors, we find evidence of both vulnerability and of resilience.
                                                    – B. Kahana, Z. Harel, and E. Kahana (2005)

Before health-care and social-service providers can effectively help survivors, they need to appreciate how survivors differ from people who have not been exposed to a mass atrocity. Prolonged victimization has a psychological affect on the body and mind. As a social worker, I view myself as a generalist and draw upon theoretical frameworks and practice information from diverse disciplines such as social work, medicine, psychology, sociology, and gerontology. I believe it is important to understand the latest developments in the area of trauma research to identify what is relevant and apply it in practice.

Prolonged victimization, however, affects survivors differently. Many have post-traumatic stress (PTS) symptoms, such as depression and anxiety, but do not suffer from full-blown PTSD. A number of studies confirm this observation (Cassel & Suedfeld, 2006), and I notice the same phenomenon in my own practice. Knowing the difference between post-traumatic symptoms and PTSD helps the social worker determine whether to respond with a psycho-social intervention or refer the survivor for medical and/or psychiatric treatment.

In addition to the vulnerabilities, it is necessary to be knowledgeable about health-enhancing factors that help survivors to cope with life's challenges. New information about the impact of trauma on Holocaust survivors is emerging. During the first decades after the war, the focus was on survivors' psychological, physical, and social maladaptation.

Today, more attention is paid to survivors' adaptation, resilience, and strengths. Unfortunately, many studies still focus exclusively on psychopathology while others focus exclusively on resilience and adaptive behaviours. The result is a split 'between positive and negative mental health conceptions, between salutogenic asset thinking and pathogenic disease orientation, often caused by the defenders of a pure sociological or pure medical model in a struggle for territorial monopolies and resources' (Ruiz cited in Almedom, 2005:262). This rift renders a disservice to survivors because it attempts to lump them together in an 'either-or perspective' (Kellerman, 2009), which limits our practice interventions. For example, if we assume that all survivors have chronic PTSD and focus exclusively on their debilitating symptoms, we may fail to assess their ability to cope with their current life situation and / or function socially.

By enhancing my understanding of survivorship, I am able to create and apply a broader range of approaches and interventions to address survivors' needs. Fortunately, there is a wealth of new information from different disciplines that describe both the positive and negative aftermath of trauma. This broader spectrum enables me to be more flexible in my practice. I utilize a balanced perspective that acknowledges survivors' resilience and strengths as well as their physical and psychological vulnerabilities. These states coexist in the majority of individuals I come across. Shmotkin's integrative model of resilience and vulnerability, which is discussed below, corroborates my observation (Shmotkin et al., 2011). When service providers maintain a balanced perspective about psychological effects, they are able to recognize post-traumatic vulnerabilities and use appropriate interventions and / or recognize the role of resilience and modify their approach. Consequently, I include in this discussion both the negative and positive psychological consequences of prolonged victimization as well as the trauma concepts that I find relevant to practice.

TRAUMA THEORY AND PRACTICE

In their comparative study of Holocaust survivors and immigrants in the United States and Israel, Kahana, Harel, and Kahana (2005) found that 'the mental health of the survivors was clearly adversely affected by their traumatic experiences' (98). Psychologist Eva Fogelman (1990) states 'regardless of how one has adjusted, the memory interferes with daily life to a lesser or greater degree' (39). Traumatic memory reverberates throughout an individual's life cycle, often triggered by events such as marriage, divorce, birth, death, illness, and / or old age (Herman, 1992). The Holocaust left an indelible imprint on the conscious and unconscious minds of its survivors. Laufer (1988) suggests that the 'war-self' is 'never able to free itself from the premature encounter with death, or its preoccupation with death and survival' (49). Some feel tainted with death (Lifton, 1968) because boundaries between life and death merged, especially in the ghettos and concentration camps. In the words of Elie Wiesel, Nobel laureate and Holocaust survivor: 'For the survivor death is not the problem. Death was an everyday occurrence. We learned to live with death. The problem is to adjust to life, to living. You must teach us about living' (Krell, 1989:216).

The resolution of trauma for survivors is never final, and recovery is never complete (Herman, 1992). Healing can be difficult because it requires accomplishing psychic tasks such as creating a sense of rootedness, belonging, and continuity with the past; working through losses, guilt, rage, and shame; and meaningfully integrating the experience into the totality of life (Danieli, 1981). The therapeutic goal attempts to ensure that the traumatic event no longer commands a central place in survivors' lives (Herman, 1992). Integrating Holocaust experiences may not be a realistic goal, however, because it may take more than one lifetime or generation to grieve the magnitude of a person's losses. In fact, Danieli (1981) asserts it should not be surprising that ageing survivors are unable to integrate the Holocaust into the totality of their life experience. 'Humanity, Western culture, and society in general have not yet integrated the Holocaust ... to expect survivors, who are hindered by a variety of factors, to accomplish this task in their old age with their diminishing capacities, may be expecting the impossible' (200).

Post-Traumatic Stress Disorder

During the last three decades, thousands of articles have been written about the stress responses of individuals who are exposed to terrifying, uncontrollable event(s) that overwhelm their sense of security and safety. People who are exposed to such events are at increased risk of developing PTSD (Yehuda, 2002), which is the most commonly used diagnosis. In 1980 PTSD was included in the DSM-III, the Diagnostic and Statistical Manual of Mental Disorders of the American Psychiatric Association.

The DSM-IV (American Psychiatric Association, 2000) lists the main elements of PTSD: 'The person experienced, witnessed, or was confronted with an event or events that involved actual or threatened death or serious injury, or a threat to the physical integrity of self or others, and the person's response involved intense fear, helplessness, or horror' (209). These reactions can be psychological as well as physical. The cardinal symptoms of PTSD include:

1. re-experiencing the traumatic event through intrusive recollections, nightmares, flashbacks, internal and / or environmental triggers;
2. avoiding any reminders of the traumatic event(s) and / or emotional numbing evidenced by behaviours such as diminished interest, detachment from others, restricted feelings, and inability to recall aspects of the trauma; and
3. increased physiological arousal resulting in sleep disturbances, irritability, outbursts of anger, impaired concentration, hypervigilance, and exaggerated startle responses.

PTSD is diagnosed when these symptoms last more than one month and cause impairment in areas such as one's job and social relationships. If symptoms last less than three months, the condition is diagnosed as acute PTSD; if the symptoms last longer, the condition is diagnosed as chronic PTSD. Delayed-onset PTSD is diagnosed when symptoms develop six months or more after the traumatic event.

Initially, Holocaust survivors were not included among populations who experienced PTSD (Kellerman, 2009). References to PTSD were also absent from the vast literature on Holocaust survivors published during the 1980s (Yehuda & Giller, 1994). Kellerman (2009) observes that a shift became apparent in the early 1990s; since then, 'clinicians and researchers ... have become less opposed to diagnosing Holocaust survivors with PTSD' (35). He attributes this change to the lobbying efforts of Dr Henry Krystal, one of the leading pioneers in treating Holocaust survivors, and to Drs Rachel Yehuda and Earl Giller.

Researchers have now discovered that between 39 per cent and 65 per cent of Holocaust survivors develop PTSD. Yehuda et al. (1998) state that traumatic 'events associated with torture or prolonged victimization are associated with the highest estimates for chronic PTSD' (1306). Chronic PTSD is evident in 50 per cent of prisoners of war and concentration-camp survivors, in contrast to about 4 per cent of survivors of natural disasters (Yehuda et al., 1998). Kellerman (2009), citing Dasberg, reports that between 39 per cent and 65 per cent of elderly Holocaust survivors developed PTSD fifty years after the end of the Holocaust. Yehuda et al. (1998) point out, however, that PTSD is not an inevitable outcome of severe and prolonged traumatic events because a large number of individuals recover and do not develop the disorder.

Complex Post-Traumatic Stress Disorder

Soon after PTSD was included in the DSM-III, many clinicians realized that the new diagnosis did not encompass the experience of all traumatized individuals (Sykes Wylie, March / April 2010). In response, Judith Herman and Bessel van der Kolk proposed a new diagnostic concept, 'complex PTSD' or 'disorders of extreme stress not otherwise specified (DESNOS),' to address the experiences and personality changes of survivors of prolonged and repeated trauma, which includes: 'victims of political repression, genocide, "ethnic cleansing," torture, or displacement' (Courtois & Ford, 2009:17). Although complex PTSD did not make its way into the DSM-IV as a separate diagnostic entity, it appears as an associated feature of PTSD. The cardinal symptoms as described in Courtois et al. (2009:85–6) are:

1. 'Alterations in the regulation of affective impulses,' including overwhelming emotional distress, self-destructiveness, difficulty modulating anger;
2. 'Alterations in attention and consciousness,' resulting in amnesias and dissociative episodes and depersonalization;
3. 'Alterations in self-perception,' such as impaired self-concept, feelings of shame, guilt, self blame, being damaged;
4. 'Alterations in perception of the perpetrator,' such as taking on the perpetrator's views or feeling a sympathetic bond with the perpetrator;
5. 'Alterations in relationship to others,' which includes an inability to trust or feel intimate with others;
6. 'Somatization and / or medical problems' that relate to the type of abuse suffered and resulting physical damage; pain or physical symptoms that cannot be medically explained; and
7. 'Alterations in systems of meaning,' including sense of hopelessness and despair, loss of faith.

Complex psychological trauma differs from PTSD in that traumatic experiences are ongoing and repetitive rather than time-limited. This diagnosis is especially relevant to survivors of war and may apply to survivors of genocide who experience numerous psychological and physical indignities over an extended period. Kahana, Kahana, Harel, and Rosner (1988:59) identify five environmental aspects of prolonged exposure to war which distinguish it from other man-made disasters:

1. 'The total life experience is disrupted' with conditions that have a surrealistic existence, 'unanchored in familiar elements of reality.'
2. 'The new environment is extremely hostile, threatening, and dangerous.'
3. 'Opportunities to remove or act upon the stressor environment are severely limited.'
4. 'There is no predictable end to the experience.'
5. 'The pain and suffering associated with the experience appear to be meaningless and without rational explanation.'

Other Disorders Linked to PTSD

PTSD may overlap with a number of other disorders listed in the DSM-IV-TR. These include: Major Depressive Disorder, Substance-Related Disorders, Panic Disorder, Agoraphobia, Obsessive-Compulsive Disorder, Generalized Anxiety Disorder, Social Phobia, Specific Phobia, and Bipolar Disorder (American Psychiatric Association, 2000).

Kellerman (2009) points out that the associated symptom of PTSD most common to Holocaust survivors is depression. He suggests that chronic PTSD, with depression as a frequent associated symptom, is the most suitable diagnosis for a clinical population of survivors. I have also observed generalized anxiety and hyperarousal symptoms, such as irritability and outbursts of anger, among the survivors with whom I have worked. Individuals who experience massive trauma may be filled with anger and rage and can behave aggressively (this is discussed further in chapter 15). An interesting phenomenon is the low incidence of substance abuse in this population (Yehuda et al., 1996).

Yehuda et al. (1994) studied depressive symptoms in non-treatment-seeking Holocaust survivors with and without PTSD. They found that Holocaust survivors with PTSD also showed a greater degree of depression and a wider array of depressive symptoms. A more recent study in a non-psychiatric primary-care clinic contrasted depressed survivors, non-depressed survivors, and older depressed non-survivors (Trappler et al., 2007). It found that the prevalence of depression and PTSD was very high among survivors; depressed survivors had significantly worse psychological and social functioning than depressed non-survivors; and depressed survivors had more PTSD symptoms than non-depressed survivors. Severely depressed survivors are at high risk for suicidal ideation and suicide attempts (Kellerman, 2009).

Limitations of a PTSD Diagnosis

As important as PTSD is in identifying the symptoms associated with traumatic events, it has its critics. Some authors say that research became more focused and at the same time more limited to psychopathology after PTSD was introduced as a diagnostic category (Brom et al., 2002). According to Brom et al. (2002), 'the almost automatic association between trauma and PTSD has diverted attention from the possibility that totally different responses or response patterns, such as personality changes, exist as well' (198). Kellerman (2009) discusses the limitations of applying any diagnostic label, including PTSD, when describing a mixed clinical population. He points out that trauma evokes a wide variety of psychological symptoms 'and responses to trauma should perhaps be better understood within a spectrum of conditions rather than as a single, well-defined disorder' (41). He describes the following clinical manifestations of Holocaust trauma observed in survivors: sleep disturbances, intrusive memories, anxiety, and complicated grief. Depressive symptoms include excessive crying, self-reproach, helplessness, overt pessimism, suicidal ideation and suicide attempts, cognitive problems, concentration difficulties, forgetfulness, irritability, loss of appetite, lack of energy, aches and pains, and fatigue.

It is important to keep in mind that a diagnosis of PTSD is only one possible response to traumatic exposure. It presents a clinical profile that does not take into account individual differences, nor does it incorporate a biographical summary of the survivor's trauma history. In addition, this diagnosis does not assess how different cultures respond to catastrophic events (Wilson & Tang, 2007). Consequently, using PTSD as a primary diagnosis emphasizes pathology and does not acknowledge the ability to function socially which may exist alongside the psychiatric symptoms, even within a clinical population. Encouraging active involvement in social activities can help alleviate post-traumatic symptoms. The following case summary exemplifies this point.

* * *

Mr G., a seventy-five-year-old survivor of the Łódź Ghetto and Auschwitz, began to exhibit post-traumatic depressive symptoms after his retirement. His work had provided him with structure and his 'good provider role' enhanced his self-worth and self-esteem. After retiring, however, he began to ask himself: 'Who am I?' When his depressive symptoms intensified, his family doctor referred him to the psychogeriatric clinic of a local hospital for evaluation. The psychiatrist diagnosed chronic PTSD with co-morbid depression manifested by sleeplessness, difficulty concentrating, and severe anhedonia. Mr G. was treated with medication that did not alleviate his depression. Subsequently, his daughter referred him to the Drop-in Centre (discussed in chapter 11). When Mr G. entered the program, it was evident he was clinically depressed. He exhibited a sad and flat affect, had concentration difficulties, was irritable, and did not interact with the other members. He was prone to anxiety manifested by excessive worry. During his bio-psycho-social assessment, however, I learned he was coping well with his traumatic Holocaust experiences. For example, he was able to speak about them with his wife (also a survivor), his children, and his grandchildren. He had also been an active member of a *landsmanschaft* where he found his sense of community and belonging. However, he stopped being active after his retirement. With the support of group members and individual counselling, Mr G. was encouraged to replace work with new meaningful activities. He continued to attend the program and began to engage in new activities of daily living. For example, he helped his wife with their weekly shopping, forced himself to socialize with his friends at the local shopping centre, and entertained his children and grandchildren at Friday night family dinners. He became active in his *landsmanschaft* again and helped organize many of its functions. He and his wife began to spend several months during the winter in Florida. As he began to adjust to his new life stage, his depression eventually diminished, and he was able to discontinue medication.

* * *

Practice Implications for Health-Care and Social-Service Providers

Exploring PTSD When Diagnosing Symptoms

As previously noted, Holocaust survivors are approaching social-service agencies more frequently for assistance. Many are doing so for the first time. It is therefore important that social workers have knowledge about PTSD because survivors may describe symptoms such as intrusive memories, sleeplessness, nightmares, anxiety, and difficulty concentrating. They may benefit from a referral to a community psycho-social program, a specialized clinic for a geriatric assessment (discussed below), or a medical practitioner for pharmacological treatment. I notice that some survivors have never been examined by a medical doctor or cannot find a family doctor to treat them. This can be exacerbated if there is a shortage or unavailability of general practitioners.

PTSD symptoms in older persons are often overlooked, misunderstood, misdiagnosed, and / or incorrectly treated (Graziano, 2003). 'PTSD is often misdiagnosed as schizophrenia, alcoholism, antisocial personality disorder, or depression' (Graziano, 2003:7). Yehuda (2002) explains that, since trauma survivors are more likely to visit medical practitioners for help in alleviating symptoms, the latter play an important role in identifying and treating PTSD. Unfortunately, they often misdiagnose PTSD because of its comorbidity with other symptoms, especially depression and anxiety. She explains that medical practitioners are often reluctant to ask their patients questions about distressing, shameful, or secretive events that may be underlying their depression and anxiety (for example, heart palpitations, shortness of breath, tremors, nausea, mood swings, unexplained pain, and so on). Patients usually do not mention these issues without prompting. However, when patients are provided with the opportunity to disclose these events, their otherwise unexplained physical symptoms and / or behaviours can be legitimized and treated appropriately.

Focusing exclusively on psychological symptoms and not linking them to historical traumatic events omits important biographical information and may lead to a misdiagnosis of PTSD. The following case demonstrates the importance of medical practitioners asking Holocaust survivors about their war experiences and recording them in their files.

* * *

Mrs R. was referred to a group I was organizing by a social worker in a local hospital. Her psychiatric evaluation indicated symptoms of anxiety, depression, sleep disturbances, and hallucinations. She was treated with psychiatric medication. There was no mention of her war history in her referral to the program, although she was a Holocaust survivor. Mrs R.'s symptoms were caused by flashbacks of her traumatic experiences in the Warsaw Ghetto, Majdanek, and Auschwitz but were misdiagnosed as hallucinations. When I asked her why she did not describe the content of her flashbacks to her doctor, she responded, 'I was not asked.'

* * *

Health professionals must be knowledgeable about symptoms that can be caused by traumatic exposure and investigate this possibility because ageing survivor patients may not volunteer information about their past. Within the safety of the group, Mrs R. spoke for the first time about what she went through during the Holocaust. Eventually her flashbacks and symptoms diminished and she was able to discontinue medication. This case summary reinforces the importance of exploring if an individual has a traumatic history to avoid misdiagnosing PTSD symptoms as something else.

Investigating Other Medical Conditions Which May Appear as Post-Traumatic Stress Symptoms

It is important to refer survivors to medical practitioners for examination to rule out medical conditions that may appear as post-traumatic symptoms. This is especially important for survivors who have never been examined by a doctor. Some medical conditions may be causing or contributing to their symptoms. For example, thyroid problems, urinary infections, drug interactions, and vitamin deficiencies can cause confusion. Signs of dementia (such as personality and mood changes, impaired concentration and memory, diminished interest, social isolation) can be misconstrued as PTS symptoms in survivors. I also notice that survivors' depression may be due to present-day challenges and physiological changes associated with ageing. All of these factors must be considered because not all survivor symptoms are related to post-traumatic stress.

I refer individuals to community walk-in clinics if they do not have a medical practitioner. In addition, if they are open to it, I send them for a geriatric assessment at a local hospital. Many hospitals have outpatient geriatric assessment clinics with multidisciplinary teams that include geriatricians, nurses, occupational and physiotherapists, and social workers – all dedicated to geriatric medicine. For example, workers at the Community Geriatric Assessment Clinic of the Sir Mortimer B. Davis – Jewish General Hospital (JGH) (Jewish General Hospital, Division of Geriatric Medicine, 2011) conduct home visits that benefit Holocaust survivors whose traumatic memories may be triggered in a hospital setting. Assessments are also done in conjunction with psychogeriatric and memory clinics. The Jewish General Hospital / McGill Memory Clinic is a specialized diagnostic service for the evaluation and treatment of dementia. It may be necessary to arrange accompaniment to these clinics, especially for survivors who have no family to support them. Canada has a universal health-care insurance plan that may provide these services free of charge.

Determining Eligibility for Services May Trigger Emotional Arousal in Survivors with PTS or PTSD

The Claims Conference allocates funds from the German government and other sources to agencies around the world for specialized services and programs. Some of these funds provide emergency assistance to qualifying survivors. When survivors contact agencies by telephone to inquire about these programs, service providers may ask questions about their financial situation and war experiences to assess their eligibility. Questions about war experiences may trigger emotional arousal in survivors regardless of whether they have been diagnosed with PTS or PTSD. However, these symptoms are more pronounced in survivors who have PTSD. They may have difficulty modulating their emotions when they get off the telephone, especially if they live alone and have no one to talk to about their interview experience. Service providers must identify these vulnerable survivors and should not ask them to disclose information about their war experiences over the telephone.

A survivor's state of readiness to talk about the Holocaust can be assessed in the following manner. After providing a brief overview of the program or fund, a worker should first inquire about the survivor's financial eligibility. If the survivor qualifies, the worker should then ask permission to move on to questions about his / her Holocaust experience(s), for example: 'I'd like to ask you some questions about where you were during the Holocaust. Is this all right with you? Are you comfortable doing this over the telephone?' If the survivor hesitates and is silent, or makes comments such as 'It's hard for me to talk about it,' 'I've never told anyone about my experiences,' or 'I've been diagnosed with PTSD,' then the worker should not proceed over the telephone. Instead, a face-to-face meeting should be scheduled, either at the agency or in the survivor's home, to continue the eligibility assessment. It is also important to note that many survivors are able to answer these questions over the telephone with minimal difficulty.

Interaction between Trauma and Ageing

There is evidence that a large number of older persons experience harmful physical, social, and psychological effects from exposure to mass atrocities (Cook, 2002). As lifespans increase, a growing number of twentieth-century mass atrocity survivors are reaching the last stage of their lives. This 'has led some researchers to call traumatic exposure and its effects "hidden variables" in the lives of older adults' (Cook, 2002:149). Several articles discuss the lack of information available about the impact of trauma on older persons (Graziano, 2003; Lapp et al., 2011). Although this may be true in the gerontological literature, there is considerable information available in other disciplines, especially psychology and sociology, about ageing Holocaust survivors. This information needs to be incorporated into the gerontological literature to help service providers improve their understanding and skills.

There is conflicting evidence about the vulnerability of older people to traumatic events that occurred decades earlier (Kahana, Harel, & Kahana, 2005). However, I believe there is enough research and observations in the fields of psychology, social work, and medicine that identify common issues which practitioners should be aware of. Although health-care and social-service professionals are often the first in the system to meet with these older survivors, they may be unfamiliar with some of the behaviours and symptoms caused by their traumatic exposure. Much of the information about the association between trauma and ageing originates from studies of Holocaust survivors and combat veterans. In chapter 7 I discuss the impacts of ageing that are specific to Holocaust survivors. In this chapter I discuss common issues that may inform the practice of service providers when working with older adults who have trauma histories.

Developmental Issues Related to Ageing

The normal changes associated with the ageing process affect trauma survivors differently. Retirement, death of a spouse, family members, and friends, loss of autonomy, illness, relocation, and limited financial resources may cause feelings of powerlessness. In turn, these feelings may awaken or exacerbate post-traumatic-stress symptoms caused by the survivor's trauma history. They can manifest as intrusive recollections, sleep disturbances, and increased anxiety (Brodsky Cohen, 1991; Danieli, 1994a, 1994b; Ehrlich, 1988; Giberovitch, 1995, 1999; Kahana, Harel, & Kahana, 2005; Rosenbloom, 1983, 1985; Safford, 1995; Sherwood et al., 2004). For example, entering a hospital or long-term residence, becoming disabled, or developing dementia may trigger additional distress originating in the survivor's traumatic experience.

Delayed-Onset PTSD

Individuals who coped adequately during years of symptom-free living may suddenly, in the last phase of their lives, experience post-traumatic symptoms such as intrusive memories and nightmares about their wartime trauma. This is referred to as delayed-onset PTSD. This term was coined to describe Vietnam War veterans who developed the first onset of PTSD symptoms in later life (Colerick Clipp & Elder, 1996). Age-associated losses, a weakening of defences or coping skills, a loss of structure provided by work, or environmental triggers can reactivate memories that were dormant for years (Aarts et al., 1996).

Environmental Triggers

Being exposed to environmental triggers, which are reminders of the original trauma, can activate traumatic memories and unresolved conflicts. Colerick Clipp and Elder (1996) describe a fifty-five-year-old veteran who developed PTSD after he saw a deceased ten-year-old boy in the emergency room. This incident reminded him of an incident in the South Pacific where he was forced to shoot a boy, also aged ten or so, because he suspected the Japanese had wired the child as a human bomb. Chapter 14 discusses a variety of situations and events that may trigger memories of persecution in Holocaust survivors.

Identifying Older Adults at Risk for Re-emergence
of Traumatic Stress Symptoms

In addition to becoming acquainted with potential vulnerabilities of ageing for trauma survivors, it is important to identify these individuals since they may not self-disclose. Graziano (2003) identifies older adults who may be at risk for the re-emergence of traumatic stress symptoms. Her partial list includes: survivors of interpersonal violence; individuals who served in combat, including prisoners of war; immigrants from countries where they experienced war, ethnic cleansing, political torture, and other forms of violence; and survivors of natural and human-made disasters.

Regardless of the setting, service providers encounter older trauma survivors on a daily basis. It is clear from the literature that vulnerabilities associated with ageing may be re-traumatizing for many individuals. Knowing about the association between ageing and trauma helps us to identify individuals who may be at risk in different settings and helps us respond better to their needs. In the process we learn about the indomitable human spirit and its ability to survive and thrive.

NEUROSCIENCE DISCOVERIES

The Neurobiology of Trauma

Over the last two decades neuroscience research has shown that exposure to extreme stress affects brain function. PTSD produces long-term neurobiological changes in the brain (van der Kolk, 1996a; 2006). Imaging technologies such as Magnetic Resonance Imaging (MRI), Positron Emission Tomography (PET scan), and Functional Magnetic Resonance Imaging (fMRI) localize parts of the brain, primarily the amygdala and hippocampus areas (associated with fear and memory), which are affected by traumatic stress.

Neuropsychology and neuroimaging research demonstrate that traumatized individuals have difficulty modulating their intense emotions. When confronted with a life-threatening traumatic event, the brain's limbic system (hypothalamus, hippocampus, amygdala, and other parts) and the sympathetic nervous system release hormones that prepare the body to fight or flee to deal with the stressor. A number of physiological responses occur in the body: muscles tense; heart rate accelerates, blood pressure rises, and breathing quickens; vision and hearing become more acute; and the adrenal glands secrete hormones which fuel the flight or fight response. This prepares the body to respond to the traumatic event. When the threat is perceived as extreme or prolonged, and running away is not possible, a third response may occur. This is described as freezing or 'going dead,' which numbs the body so it feels less pain when faced with imminent death (Rothschild, 2000:11). This may explain the psychic numbing and catatonic state observed in some concentration- and death-camp inmates. They were called *muselmen* – the walking dead – and most died soon after entering this state.

People who freeze during a traumatic event have greater difficulty coming to terms with it than those who fought back or escaped (Rothschild, 2003). They are also more apt to develop PTSD. Traumatic memories are believed to be stored in the unconscious non-verbal implicit memory system of the brain as emotional states, physical sensations, and visual and auditory images (van der Kolk, 1996b). These memories tend 'to be dissociated, and to be stored initially as sensory fragments that have no linguistic components' (van der Kolk, 1996b:289). Implicit memories are not specific to the time and space in which they originally happened. 'They seem to float freely, often invading the present' (Rothschild, 2003:11). This may explain why many Holocaust survivors are unable to verbalize traumatic experiences that may be trapped in their implicit memory. Consequently, they may have strong automatic reactions to triggers or cues in their present environment that cause them to re-experience their original traumatic event(s) as flashbacks or intrusive images.

For traumatic memory to be integrated, it must make its way to the conscious, explicit, declarative part of the brain. The explicit memory 'enables the telling of the story of one's life, narrating events, putting experiences into words, constructing a chronology, [and] extracting a meaning' (Rothschild, 2000:29). Byington (2007) describes this process as having three stages. In the first stage, individuals are taught to calm their arousal levels and feel safe in their environment. The second stage consists of moving the memories from implicit to explicit storage by weaving the sensory fragments together into a personal narrative. The last stage consists of finding and attaching meaning to the experience. The trauma-recovery model discussed in chapter 11 describes interventions and activities that support this process.

These findings underscore the importance of creating opportunities for survivors to talk about their past through oral-history projects, memoir writing, and intergenerational dialogue programs. In *Opening Up: The Healing Power of Confiding in Others*, clinical psychologist James Pennebaker (1990) confirms that oral testimony is a psychologically beneficial experience for most survivors. His research found that survivors who participated in oral-history projects were significantly healthier the year after the interview than before.

The Brain's Plasticity

Neuroscience research reveals important information about the brain's plasticity. Until the 1980s and early 1990s, scientists believed the brain became hardened or static once it reached maturity. Neuroscience research during the past twenty-five years demonstrates otherwise. Farmer (2009) discusses the two elements of this plasticity: the brain changes throughout the life cycle and it is altered and shaped by ongoing experiences. This is especially evident in individuals who suffer damage from PTSD. However, the brain can continue to regenerate and rewire itself in response to environmental factors such as social support. Interpersonal relationships with family, friends, and social-service professionals can create new synaptic connections that change neural circuits in the brain and help repair the damage.

Implications for the Therapeutic Relationship

Dan Siegel's (2006) field of interpersonal neurobiology emphasizes the social nature of the brain and demonstrates the importance of connections to other people to regulate the body and balance emotional states. As he puts it: 'The structure of our neural architecture reveals that we need connections to other people to feel in balance and to develop well' (Siegel, 2006:254). This research bridges the gap between neuroscience and clinical practice. It has clinical implications that can significantly affect the therapeutic relationship. As health-care and mental-health professionals, we understand the importance of establishing a safe and trusting therapeutic relationship (discussed in chapter 13) with individuals who turn to us for assistance in dealing with their difficult challenges. The 'neuroscientific revolution' provides scientific support for our focus on this therapeutic alliance. In the words of Rosemary Farmer (2009), 'neuroscience is the missing link for understanding what makes the therapeutic relationship curative and effective' (122).

Brain-science research is also identifying therapeutic interventions that may influence the brain's ability to form new connections. One such example is the emerging social-cognitive neuroscience research on empathy and the role of mirror neurons (Gerdes & Segal, 2011). Mirror neurons are a class of cells in the brain that fire equally when an individual performs an action and when they observe someone else perform the same action. Neuroscientists believe that mirroring helps us understand the intentions of others and connect emotionally with them (Farmer, 2009).

In the therapeutic relationship, this consists of our connecting with individuals and them with us. As we listen intently to their story, we communicate the message that we are joined with them. We observe the unfolding of their subjective experience by noticing their tone of voice, words, and body language. As we empathize with them, our words and body language show that their story has touched us and we understand their feelings. This process entails 'putting ourselves into our clients' shoes' and feeling their feelings without being overwhelmed by them. During this interactive experience, individuals 'feel felt' and 'may establish new neural net firing patterns that can lead to neural plastic changes' which help them to modulate their intense feelings and enhance well-being (Siegel, 2006:255–6). As Gerdes and Segal (2011) state: 'Clients experiencing empathy through treatment have improved outcomes' (141).

As a practitioner, I observe that empathic listening skills are at times more important than the type of therapeutic approach used. Survivors respond positively to a relationship that is warm, caring, and authentic. These attributes, I wish to add, are not exclusive to mental-health professionals. In our Drop-in Centre, survivors feel cared for and listened to by volunteers, students, and guests. Often I hear comments from survivors such as, 'Thank you for listening to me. I know you care.' Most of the time, empathic listening works to calm their arousal, as often occurs when survivors return to the program after a week's absence. Finally, neuroscience research has confirmed the effectiveness of this therapeutic skill.

Service providers benefit from knowing about the workings of the brain in a number of ways. First, it enhances our knowledge about the impact of trauma on the body and mind and our understanding of human behaviour. Research from neuroscience helps us to understand that PTSD produces long-term neurobiological changes in the brain, especially hyper-arousal. Researchers can actually see the parts of the brain that have been affected by the emotional states of the individuals we work with. Also, as Siegel (Sykes Wylie, 2004) suggests, when we share this information with our clients, it is comforting and therapeutic. It also empowers them. For example, when survivors tell me about their intrusive recollections, I respond now by noting that 'brain science confirms what you are experiencing.' This is more powerful and effective than the kind of statement I used to make: 'Your responses are a normal and natural for people who survived the atrocities you did; and others are also experiencing these symptoms.' Survivors feel better knowing there is actual neurobiological proof. We can also share information about brain science with survivors' families. Survivors feel validated by such information, which also helps adult children be more sensitive to their parents' symptoms, such as chronic anxiety.

Second, this knowledge guides us to serve our clients better by paying attention to the skills we use and integrating them more mindfully into practice. We become more cautious when asking survivors about their war experiences, especially those who come into our offices already in an agitated state. For example, during trauma work, we can help calm their arousal by using and teaching relaxation techniques (discussed in chapter 13). We also understand the importance of empathy. The scientific information about mirror neurons generating new synaptic connections in the brain encourages us to pay more attention to the benefits of the therapeutic relationship, especially empathic listening. Practitioners have always used empathic skills to join with clients and demonstrate an understanding of their feelings. However, the science behind this intervention is new: the use of empathic skills can actually generate new synaptic connections in the brain. This information supports empathic connection with individuals and motivates exploration of other contexts, such as groups, in which it can be applied. In addition, when we display empathy towards our clients, it helps them to develop their own empathic responses and apply them in their personal relationships (for example, empathic listening, acts of kindness, compassion, and so on). Finally, brain science validates the benefits of the therapeutic relationship in helping individuals handle difficult challenges by providing them with social support.

PSYCHOLOGICAL WELL-BEING IN SURVIVORS

Many survivors are emotionally and psychologically fit. Researchers and clinicians (Almedom, 2005; Kahana, Harel, & Kahana, 2005; Kellerman, 2009; Sigal, 1998) present a variety of explanations to account for the psychological well-being found in a significant number of survivors.

The Intrapsychic Dimension

Some individuals are able to distance themselves from their experiences by using defences such as intellectualization and repression to deal with their strong emotions (Helmreich, 1992; Sigal, 1998). In so doing they are able to compartmentalize their experiences and set them aside so they can engage in their activities of daily living.

Factors That Preceded Persecution

Sigal (1998) puts forth another explanation that focuses on factors that preceded persecution. Besides active wartime coping and post-war care, he suggests that pre-war personality and family environment may explain the resilient traits observed in studies of child survivors. Along these lines, Kellerman (2009) argues that, since survivors were healthy before the war and a majority recuperated well afterwards, they likely were strong and resilient to begin with. 'Thus, a robust biological constitution is often a prerequisite for both survival and longevity' (Shrira et al., 2011:68). Kahana, Harel, & Kahana (2005) point to 'selective long-term survival of those with the greatest resiliency and personality resources prior to the trauma' (105). These perspectives suggest that survivors' pre-existing personalities, resilient traits, and health had an impact on their long-term survival.

The Inoculation Effect

The inoculation effect suggests that survivors of previous trauma become stronger and better able to deal with subsequent adversity (Kahana, Harel, & Kahana, 2005; Shrira & Palgi et al., 2010). This concept is based on the observation that the majority of traumatized people show resilience and post-traumatic growth based on their strengths and coping abilities (Shrira & Palgi et al., 2010).

The Salutogenic Approach

The salutogenic approach emphasizes survivors' psychological strength, self-confidence, courage, insight, and growth in overcoming traumatic experiences (Cassel & Suedfeld, 2006). Aaron Antonovsky (1993), a medical sociologist, developed the salutogenic theoretical model (origins of health) in 1979 as a complement to the pathogenic orientation (disease causing) that dominated biomedical and social-science disease research at the time. He identified the 'generalized resistance resources' individuals across cultures use to cope successfully with their traumatic experiences. These resources include: 'individual identity (ego), intelligence / knowledge, social ties, sense of control, material assets, cultural stability, stable values and beliefs, genetic predispositions and a sense of coherence (SOC)' (Almedom, 2005:255).

The Long-Term Healing Process

Positive long-term outcomes may be attributed to the long-term healing process, which is viewed differently by clinical psychologists and social scientists. For example, whereas clinical psychologists may attribute these positive outcomes to the regenerative powers of the ego, sociologists or social psychologists point to the healing powers of social integration and support, and / or finding meaning in adversity (Kahana, Harel, & Kahana, 2005).

Environmental Factors and Supportive Social and Cultural Environments

These factors enhance survivors' psychological well-being and adaptation and may mitigate the impact of their traumatic experiences. They are discussed in chapter 6.

Personality Traits

Survivors' psychological well-being may be explained by personality traits: expectation of personal efficacy; hardiness; and resilience. Expectation of personal efficacy, or mastery, influences an individual's ability to handle difficult situations (Bandura, 1977). These individuals are confident in their ability to control their environment. Hardiness is another personality trait that buffers the effects of stressful events (Kobasa et al., 1982). Hardy individuals are committed to find meaning and purpose in life; believe in their ability to influence events by using their imagination, knowledge, and skills; and feel confident that they can transform themselves by learning and growing from their experiences. These hardy personality traits can be observed in Holocaust survivors during their journey of recovery in the post-war years (discussed in chapters 2 and 4). The third personality trait, resilience, is discussed below.

Resilience

Resilience is the ability of a person, group, or community 'to overcome adversity by using a variety of adaptive behaviors' (Cohen et al., 2010:531). Ayalon (2005), citing the literature, discusses individual and social resources associated with resilience. Individual characteristics include intelligence; positive temperament; sociability; communication skills; beliefs in internal control; self-efficacy; a sense of coherence, hardiness, and optimism; and active problem solving. Social factors include 'positive parent-child attachment, parental warmth, family cohesion, close relationships with caring adults, social support, nonpunitive social environments, and supportive communities' (349–50). She also identifies factors specific to the resilience of Holocaust survivors that include personality characteristics, war experience and conditions, and post-war adaptation, especially the social environment.

During the last decade there have been 'many studies attesting to the resilience of survivors of trauma, genocide, and persecution' (Cassel & Suedfeld, 2006:223; Suedfeld et al., 2005). Rather than a trait, Greene and Graham (2009) define resilience as a process that evolves over time; it encompasses the life course and the social structures and historical events that individuals experience. They identify adaptive pre-war, wartime, and post-war behaviours that contribute to survivors' resilience. The factors they cite include: coming from a warm and supportive pre-war family environment; engaging in resilient behaviours during the war such as surviving in groups and helping each other; and rebuilding their lives after the war by creating families, developing careers, and leading productive lives. Kahana, Harel, and Kahana (2005) point to the resilience of survivors in areas such as social functioning and achievements. These achievements include transmission of humanitarian values and a commitment to bear witness to the Holocaust 'with the explicit purpose of protecting humankind from repeated acts of genocide or experiences of inhumanity' (140).

AN INTEGRATIVE MODEL OF RESILIENCE AND VULNERABILITY

Based on empirical findings from large community samples of Holocaust survivors, Dov Shmotkin's research concludes: 'Impairment and suffering that follow trauma do not preclude concurrently restorative and successful adjustment' (Shmotkin et al., 2011). Using resilience as a theoretical construct, this model posits that 'the resilience of older survivors is manifested in a wide range of capabilities that enable them to lead basically normal lives as compared with people who did not experience the Holocaust' (Shmotkin et al., 2011:8). Survivors rebuilt their lives and many reached old age. This demonstrates that their survival skills and accomplishments may have facilitated their ability to cope with late-life challenges. Studies of survivors who live to old age (75+) indicate that they do not differ from control groups in physical and cognitive functioning (Shrira et al., 2011; Shmotkin et al., 2011). Their durability is also reflected in mortality studies that find that survivors in late life showed mortality risks similar to those of their non-survivor counterparts. On the other hand, this research demonstrates that older survivors' psycho-social vulnerabilities, which manifest in post-traumatic symptoms such as intrusive memories, sleep disturbances, and other forms of emotional distress, are often triggered by environmental factors and illness. For example, traumatic events such as the first Persian Gulf War, the terrorist attacks on the United States on 11 September 2001, and developing cancer caused greater distress in Holocaust survivors than in other individuals their age who did not experience the Holocaust (Shmotkin et al., 2011). Other vulnerabilities consist of the difficulty in experiencing joy, a sense of helplessness, symptoms of PTSD, depressive symptoms, and less engagement in leisure and social activities (Shrira et al., 2011). These findings are consistent with my own observations of survivors living in the community.

6 Environmental Factors That Reduce the Impact of Trauma

When my husband was alive, every night after supper we would have our cup of tea and remember the old country, and talk about our war experiences. Who wants to listen to me today?

— Auschwitz survivor

FACTORS THAT MITIGATE SURVIVORS' TRAUMA SYMPTOMS

Social workers can assist survivors with their psycho-social adjustment by having knowledge of post-traumatic factors that may mitigate the impact of trauma. Kahana, Harel, and Kahana (1988; 2005) identified factors that influenced survivors' psychological well-being and adaptation during their studies of survivor populations in the United States, Canada, and Israel. These factors were gleaned from coping strategies which survivors employed and which aided in their recovery during the post-war years. The researchers observed that the ability of an individual to cope with extreme stress is affected not only by the nature and duration of the stress experiences but also by personality traits, cumulative life experiences, and current personal coping mechanisms. They also identified certain environmental factors that help survivors cope. These environmental factors include adequate economic resources; better health and functional status; availability of social-support networks; opportunity to disclose and speak about wartime experiences; altruistic tendencies; and finding and attaching meaning to survival. Each of these environmental factors is discussed below.

Adequate Economic Resources

The perception that all survivors are financially secure because they receive restitution payments from the German government is a myth. While some survivors receive monthly pensions, many others do not. The reasons are varied. Many survivors see restitution as 'blood money' from the German government, and they believe that no amount of money will ever make up for their losses. Some do not want to absolve the Germans of their collective guilt. Others refused to subject themselves to the bureaucratic red tape that was required in the post-war years to make restitution claims – specifically, the compulsory medical and psychiatric examinations which linked their mistreatment during the Holocaust to their health problems.

Studies find that many Holocaust survivors are in a worse economic situation than Canadian-born Jews (Torczyner & Brotman, 1994; Weinfeld et al., 1981). A study based on 2001 census data of the Montreal Jewish elderly (Shahar & Tobman, 2004) found that 25 per cent of survivors live below the poverty line and another 15 per cent are poor and live alone. This segment of the survivor population is particularly vulnerable.

Social-service agencies must ensure that survivors have adequate financial resources. This requires creative responses because many survivors resist financial assistance. While some consider financial assistance programs as 'charity,' others refuse to disclose their annual incomes to determine eligibility. Still others expect free services because they suffered in the Holocaust.

As discussed in chapter 3, the Claims Conference has lobbied the German government for compensation payments to Holocaust survivors, and the result has been a number of funds and services. For example, the Claims Conference allocates funds to social-service agencies for case management, home care and cleaning, emergency assistance, food and transportation programs, and day centres and socialization programs.

Standard social-service intake and assessment forms must be adapted to identify survivors who may be eligible for these funds. Then case managers can help survivors access services of which they may be unaware, along with Holocaust-related government pensions and restitution funds.

Adequate Health and Functional Status

While many survivors accept services available to them when they lose their independence, others resist, saying: 'I have managed on my own until now and will continue to do so.' However, once we explain that these services, far from taking away their independence, will allow them to remain autonomous and at home, they sometimes accept them. Examples of such services include home care (meal preparation, light housekeeping, cleaning, errands, bathing assistance, and so on), meals-on-wheels, and transportation assistance.

Proper nutrition is a vital element in maintaining a healthy lifestyle. Many frailer survivors, especially those with limited mobility, find it challenging to prepare meals that require grocery shopping and standing in the kitchen. It is easier for them to open a can or buy commercially processed foods, which often lack adequate nutrition. Fresh or frozen meals-on-wheels is a healthier alternative. For those with limited financial resources, this service is usually available on a sliding scale.

The Claims Conference provides allocations to social-service agencies around the world for home-care services. It is important to share information about these services with survivors, their families, and referring agencies. Many survivors should remain in their homes as long as possible because moving to a residence or institution may trigger memories of persecution during the Holocaust. These triggering events are discussed in chapter 14.

There are also survivor-related medical conditions that have an impact on current health. Research demonstrates that trauma affects people on multiple levels of biological functioning (van der Kolk, 1996a). Individuals with post-traumatic-stress disorder have a variety of health problems that include the cardiovascular, neurological, and gastrointestinal systems. Individuals may also experience somatic symptoms and physical illnesses, especially hypertension, asthma, and chronic pain (Yehuda, 2002). A number of researchers (Eitinger, 1981; Hoppe, 1971; Matussek, 1975; Sigal & Weinfeld, 1989) documented damage to survivors' health resulting from their maltreatment. For example, a study conducted in Israel (Marcus & Menczel, 2007) with European-born Jewish women sixty years or older found that female Holocaust survivors had a higher prevalence of osteoporosis. During the war, these women experienced long periods of malnutrition, protein and vitamin deficiency, lack of exposure to sunlight, and lack of physical activity, all factors that influence bone density. The study's researchers recommended that female survivors should be screened to determine their bone mineral density (BMD) levels so appropriate treatments can be implemented to minimize fractures.

There is also anecdotal evidence that survivors were exposed to diseases in the camps and ghettos, or while in hiding, which have remained dormant for many years. These diseases are appearing later in life when immune functioning decreases and/or a health crisis occurs. For example, an oncologist in Los Angeles warned members of a survivors' club about the emergence of tuberculosis in some survivors (Kinsler, 1995). When my late mother had a heart attack and was admitted to a hospital that treats a large number of Holocaust survivors, she developed internal bleeding. Her doctor suspected that the bleeding was caused by a chronic viral hepatitis. He told us that this disease is detected in a number of survivors who had lived in cramped quarters in concentration camps. Hepatitis can be asymptomatic and undetected for years, even while slow and progressive liver damage is occurring.

Survivors and their families must be informed about these medical conditions so that measures may be taken to minimize the consequences.

Availability of Social-Support Networks

Social support is important because survivor families are generally small, with little, or no, extended relations. In addition, many survivors are not integrated into the general community because they created their own organizational support networks where they found a sense of belonging with peers. In recent years, however, these organizations' activities have diminished, and many no longer exist owing to members' inability to remain active, relocation, and death. This important loss of community causes many survivors to feel lonely and isolated, which, in turn, may lead to depression and/or dwelling on past horrors.

The quality of life for an isolated survivor can be improved by creating a new network of relationships and activities that provide physical, intellectual, and social stimulation. Creative responses include developing social-support groups that fulfil survivors' needs for socialization with peers and foster a sense of community and belonging. These groups exist in different parts of the world (Dasberg, 1995; David, 2002; Fried & Waxman, 1988; Giberovitch, 2006; Guttmann, 1995; Hassan, 1995; 2003). Several types of groups are described in chapter 10. In chapter 11, and throughout this book, I discuss the Drop-in Centre for Holocaust Survivors that replaced the disappearing *landsmanschaften* in Montreal.

Opportunity to Disclose Wartime Experiences

Kahana, Harel, and Kahana (1988) concluded that survivors who were able to share their experiences with their spouse, children, and other family members had higher levels of psychological well-being. They also observed that survivors who were married to survivor spouses had greater opportunities to share their experiences. For example, Mrs B. told me: 'When my husband was alive, every night after supper we would have our cup of tea and remember the old country, and talk about our war experiences. Who wants to listen to me today? My daughter cannot bear to hear my stories and my grandchildren live far away.'

There are numerous ways that we, as service providers, can offer opportunities for survivors to talk about the Holocaust. For example, the Drop-in Centre's newsletter, *Never Again*, prints survivors' recollections of pre-war, wartime, and post-war experiences, and serves as a vehicle for their poetry and reflections. We organize intergenerational programs with high school and university students (discussed in chapter 12). Some of our members were chosen to accompany the March of the Living (see chapter 12) in Poland and Israel and many of our members' testimonies appear in newspapers and magazines around Montreal. We also organized an intergenerational memoirs project and published the book *Preserving Our Memories: Passing on the Legacy* (Gelbart & Giberovitch, 2006).

There are many organizations that publish survivors' memoirs and film survivors' testimonies. It is important for service providers to be knowledgeable about such resources so we can refer survivors to them. For example, the Azrieli Foundation, in association with York University's Centre for Jewish Studies, publishes the memoirs of Canadian survivors. These books are available at no cost to schools, libraries, Holocaust-education programs, and events sponsored by the foundation. In 2008, in cooperation with a number of organizations around the world, the Claims Conference launched its Worldwide Shoah Memoirs Collection that collects survivors' unpublished memoirs. Documents in this electronic collection are made available to individuals and organizations researching and documenting the Holocaust (Claims Conference, 2007–8). Yad Vashem and the Holocaust Survivors' Memoirs Project, with the assistance of the World Federation of Bergen-Belsen Associations, publish Holocaust survivors' memoirs in English. Its goal is to collect and preserve survivors autobiographical accounts and make them available to interested readers. In the province of Quebec, survivors participate in several video projects, which include the Witness-to-History program at the Montreal Holocaust Memorial Centre (MHMC) and the Living Testimony project at McGill University. Until the program ended in July 2012, Holocaust survivors participated in Concordia University's CURA project (Life Stories of Montrealers Displaced by War, Genocide, and Other Human Rights Violations), which used oral-history methodology to explore survivors' past and social memories of trauma and displacement.

Many survivors I work with achieve some peace of mind after writing their memoirs or participating in oral-history projects. Some say they can now die in peace, having honoured the commitment they made to bear witness. Written and / or oral disclosure enables them to honour the memory of their murdered families, friends, and extinguished communities by documenting their story to ensure that they will never be forgotten.

As service providers, we play an important healing role when we are willing to listen to and validate survivors' experiences. In so doing, we offer them the opportunity to give a voice to the unspeakable. In my work over the years with hundreds of survivors, the most consistent remark I hear after I listen to their trauma history is: 'Thank you for listening to me.' A survivor needs to feel that they have been heard and believed. Although they have been in contact with psychiatrists, therapists, social workers, and other health-care professionals, many survivors have not found service providers who show an interest and ask them about the Holocaust. Consequently, they have not been able to disclose their past, even after dropping hints about their persecution.

It is important to note, however, that not all survivors want to disclose their trauma history. Many refuse to talk about the past and avoid any situation that may trigger memories of it. For them, silence is an effective coping mechanism and must be respected. Some survivors deteriorate psychologically when pushed to self-disclose and are left with distressing recollections they cannot repress again. Health-care workers should respect survivors who have coped effectively by repressing their memories.

Sometimes I receive telephone calls from adult children who ask me to call their parent and encourage them to participate in a community documentation project. In one such case, the daughter of a survivor watched a television program about the importance of video testimony and she persuaded her mother to participate. Her mother agreed because she wanted to please her daughter. Unfortunately, the experience released repressed memories that overwhelmed the survivor parent and caused depression, anxiety, and nightmares.

Today, survivors increasingly volunteer to give video testimony – even though some are not appropriate candidates. A skilful intake process can help eliminate unsuitable individuals. The literature on direct therapeutic-exposure techniques in the treatment of post-traumatic-stress disorder (Litz et al., 1990) suggests practical guidelines to employ when deciding which individuals may be unsuitable for such interviews. Litz and colleagues (1990) identify several criteria in this regard, which include psychiatric disorders, poor cognitive functioning, unresolved life crisis, poor physical health, inadequate motivation to disclose, and inability to describe the traumatic events.

Altruistic Tendencies

The majority of survivors with whom I work have a history of volunteerism and communal involvement, many from the time of their arrival in Montreal. It is a natural transition for older survivors because they experienced some sort of organizational affiliation in their pre-war years (Giberovitch, 1988; 1994). Imbued with a strong sense of tradition, culture, and communal involvement, they brought this Old World heritage into their new environments. Some survivors also believe that, because they survived, they have a responsibility to give back to their peers and community. Volunteering gives many survivors a sense of meaning and purpose in their lives.

Finding and Attaching Meaning to Survival

In recent years, meaning making is 'emerging as a core construct in addressing trauma and violent loss' (Neimeyer cited in Armour, 2010:441). In fact, Witztum and Malkinson (2009) point out that the reconstruction of meaning may well be 'the central dynamic force during and after an event of loss' (136). People find meaning in different ways. Some find gratification in interpersonal relationships or through work while others find it through volunteer activities, altruism, spirituality, creative endeavours, and involvement in social and political causes. For Holocaust survivors, there is an added dimension: finding meaning in survival. Many survivors find a sense of purpose and meaning in life by bearing witness to the atrocities they endured. In doing so, they control their feelings of helplessness and despair.

In recent years, there has been an urgency to bear witness that is prompted, in part, by the Holocaust-denial movement. Many survivors, as first-hand witnesses to the depths of human depravity, feel an obligation to set the historical record straight by educating others. Teaching others, especially subsequent generations, about genocide's consequences has a therapeutic effect for survivors. They write memoirs, books, and articles, and participate in interviews, lectures, conferences, and documentation projects. One child survivor, who had never spoken about her ordeals, became angry when she read a newspaper interview with a Holocaust denier who promoted hatred against Jews. Her anger motivated her to take action. She thereby overcame her feelings of powerlessness. Now she speaks to community groups and students in different educational settings. For a description of interventions that help survivors find meaning and purpose, see chapter 13.

7 Other Issues Unique to Survivors

... and their last word was: Remember us, don't let them forget. And this we keep holy.

– Survivor from Wolyn, Poland

Survivors are often labelled as 'paranoid' or 'depressed,' a tendency that causes health-care providers to overlook their current social environment and health conditions. Survivors do not live in a social vacuum. As members of an ageing society, they are faced with the same issues as other older adults, such as financial security, adequate housing, transportation and mobility, availability of health services, and physical and psychological changes. However, it is important to understand issues unique to Holocaust survivors that arise from their war experiences. Some of these behaviours and challenges developed during the war, or soon after, while others appear as they age. Below is a summary of issues unique to survivors.

COMMON ISSUES

Impact of the Past

Differences between Survivors and Non-Survivors in Focusing on the Past

Focusing on past traumatic events is a unique difference between the memories of Holocaust survivors and non-survivors (Krell, 1992). For older adults who have not lived through extreme trauma, their trip down memory lane may be pleasant and non-threatening (Krell, 1992). Conversely, when Holocaust survivors reflect on the past, they remember forced separations, the last time they saw their family members alive, terror, death, destruction, and hunger. Even their pre-war memories are tainted with sadness, a fact that is particularly true of survivors from Eastern Europe, where entire communities – family, friends, homes, and institutions – were destroyed. In this regard, Holocaust survivors are different from other populations who underwent genocide. Although they survived, their world was obliterated. Their past has become intangible and exists only as painful memories.

Lack of Objects That Serve as Reminders

Most survivors have no pictures, heirlooms, or mementos of their pre-war existence. These 'treasures' were either taken from them upon arrival at a death camp or pillaged from the homes they left behind. Hence, their past exists only in memories of the pre-war communities where they lived. When I conducted my master's research, I was astonished by the wealth of documentary material I found in their possession. They collected newspaper and magazine articles, maps, *yizker bicher* (memorial books), and numerous books about their hometowns. Some people collected and preserved every bit of information about their *heim* (home) and referred to all of it as 'treasures.' In so doing, they attempted to reconstruct tangible evidence of their world, as it once existed.

Opening Up about Traumatic Experiences

There are many reasons why survivors are talking more about their traumatic past today. For example:

1. The 'conspiracy of silence' has dissipated and they are exposed to an abundance of literature, television, and radio programs about the Holocaust. For example, there is a proliferation of Holocaust films, which include *Schindler's List*, *The Boy in the Striped Pyjamas*, *The Reader*, *Defiance*, and *Sarah's Key*. The topic is no longer taboo. When survivors give feedback about these films, their comments often are along the lines of 'my experience was much worse.'
2. As death approaches, many feel the urgency to share their past and that of their murdered families and friends. Survivors view themselves as the last remnants of a soon-to-be-extinct population of firsthand witnesses. Many feel an obligation to pass on their legacies.
3. The growth of the Holocaust-denial movement around the world creates an urgency to bear witness. Many survivors live with the

'holy mission' to memorialize their dead and not allow the world to forget what happened. They become angry when they read about Iran's Holocaust-denial website or hear historical distortions such as the claim that Auschwitz inmates died from disease and were not exterminated in gas chambers. As a result, they feel a responsibility to speak up and keep the record accurate.

4. Environmental triggers often rekindle vulnerable feelings and repressed memories. These include threats to the state of Israel, anti-Semitic incidents, other genocides, terrorist bombings, and catastrophes. Survivors respond to threats and environmental triggers in different ways. Some become enraged and remain vigilant while others lapse into anxiety and depression. Many fear that their children may be threatened or harmed.

5. Many second-generation offspring are asking their parents about their experiences during the Holocaust. While some want to learn about their family history, others are attempting to understand the impact of the Holocaust legacy. Some record their parents' memories on audio and videotapes. Others translate their parents' memoirs from their mother tongues into English. Still others participate with parents in Holocaust-related activities such as conferences, lectures, courses, and community commemorations. In some instances, three generations of the same family make pilgrimages to European hometowns and death camps. The ability to share the Holocaust legacy often brings families closer. As adult offspring of survivors explore their roots, they create a continuity of life between those who were murdered and those who survived.

6. The grandchildren of survivors are interviewing their grandparents as part of class assignments related to the Holocaust. In some instances, survivors are invited to classrooms as guest speakers. Grandchildren often help families communicate more effectively and, in families that have not talked about the Holocaust, the second generation often learns about their parents' experiences by reading their children's projects.

7. New restitution and social-security programs require survivors to fill out forms providing testimony of their war experiences to qualify for benefits.

Fulfilling Their 'Holy Mission'

During my master's research, survivors repeatedly told me that they had promised the 'martyrs' who were killed in the Holocaust that they would never allow the world to forget what happened to them. This promise became a 'holy mission' for some, one that compels them to bear witness repeatedly to the tragedy. Their behaviour may be misinterpreted as compulsive rather than viewed as a commitment to keep the memory of the dead alive. They take this responsibility very seriously. Mr W., from the Federation of Wolynian Jews, explained this 'holy' commitment as follows:

> This is the mission of the survivors. In my point of view, this is all our mission because who stay alive this means he's got a mission from God to not let the world forget what happened to our people ... because if you take the main driving words of our martyrs when they went to the graves. They forced them to dig their own graves, and their last word was: Remember us, don't let [them] forget. And this we keep holy. And this we think we are living to preserve and to keep holy. Their last wish, to remember and not to forget. (Giberovitch, 1988:73)

Terrence Des Pres (1976) points out that the responsibility to bear witness began during the Holocaust. Despite the risk of being caught and killed, camp internees documented the atrocities perpetrated against innocent victims in memoirs and diaries, which they hid. Survivors' ongoing loyalty to the dead reinforces their commitment to bear witness to the atrocities committed against them. In so doing, they give them a voice and ensure they will not be forgotten. People facing extinction often requested, 'Whoever comes through will take with him the burden of speaking for the others. Someone will survive and death will not be absolute' (Des Pres, 1976:40). Many survivors continue to honour this special mission.

Survivor Guilt

Survivor guilt comes in a variety of forms. Some feel guilty they survived when others did not. Others feel guilty for not having protected or saved someone close to them. Still others feel guilty for having escaped and leaving family members behind. Russian survivors feel guilty when they talk about their suffering because ghetto, concentration, and death-camp survivors suffered more than they did.

Carmelly (1975) identifies two types of guilt carriers: active and passive. The active guilt carrier may feel guilty because she or he committed 'morally unacceptable acts' (140) that endangered the lives of others. The passive guilt carrier feels guilty to have survived when so many others did not. For example, a survivor, who managed to escape, relived his guilt about his family's murder on a daily basis. His family was forced into a synagogue that was set on fire. He was haunted by their screams.

Chodoff (1981) discusses 'guilty feelings which are not related to particular misdeeds, fancied or real, but which are experienced as nonspecific, vague and pervasive conviction of having done something wrong and shameful, even though this feeling cannot be attached to a remembered episode' (5).

Bereavement and Loss

Traumatic Grief

For most survivors, grieving their losses is a life-long process. In the usual grieving process, individuals deal with one death at a time. By participating in mourning rituals, they are able to work through their grief. Many survivors, however, did not have an opportunity to grieve their losses for three reasons. First, there was no opportunity to bury their dead, since the corpses were either buried in mass graves or burned in crematoria. Second, most survivors, particularly those from Eastern Europe, had no homes to return to. There remained little tangible evidence of their pre-war existence and their families, homes, and religious, communal, and educational institutions were all gone. Third, most survivors were unable to participate in mourning rituals such as making funeral arrangements, sitting *shiva*, and arranging for a gravestone.

In *Grief and Loss*, Katherine Walsh (2012) uses the term 'traumatic grief' to identify the variety of 'complicated grief reactions' associated with trauma and loss (121). She points out the importance of service providers being attuned to the traumatic events that affect our clients' lives. This information should inform our practice and the type of interventions we provide.

Prolonged Grief and Mourning

The death of a spouse, family member, or friend with a link to their past may trigger a memory of the Holocaust and cause excessive grieving. Mourning is a cumulative process where the survivor grieves not only the deceased but also all others who were killed in the Holocaust and the era the deceased person symbolized.

For example, once survivors discovered that family members had been murdered, they formed new intimate attachments and married very quickly. These marriages were usually with a person they knew before the war, someone who experienced similar circumstances or who knew a member of their family. Consequently, when their spouse dies, the survivor is mourning not only their spouse but also the whole way of life that person represented. The spouse was a link to a bygone era which was so violently destroyed. I often hear comments like: 'She / he was everyone to me, my mother, father, sister, brother, aunt, uncle, cousins.'

Death of a spouse may also lead to disengagement from activities, anxiety, and depression. Researchers found that survivors who married other survivors had better opportunities to be understood by their mates (Kahana, Harel, & Kahana, 1988). In fact, these studies conclude that having a spouse who is also a Holocaust survivor is an important determinant of psychological well-being. Many people I provide services to have described the security they feel with a mate who has gone through similar experiences, someone who may even have seen them in the most degrading situations. They validate each other's stories. With the death of an important support person who provided an outlet for sharing memories, many survivors become focused on the past.

The Missing Grave

Gravesites hold great significance in Judaism. In pre-war Europe, the deceased continued to play important roles in the lives of the living. As noted in chapter 2, graves of loved ones were visited regularly at times of crisis, during happy occasions, and before holidays, especially Rosh Hashanah and Yom Kippur.

The missing grave hampers the mourning process. Often the death of a loved one is not accepted because there is no tangible evidence of their death (Szatmari, 1968). This causes some survivors to live with the hope that a family member or friend survived. Some describe looking for familiar faces in crowds. Others search for family members by placing notices in newspapers and on bulletin boards at survivor conferences. Still others look through telephone books for familiar names whenever they travel.

Anniversary Reactions

Some survivors go through intense psychological distress before or on the actual anniversary of a significant event such as the liquidation of a hometown and / or ghetto or deportation to a death camp. It was on these dates that they saw their family members for the last time. Sometimes the anniversaries coincide with Jewish holidays. For example, the Warsaw Ghetto uprising and liquidation took place before Passover. The Łódź Ghetto was liquidated in August, just before the Jewish High Holidays. Hungary was occupied in the spring of 1944 and deportations began around Passover.

Jewish holidays may be linked with the mourning process and can be a difficult time. There are also few extended family members with whom to celebrate holidays, which is especially the case for those survivors whose children live out of town. Therefore, outreach to widowed and single survivors with no children, especially around the holidays, is important. Some communities hold dinners in synagogues and community centres to which survivors can be referred.

Some survivors created rituals to honour the memory of their family members or go to synagogue and say *kaddish*, the prayer for the dead. Others light memorial candles every year on the exact date of a death, if it is known, or on a symbolic date such as the 27th day of *Nissan* (Hebrew lunar calendar) – the annual Holocaust Remembrance Day designated by the Israeli government in 1953.

Significance of Family

Family is of great significance for Holocaust survivors because so many members of their families were killed. In Montreal, most survivors are sole surviving members of pre-war families. They created new families quickly, many in the DP camps of Europe. They married other survivors, usually someone with a link to their past, and brought forth a new generation.

Most survivors have a strong sense of family and bonds are strong. Children and grandchildren are deeply loved and considered precious. When asked what makes them most happy, many respond with: 'Spending time with my children and grandchildren.' Closeness, however, may manifest in overprotection, causing some offspring to distance themselves. Most sons and daughters are named after murdered family members. Although this is customary in Judaism, being a replacement for someone who was so brutally murdered has implications. In many instances, children live with the responsibility of compensating for their parents' losses and shielding them from disappointments, leading them to subjugate their own feelings and needs.

Support groups help adult offspring of survivors share feelings, thoughts, and concerns related to their legacies. Once they explore the effect that the Holocaust has had on their lives, many are able to involve themselves in Holocaust-related activities.

Religious Faith after the Holocaust

In the area of religious faith, survivors have varying beliefs and practices. Some devout survivors felt abandoned by God during the Holocaust and turned away from their Jewish roots and heritage. In fact, I met several offspring of survivors who did not learn that their parents had been Jewish until they reached their teenage years. Although initially confused about their identities, they went on to explore their Jewish roots in meaningful ways.

Other orthodox Jews became secular, participating in cultural rituals and traditions. Still others felt that God had helped them to survive and returned to their religious roots. In the words of one survivor: 'It was a miracle that I survived.' One woman, from a religious background, became a member of Lubavitch, one of the largest Chasidic movements in Orthodox Judaism. She remained religious because she believed that the non-Jewish world would never accept Jews. Some survivors dropped religious rituals but remain altruistic, support Israel, are committed to family and community, and involve themselves in Holocaust-related activities. Mrs S. came from a religious home in pre-war Poland. After the war she lost faith in God and never stepped into a synagogue. However, she lived her life committed to helping others in whatever ways she could.

As survivors are getting ready to die, some return to their religious beliefs and roots. They do this in different ways. Some attend synagogue services and others participate in the rituals of Judaism within the privacy of their homes. I met a man who puts on *tefillin* (small leather box containing Hebrew texts) and prays every morning at home, but has never stepped into a synagogue.

I know some survivors who enter a synagogue only once a year to attend a Holocaust Commemoration Service where they say *kaddish* for their murdered family members. They come early to sit and reflect upon their losses.

Significance of Food

Food is of fundamental significance in the lives of survivors (Sindler et al., 2004). Some stockpile food in case of an emergency. Others refuse to throw away food. Still others refuse to eat any foods that remind them of the war. For example, a man who hid during the war ate raw potatoes to survive; afterwards, he would not eat potatoes; he refuses to do so to this day. Bread symbolizes life and some survivors will not discard it even if it has turned mouldy; instead, they remove the mould on the bread before eating it. In one group, members brought an assortment of breads to share at a final session. Some people hide food in their pockets and purses.

Most survivors derive pleasure in having a refrigerator and table full of food, especially at family get-togethers. Survivors also use food to show appreciation and love. They frequently give baked goods and jams as gifts.

ISSUES ARISING FROM THE AGEING PROCESS

For many survivors, their senior years are a period of growth and satisfaction evidenced in a variety of ways. Many engage in leisure activities such as travel and in intellectual, physical, social, and creative pursuits. For instance, some survivors spend winters in warm climates. Others remain active by attending adult-education courses, participating in exercise, dance, swim, and art classes, and / or volunteering and engaging in a variety of organizational activities. This diversity in survivors' lifestyles and coping mechanisms leads me to caution against assuming that old age is traumatic for all survivors. While this may be true for a segment of the survivor population, for many it is not.

Some survivors, however, have difficulty adapting to the challenges of ageing. Past vulnerabilities are emerging which require understanding and a compassionate response. For example, coping with losses is a core challenge during the ageing process. Stressful life events, such as retirement, death of a spouse, family members, and friends, loss of autonomy, illness, relocation to a new residence, and lack of financial security, may cause feelings of powerlessness. These changes and associated feelings can activate, or exacerbate, symptoms of post-traumatic stress which may manifest as intrusive recollections, sleep disturbances, and increased anxiety (Brodsky Cohen, 1991; Danieli, 1994a, 1994b; David & Pelly, 2003; Ehrlich, 1988; Giberovitch, 1995, 1999; Rosenbloom, 1983, 1985; Safford, 1995; Sherwood et al., 2004). In short, survivors' current losses are often reminders of their wartime experiences and accompanying feelings of grief, vulnerability, dependency, and helplessness. Such responses are most acute for elder Holocaust survivors who live alone (Torczyner & Brotman, 1994).

The developmental, cognitive, and psychological aspects of ageing are also challenging. There are fewer distractions during this stage of life, which provides more time to reflect on the past. Many Holocaust survivors relive their original trauma, both cognitively and emotionally. Some knowledge of the psycho-social tasks involved in ageing may be helpful in understanding the reasons for this. These tasks include: reflecting upon and re-examining one's life; accepting all that has happened and integrating these experiences into the totality of one's life; resolving emotional conflict such as guilt and 'unfinished business'; and finding personal meaning (Erikson, cited in McInnis-Dittrich, 2009; Melendez et al., 2008). Cognitively, when memories are reinforced by strong emotions, they are deeply embedded in secondary or long-term memory and more easily accessed (McInnis-Dittrich, 2009). As protective defences or coping mechanisms weaken, survivors are no longer able to ward off symptoms such as intrusive memories, sleep disturbances, anxiety, and depression (Colerick Clipp & Elder, 1996; Aarts et al., 1996). This normal process of ageing leads to a focus on the past and the desire to talk about it which, for some survivors, generates feelings of vulnerability associated with their wartime experiences.

Survivor Responses to Their Loss of Independence

Since survivors are not a homogeneous group, they respond to losing their independence in different ways. For some, declining physical health may restrict activities with family and peers and lead to disengagement that causes loneliness, depression, and focusing on past traumas. Others view a decline in health as a challenge to overcome. Still others find it difficult to accept the challenges of ageing, especially physical and cognitive deterioration.

Thirty-five survivors in the Drop-in Centre revealed how they cope with their loss of autonomy:

- 'Living one day at a time';
- 'Accepting and adjusting to the changes, especially the physical limitations';
- 'Being strong and helping myself';
- 'Asking for help from my children';
- 'Pacing myself';
- 'Staying optimistic by giving myself pep-talks';

- 'Being grateful that my mind works';
- 'Staying healthy by eating properly and doing brain exercises';
- 'Believing that God does not give me more than I can handle'; and
- 'Volunteering.'

Over the years I have observed that survivors have a number of traits in common.

A Strong Survival Instinct

Some survivors view their declining health as a challenge to overcome. They have a tenacious survival instinct manifested by a determination to recover when severely ill. Knowing that they survived worse, they are prepared to 'fight' any new challenge; they exhibit an overwhelming ability to persevere and not give in to the illness. Mrs T., a survivor of Bergen-Belsen, suffered from severe angina. Formerly an active person, she learned to adapt to her illness and attend to her activities of daily living. Mrs G. continues to pace herself and go on with her daily activities even though her cancer has metastasized. Mrs V. has osteoporosis, which required two hip-replacement surgeries within a short time. When she recovered, she broke her shoulder, again requiring a long convalescence. She is determined to get well again.

A Determination to Withstand Tremendous Physical Pain

Many survivors live with diseases such as osteoarthritis or angina but rarely complain about their pain. Many continue to fight debilitating illnesses and are unwilling to give up. Even when severely ill they do not lose their will to live. Life is too precious for them. Mrs Y. has rheumatoid arthritis which is so severe that she often cannot sleep because of the pain. Yet she refuses to be sidelined by this autoimmune disease. She prepares salves to relieve her pain and takes medication. She declines offers of help to clean her apartment. She says that performing menial cleaning tasks helps her to exercise and keep her 'depressing thoughts' under control.

An Acceptance of Their Present Situation, No Matter How Difficult

One woman said, 'I have been given these past sixty years as a gift. I have nothing to complain about. After the concentration camp, I didn't think I would live this long.' Another woman, whose house had just burned to the ground, said, 'I have survived worse. No one is hurt and I am alive.' A survivor in a group program said, 'I do not dwell on my suffering. I try to be happy, focus on the positive, take things in stride, and adjust.' A discussion in a group program that focused on members' increased frailties prompted one member to say: 'We are soldiers! We should rename our group Drop-in Centre Fighters!'

A Wish to Live Independently in the Community

Many survivors live independently in the community in spite of periodic mental health upsets. Mrs B., a Holocaust survivor of the Radom Ghetto, Auschwitz, and several labour camps, lost her husband and sister in the same year. Just before her husband's death, she suffered a paranoid episode and was admitted to the psychiatric emergency department of a large hospital. The episode was precipitated by her overwhelming despair as she faced the impending loss of her husband. However, Mrs B. mobilized her coping mechanisms and was released the same day, requiring no medication.

A Desire to Maintain Control over Their Environment

Some survivors find it hard to lose their independence and struggle to maintain control over their environment. These survivors battle fiercely to remain in their homes in spite of significant challenges such as mobility problems, terminal illnesses, deafness, and blindness. They may refuse help from service providers and / or their children. Some refuse to use a cane or walker or wear a hearing aid. Others are afraid to go out alone or afraid they will fall, especially during winter. In the words of one woman, 'I'm tired of being sick. My eyes and mind can do everything but my body does less.'

A Tendency to Adapt to Changing Circumstances by Seeking Solutions

Mr N., a widower, suffered a stroke resulting in a loss of mobility. He was referred to a rehabilitation hospital where he works diligently to reclaim the use of his left arm. Realizing that he may no longer be able to live on his own, his social worker is helping him explore different living arrangements.

A Desire to Give Back to the Community

Some survivors, who receive social services, feel obliged to give back to their peers and community. They look for meaningful ways to do so. For many years Mrs N. received home-care services for her husband from a social-service agency. After he died, she volunteered to visit a homebound survivor who needed a break from her caregiving responsibilities. Another survivor provides Russian translation for an agency service.

An Ability to Appreciate the Simple Pleasures of Life

Some survivors learn to pace themselves and live one day at a time. They enjoy the simple pleasures of life such as family, friends, health, and a refrigerator filled with food. They take nothing for granted and value their friendships.

An Ability to Keep Their Sense of Humour in Spite of Tremendous Hardships

Mrs E. fell in her apartment, which caused multiple bruises and a severe limp. When describing her mishap, she said, 'I didn't break the floor.' She refused to dwell on her incapacities and was happy just to be alive.

Retirement

Retired survivors, particularly men, may be vulnerable to past memories. Hard work occupied their minds and kept intrusive feelings and memories away. Work also gave structure, meaning, and purpose to their lives. With more free time, some are flooded with memories, anxiety, and depression related to their past. Survivors, for the most part, did not develop hobbies or plan for their retirement. They are especially vulnerable to depression when retirement is combined with death of a spouse.

It is important to encourage survivors to become involved in meaningful activities. Some volunteer in Holocaust-related activities. Others take courses and attend social programs. Sometimes their children accompany them to these programs.

With retirement, marital discord may emerge between the partners. At the end of the war, when survivors learned they were the sole surviving members of their families, most remarried other survivors in a hurry. They disregarded the usual criteria for picking a mate (love, common interests, social status). They married to appease loneliness and create new family. In spite of this, however, Holocaust survivors have a very low divorce rate.

Social Service and Health Care

Factors That Contribute to Survivors' Vulnerability in the Community

In general, survivors have fewer extended family members than the average older adult. Many survivors are sole remaining members of pre-war nuclear and extended families. Some survivors, whose first families were murdered in the Holocaust, may have remarried after the war but others did not, or could not, have children. This lack of family support contributes to their vulnerability in the community, which is further compounded by language difficulties. Older survivors had more difficulty adjusting to their new environment and many did not learn the language(s) of their adopted communities. Consequently, many communicate in their mother tongues (such as Yiddish, Hungarian, Romanian, Russian). The inability to communicate makes it hard for them to request social services.

Creative solutions entail hiring staff persons who understand the cultural history of these survivors and can communicate with them in their mother tongues. For example, in 2006, CJCS intake workers spoke several languages, including Yiddish, Russian, Hebrew, and French. When funds became available from the Hungarian Gold Train Settlement program, the agency hired Kathy Viragh, a native Hungarian, to work specifically with Hungarian survivors. The ability to speak their language enabled Kathy to reach out to this community and identify vulnerable survivors requiring assistance, many of whom were in their nineties.

Some survivors fear and mistrust government bureaucracy. Others seek assistance only from Jewish agencies. This may pose service-delivery problems. For example, in the province of Quebec, most health and social services are provided by government agencies. Some survivors refuse to approach these agencies because they do not trust non-Jewish workers or fear being identified in a central registry. One survivor, when asked to fill out a form and answer questions in a government office, relived her interrogation by the Gestapo and became afraid. Another survivor refused to complete a government application form for health insurance. Sometimes these feelings of mistrust can be mitigated if a trusted individual accompanies the survivor to the government agency.

Understanding Survivors' Resistance to Assistance

Until recently, survivors rarely sought mental-health or social-service assistance. Illness or a personal crisis now brings increasing numbers of them into the system involuntarily where they become dependent on service providers for help. Others may lack knowledge of available resources and do not know how to access and negotiate the system.

The reasons for survivors' reluctance to accept help are varied. Many survivors' lives are intricately interwoven with values inculcated in their pre-war communities. These values influence their attitudes towards seeking help. Some survivors adhere to the Old World ethic of self-reliance and are proud, particularly concerning financial matters. For example, a cognitively competent child survivor lived on his monthly restitution pension of $400 from the German government. Although he was eligible for local government welfare, he refused to apply for it because his father, a rabbi in pre-war Europe, used to invite less fortunate members of the community to their home for Sabbath dinners. He remembers his family's pity towards these guests. He did not want pity. I worked with him to reframe his thinking and helped him apply for assistance. Eventually he accepted a disability pension and moved into low-cost housing.

Some survivors refuse mental-health intervention. Many survivors from Eastern Europe believe that only people who are insane seek such help. They often decline psychiatric referrals. Those who accept them may experience feelings of helplessness, dependency, and shame. These feelings can be reframed by presenting the act of seeking help as a sign of strength and courage.

Other reasons survivors stay away from community assistance include anger towards the general Jewish community for being complacent during the war while millions were being murdered; the host community's negative reactions and attitudes when they arrived; and the minimal help provided when they immigrated.

Fear and mistrust of authority figures (such as police officers, customs agents, and government officials) are often observed in survivors. During the war, people in positions of power frequently wore uniforms and may have mistreated or harmed them. Consequently, survivors may fear and mistrust social-service providers. The power differential between worker and client makes them uncomfortable and seeking help generates feelings of helplessness, dependency, and shame. Survivors may also avoid professional assistance because some practitioners participated in a 'conspiracy of silence' during the post-war period, often ignoring their war stories or accusing them of exaggeration (Danieli, 1988).

Significance of Illness

Some survivors stay away from medical intervention because they associate illness and hospitalization with death. During the Holocaust the weak, infirm, and old were sent to the gas chambers because they were unable to work as slave labourers for their captors. Many survivors I have worked with over the years stay away from medical doctors and rely on home remedies from the 'old country' when they are ill.

A medical crisis may bring them into the system involuntarily and trigger repressed memories. Mr D., an eighty-five-year-old Auschwitz survivor, required immediate surgery for colon cancer. As I sat with him for his pre-admission tests, his memories of persecution surfaced. He described his deportation from the Łódź Ghetto, the train ride to Auschwitz in cattle cars, and the selection process. Cohen (1977) explains that feelings of helplessness and persecution may surface in the setting of a hospital where the patient is helpless and dependent on medical personnel. In such cases, it is important to get survivors' permission to inform hospital staff of their vulnerabilities so they can be treated with sensitivity.

In addition to hospitals, re-traumatization may also occur in social-service agencies and long-term-care facilities (David & Pelly, 2003; Edelstein, 1981; Shour, 1990; Zilberfein & Eskin 1992).

Attitudes towards Doctors

Doctors' appointments, tests, hospitalization, and surgery may induce anxiety, depression, and nightmares (David & Pelly, 2003; Ehrlich, 2004; Rosenbloom, 1985). Medical personnel need to be sensitive to a patient's history and understand their individual needs. Knowing about the nature and duration of their persecution may give a clue to a survivor's potential response during a medical intervention. It is important that physicians have an understanding of survivors because they are often the contact point in the system for patients who have been admitted to the hospital involuntarily as a result of a medical emergency.

Attitudes towards doctors vacillate between reverence and mistrust. In pre-war Europe, doctors were respected as learned men and held positions of stature in their communities. Conversely, during the war, doctors became associated with death. In the death camps they selected who would live or die, supervised the murders in the gas chambers, and conducted gruesome medical experiments. Some survivors delay seeing doctors until they have an extremely serious medical emergency.

One participant in a support group had medical experiments conducted on her and her twin sister when they were young children. She survived but her sister did not. This ordeal causes her to have a recurring nightmare where a snake is cut into small pieces and placed in a jar. Consequently, she stays away from medical doctors and seeks out natural therapies instead.

Holocaust Survivors and Alzheimer's Disease

Alzheimer's disease and related disorders (ADRD) are particularly difficult for Holocaust survivors because, as they lose their short-term memory, they focus on traumatic past memories. Family members are heartbroken to see them relive their traumatic past mentally and emotionally. I witnessed a number of individuals who were locked in their traumatic memories and all attempts to comfort and reassure them failed. Eventually they were relieved of their pain when their memories regressed further back into their youth. Many communities have programs and services designed to assist individuals diagnosed with ADRD and those who care for them.

Caregiving and Placement

Impact on Survivors

Occasionally I meet couples where one of the spouses, usually the female, is wearing her / himself out in an intensive caregiving role. Survivors have a strong commitment to their marriages, even if their relationship is conflictual. They make remarks such as: 'He's alive. I have to take care of him.' Some may see the opportunity to care for a spouse as compensation for not having done the same for their parents.

Unfortunately, many survivors do not have a realistic understanding of what is involved in being a caregiver for an ageing adult because they did not have ageing parents with specific needs as role models. Consequently, as they become frailer with medical problems, they often find caregiving to be overwhelming and neglect their own needs. The social worker must help caregivers recognize that they also have to take care of themselves.

Case management is key. Social workers conduct bio-psychosocial assessments to determine presenting issues and evaluate the needs of the caregiver within their environment. It is also important, when developing an intervention plan, to give survivors permission to accept help and involve their children. Many survivors refuse help from service providers and family members. They have a strong desire to remain independent and insist that they can handle caregiving on their own. In addition, a survivor parent in a caregiving role at home may not disclose the full nature of their spouse's illness or the extent of their caregiver role to their children, especially to children who live out of town. They are trying to shield their children from responsibility and worry.

The availability of a social network is important in sharing caregiving responsibilities. Survivor spouses benefit from caregiver support groups and socialization programs. Sometimes survivors turn to friends or hire caretakers. When this is not possible, service providers should arrange for resources such as home care, respite, transportation, and day programs.

Caregiving survivors often refuse to place a spouse in an institution, even though they are exhausted and no longer able to manage. Quite often a crisis occurs before action for placement is taken. For example, Mr L. decided to place his wife, who had middle-stage Alzheimer's disease, in an institution only after she attacked him with a knife and he began to fear for his safety. Another survivor, Mr S., was hospitalized with exhaustion and contemplated suicide before he eventually decided to institutionalize his wife.

Placement should be discussed as an option before the caregiver reaches a breaking point. A social worker can plant seeds for the idea before the burnout stage. The social worker should initiate the discussion, however, because the survivor may not want to consider it as an option for several reasons. First, there is a tremendous bond and interdependency between the couple. Second, some survivors consider placement as an act of abandonment and negatively judge those who decide to take this route. There is an unspoken 'code' in the community that a spouse does not give up on the other, no matter how difficult the situation. Consequently, an individual who decides to place their spouse may not receive the social support they so desperately need during this time of crisis. The social worker may need to mobilize social support within the health-care system. Social workers can also help the survivor save face in their community by suggesting that they tell friends that a professional worker made the decision.

Impact on Adult Children of Survivors

The caregiving needs of survivors may be an emotionally charged area for their adult children as well. Extended families are either non-existent or small, and the burden of care usually rests with the children. They may be overwhelmed by their ageing parents' needs, particularly when both parents are ill at the same time. Some children have difficulty with the role reversal that happens when parents become dependent on them. Most have trouble witnessing their parent's suffering. Intensive loyalties to parents may also create conflict within their own nuclear family. Some children put their own lives and needs on hold to care for their ageing parents. Others feel angry and resentful because they have not resolved their own issues with their parents. In this respect, survivor families are no different from the rest of the population. McPherson (1983) observes, in his discussion of intergenerational family relationships, that 'depending on the quality of the relationship during the earlier years, the onset of dependency can provide an opportunity to reward the parent for past debts, or to seek revenge for real or imagined parental injustice during childhood or adolescence' (335).

Some relationships are stuck in an unresolved parent-child dynamic where adult children feel they have no decision-making powers. In attempts to please parents and not cause them pain and suffering, children do not disclose the difficulty of their caregiving roles, set limits on their involvement, or suggest the parent move to an assisted-living residence.

Getting parents to relocate to a residence when they are no longer managing on their own is a difficult issue. Intense family loyalty causes adult children caregivers to burn out as parents lose their ability to be self-sufficient. Sometimes survivors remain in dangerous situations because their children have difficulty with role reversal and / or their inability to make decisions for their parents. For example, when Mrs B. was in her eighties, she showed signs of dementia which her daughter refused to acknowledge. The daughter had a close relationship with her mother and was unable to accept her mental deterioration. After Mrs B. left the burner of her stove on and burned her hand, her daughter realized her mother required a geriatric assessment to assess her cognitive state. Her mother was eventually placed in a long-term-care facility.

The first step to break these old parent-child dynamics is to have the child make a choice to have an adult relationship with parents and then find ways to bring this relationship about. It could be as simple as children having a conversation with parents and disclosing their difficulty with their caregiving role. Social workers can facilitate these discussions. I occasionally work with families whose adult children are no longer able to provide the level of care their parent requires. Sometimes this entails arranging outside resources (such as home-care services) to help with the parent's daily living activities. Other times it may be necessary for the parent to relocate to a residence that provides services. Some survivors resist such a move and may not consider moving until a crisis occurs. The following case summary illustrates some of these points.

* * *

While they were together, Mr G. and his wife had segregated roles where his wife was responsible for taking care of the household. After her death, Mr G., in his mid-eighties, wanted to maintain his autonomy and continue living on his own. This required his two children, one with a family of her own, to become caregivers. As the situation became increasingly more difficult, however, he refused to relocate to a residence with services. Instead, he wanted to move in with one of his children. As much as his children wanted to accommodate his request, they knew it would not work out. They continued to support their father in his apartment as they struggled with their guilty feelings around forcing him to move. Eventually Mr G. developed colon cancer and required immediate surgery. His children knew he could no longer continue to live on his own when he would be discharged from the hospital. They organized a family meeting in Mr G.'s hospital room, discussed his options, and set boundaries on their involvement. When he heard about the difficulties they were having in their caregiver roles, he agreed to move to a residence for a two-month trial period. He helped identify possible residences that his children visited and described to him. He chose one that was close to his apartment because he wanted to remain in his familiar neighbourhood. The children moved his belongings and released the apartment before Mr G. left the hospital. Once relocated, he adjusted to his new environment and signed a longer-term lease.

* * *

It is important for adult children to find someone with whom to share their feelings and emotions about their caregiving responsibilities. It may be a good friend, a family member, a professional therapist, or a caregiver-support group. Besides offering mutual support, groups also provide information and coping strategies. Caregiving-support resources exist in many communities and can be found by contacting local social-service agencies.

Environment

Impact of Hospitalization and Institutionalization

For some survivors, short-term hospitalization and long-term institutionalization may cause disorientation and trigger anxiety and nightmares of their incarceration. When inmates became sick in the camps, they were either killed immediately or sent to the 'hospital,' which had no medical treatments. Inmates were left to die, deported, or used for medical experiments. Feelings of vulnerability may become activated in the setting of a hospital where the patient is helpless and dependent on doctors, nurses, and orderlies (Cohen, 1977; Edelstein, 1981; Hirschfeld, 1977). Staff in white uniforms may be perceived as potential persecutors. Survivor patients may refuse to undergo tests or treatment. In addition, some institutionalized survivors go through a profound emptiness coupled with feelings of aloneness and abandonment when separated from their spouse.

An institutional setting may expose survivors to a range of vulnerabilities (Brandler, 2000; Cohen, 1977; Edelstein, 1981; Hirschfeld, 1977; Shour, 1990). For example, survivors may

- experience disorientation, anxiety, depression, and nightmares of persecution;
- perceive institutions as death factories where medical experiments are conducted;
- associate regulations and restrictions with the concentration camps;
- feel helpless when dependent on nurses, doctors, orderlies, and so on;
- fear loss of control over their destiny;
- fear renewed persecution (viewing persons in uniform as persecutors);
- feel anxious and / or depressed over medical procedures (such as tests or body shaving before surgery), and, for that reason, refuse to undergo tests and treatment;
- associate changes in appearance, such as weight loss, shaved head, and amputations, and bodily exposure with the concentration camps; and

- develop issues around food, such as refusal to be served by wait-resses of certain European countries, an inability to enjoy food, and saving and accumulating food in room.

In the midst of all these challenges, survivors who are institutional-ized may not have extended family to provide emotional and / or so-cial support. Also, their lack of fluency in the prevailing language may cause misunderstanding and confusion, and their fear and mistrust of government bureaucracy (in many instances, institutions are gov-ernment facilities) may trigger feelings of dread and interfere with their care.

In general, common themes in survivor testimony about the impact of institutionalization include: confinement, isolation from community, abandonment, enforced separation from family and home, deperson-alization, and loss of control over their destiny.

Ageing in Place

Maintaining a sense of control over their environment may be a more important psycho-social need for Holocaust survivors than for other older adults because their environments were so stringently con-trolled during the war. Survivors are well served by programs that focus on 'ageing in place' or 'ageing at home,' which give older adults a choice in their care and living arrangements. Holocaust survivors have more of a need to stay in their homes because the potential ad-verse effects of institutions could remind them of their persecution during the Holocaust.

Quebec health-care policy requires that older adults be maintained in their homes for as long as possible and provides health and social ser-vices to further this end. This works well for Holocaust survivors. In addition, the Claims Conference provides funds to agencies that main-tain eligible survivors at home with home-care and cleaning services, meals-on-wheels, transportation, and so on.

Death and Dying

Preparation for Death

I find that many survivors prepare meticulously for their deaths. Many have bought cemetery plots, pre-paid for funeral arrangements, and described to their children the type of casket to order. They give three reasons for this preparation: their desire not to burden children with expenses; their wish to be involved in planning details of their deaths; and the comfort they feel in knowing that family members and friends will have a tangible gravesite to visit.

PART III

Survivor Services and Programs

8 Transcending Victimization through Empowerment

The core experiences of psychological trauma are disempowerment and disconnection from others.

– J.L Herman (1992)

VICTIMIZATION

Long-term victimization under a systematic and comprehensive program of genocide adversely affected the mental and emotional well-being of many survivors. 'People who have endured horrible events suffer predictable psychological harm' (Herman, 1992:3). Although survivors differ from each other in many ways, as noted in chapter 3, they share a common wartime experience that may have affected their self-concept. All were subjected to massive human-rights abuses by racist policies that labelled them as different, turned them into outcasts, brutally uprooted them, and targeted them for extinction through mass murder. Consequently, many internalized a negative self-image and a loss of self-esteem as they began to identify with the labels ascribed to them (inferior, vermin, parasites, undesirable, and so on).

This intentional annihilation plan also destroyed everything that defined them – family, homes, and community; cultural and religious traditions and practices; vocations; and social, educational, and religious institutions. The process left many individuals feeling powerless, inferior, helpless, and insecure. Survivors' self-images were damaged further after the Holocaust when they were viewed as victims and greeted with negative attitudes where they settled. In many instances, these attitudes represented social judgments that continued to label survivors as different and inferior. In addition, some older survivors experienced loss of social status when they were uprooted and moved to different environments. For example, Mr B. said, 'Who am I in this country? In Europe I was a lawyer, respected by colleagues and the community.'

Although survivors reinvented themselves after the Holocaust and recreated families, community, culture, and institutions, their emotional and psychological wounds went unrecognized and were misunderstood. Recovery plans overlooked their psychological needs and mental-health professionals avoided asking questions about their war experiences. Consequently, many survivors were left to struggle on their own with invisible psychic wounds. The lack of resources to address survivors' psychological needs made it difficult for many to heal. This scarcity of mental-health services, both public and private, continued until ageing and associated challenges forced survivors to approach communities for help in the 1980s. In response, communities around the world began to explore survivors' unique needs and develop specialized programs for them. Eventually, in 1992, the first North American conference on the treatment and care of ageing Holocaust survivors took place in Miami, Florida (Kenigsberg & Lieblich, 1992), forty-seven years after liberation. Since then, many improvements have been made in treating survivors' psychological wounds.

Changing Self-Concept and Enhancing Self-Esteem

The psychological healing and recovery process, then, must include helping survivors redefine their self-concept and enhance their self-esteem. Appreciating and acknowledging survivors' abilities, and developing programs from a strengths perspective, helps survivors change their self-perception. It encourages them to talk openly about their wounds, gain insight into how these wounds affect their present lives, and make a decision to heal them. This approach uses the resiliency of the human spirit to recover and heal from the most severe forms of dehumanization and degradation.

Service providers can help survivors transcend victimization in different ways. The process must begin by acknowledging that surviving a mass atrocity is a significant accomplishment. This helps us to recognize and believe in survivors' strengths, capabilities, and resources. For example, many survivors are not aware of the determination, strength, and courage it took to reconstruct their lives in the post-war years and regain control over their lives. When I focus their attention on these achievements, they feel a sense of accomplishment, self-respect, and pride.

Another way to help survivors transcend their victimization is to create therapeutic environments where they feel safe to work through their grief and losses, thus reducing their emotional pain. This can be done with individuals (discussed in chapter 13) and groups (discussed in chapters 10 and 11).

Focusing on the survivor part of their psyche, rather than the helpless victim, is another important technique that helps them recognize their personal coping mechanisms. It serves two purposes. First, it helps the survivor regain confidence by acknowledging the strengths of their coping mechanisms. Survivors, under extraordinary conditions, developed skills and resources that can be mobilized to help them deal with recovery as well as present-day challenges. Second, this focus helps workers view a survivor as someone who has dealt with and will continue to adjust to changes in their life. In other words, it reinforces a perception of survivors as self-sufficient and strong rather than as dependent and fragile victims.

Helping survivors transcend victimization also involves being aware of the terminology we use to describe them. When we refer to them positively as Holocaust 'survivors,' rather than negatively as Holocaust 'victims,' we help them to see themselves differently in the world. Today I witness many survivors disclosing their survivor identity with great pride and confidence as they say, 'I am a Holocaust survivor.' By accepting this identity, they assert they have overcome oppression and are no longer victims.

EMPOWERMENT

Judith Herman (1992) states that 'the core experiences of psychological trauma are disempowerment and disconnection from others' (133). Recovery is based on empowerment and creation of trusting relationships and group structures that encourage survivors to assume personal control of their environment. Survivor initiatives as they rebuilt their lives in the post-war years helped me to recognize this phenomenon and integrate it into my practice. The Holocaust disempowered individuals socially, psychologically, and culturally by severing their connections with family and community. Consequently, immediately after liberation, they felt an urgent need to recreate their destroyed world. They made new ties, re-established old ones, and rebuilt their communities. In so doing, they reclaimed their power as they found ways to create new identifies, roles, and purpose. Their journey exemplifies the definition of empowerment put forth by Torre and cited in Cox and Parsons (1994): 'a process through which people become strong enough to participate within, share in the control of, and influence events and institutions which affect their lives. [This, in part,] necessitates that people gain particular skills, knowledge, and sufficient power to influence their lives' (18).

I take these facts into account when I design group programs and activities that support empowerment. My work with Holocaust survivors is also influenced by the empowerment principles discussed by Gutiérrez, Parsons, and Cox (1998). In their model, social-service workers should recognize that

- the relationship with their clients is a collaborative one whereby all involved share power and leadership;
- the helping process gives clients a voice and provides opportunities for them to make their own decisions, gain knowledge and skills, educate staff and each other, and participate in collective action towards social change;
- a safe and supportive environment is essential for workers and clients to work together and build trust, which fosters a sense of community;
- clients need to be understood within the context of their personal and cultural background, with respect for their unique qualities, values, and experiences, and acceptance of their definition of the problem to be worked on; and
- multiple roles on the part of workers, and involvement in organizational development on the part of clients, are twin pillars of institutional success.

Empowerment is a central tenet of strengths-based practice. Individual strengths provide the fuel and energy for empowerment (Cowger & Snively, cited in Rankin, 2006 / 2007). Indeed, the two are interrelated and cannot be separated. I begin with the attitude that every individual I come across has knowledge, assets, and wisdom. My mindset is that individuals are knowledgeable about their needs and capable of making their own choices and decisions. In other words, if service providers believe that individuals are the resilient authors of their lives, then we use interventions that support this vision. We view them as elders and historians, not clients, who have lived a unique life, and we are open to learning from them. Such an approach respects the dignity and uniqueness of each individual and creates a working relationship that is characterized by respect, trust, collaboration, and partnership. This approach also minimizes the power differential.

This philosophy, however, is not realized by giving lip service to it. It must be incorporated into practice. For example, when developing an individualized service plan, we engage survivors in the process by listening to their concerns, answering their questions, involving them in problem-solving solutions, and accepting their decisions, even if we may not agree with them. We should not lose sight that their goals are the focus of the assessment process. As long as they are cognitively competent and are not putting themselves at risk, we do not have the last word on what they need.

Empowerment practice is also congruent with the basic values of the social-work profession, which include respecting the dignity and uniqueness of each individual; maintaining a professional commitment to the individual's right to self-determination; focusing on strengths without losing sight of limitations; and involving individuals in problem solving and decision making.

Incorporating Empowerment into Clinical Practice

Empowerment Practice Components

Practice components of empowerment consist of listening to individuals to gain an understanding of their view of the presenting problem; trusting and respecting that they are the authors of their lives; solving problems collaboratively with them; educating them about post-traumatic reactions and teaching coping skills; and, if they are open to it, helping them work through traumatic memories (discussed in chapter 13). Empowering survivors also means giving them choices about which interventions to use, and permission to disagree or refuse. In the words of McInnis-Dittrich (2009): 'A sense of control over life and the ability to continue to make decisions, both long and short-term plans, are the best predictors of emotional well-being among older adults' (145).

Assessment

Helping survivors to see themselves as capable and empowered individuals begins by integrating questions that assess their strengths into an existing standardized assessment process. Ideally, the assessment is conducted in the individual's home where they are in control of their environment. Here the worker may observe photos and objects that reveal the person's interests, talents, and skills and lead to a conversation about them. Nelson-Becker et al. (2006) suggest some questions that support the strengths-evaluation process during a formal assessment. I have added some questions of my own.

- Explore common values, experiences, interests: What makes life worth living for you? What activities give you a sense of satisfaction, accomplishment, and fulfilment? What do you look forward to when you wake up in the morning? Who is important to you?
- Learn how the person has successfully coped with past difficulties: What has helped you cope with life's challenges? What has worked well for you in the past?
- Focus on the individual's internal strengths and those of their environment: What is going well for you right now? What are your strengths?
- Create a vision of the kind of life the person wants: If things could be different, what would you wish for?
- Explore the individual's achievements: What accomplishments are you most proud of?

* * *

The following case illustrates the benefits of the strengths approach. Mr G., a sixty-five-year-old survivor of seven concentration camps, was referred to me by a storefront community organization where he was often found because he had nowhere else to go. He was diagnosed with paranoid schizophrenia and was socially isolated and overmedicated. During my assessment I learned that, during his internment in the camps, he suffered severe beatings which resulted in neurological problems and a psychiatric condition manifested by paranoid ideation. My social-work interventions included referrals to the psychogeriatric clinic at a local hospital where his medication was adjusted; the psycho-geriatric day centre which he attended two days a week; and low-cost supervised housing.

During my initial home visit, I noticed some handwritten poems on the kitchen table. When I asked Mr G. about them, he told me that he wrote poetry and brought out a pile of other poems to show me. His poems described his war experiences, his pain in being the sole survivor of a large pre-war family, and his gratitude to Quebec and Canada for having provided him with a safe haven in the post-war years. I shifted my focus to his strengths and creativity, and began to view him as a poet rather than a fragile victim.

Mr G. had enough material for a book of poetry. When I asked him if he had considered compiling such a book, he said he hadn't but was excited by the idea. He asked if I would help edit it and so we began our work together. During the two sessions in which I helped him, I learned about his life in pre-war Poland and his experiences during the war. He read his poetry to me and sometimes cried. For the most part, I listened and said little because my calming presence was helping to contain his emotions. From this process I learned that since the war he had moved many times and was unable to sustain ongoing relationships. He had been seen by a number of psychiatrists but no one had asked him about his Holocaust experiences. During our participatory and collaborative process, I viewed Mr G. as an accomplished poet rather than as a person with a psychiatric condition. This approach satisfied his emotional needs, increased his self-esteem, and gave him a sense of importance. After the poems were edited to his satisfaction, I typed them and had them bound into a manuscript. We mailed copies to the Holocaust Remembrance Committee, the Canadian Jewish Congress, and the Yad Vashem Museum and Archives in Israel. In return, these organizations sent Mr G. letters acknowledging his work. This process created a positive experience that infused meaning and purpose into his life. Mr G. felt satisfied that his experiences were now preserved for future generations to read. Subsequently, I periodically contacted his psychiatrist, who informed me that Mr G. was admitted into subsidized housing and continued to attend the hospital day program. He continued to write poetry until his death.

* * *

Empowerment through Education

Having basic information about one's self and one's immediate situation is also an important component of empowerment (Cox & Parsons, 1994). The ageing process, and the accompanying losses that may trigger past vulnerabilities, can be quite frightening and may cause some people to feel helpless and powerless. These feelings can be mitigated through education. My work with survivors consists of a mutual exchange process whereby I teach them coping skills and wellness strategies and provide information about post-traumatic-stress reactions. They, in turn, teach me about their traumatic past history and the internal resources that help them to cope with present-day challenges.

During individual counselling sessions I provide survivors with articles and handouts compiled from the extensive literature on Holocaust survivors and post-traumatic stress. Sometimes we review them together and other times they take them home to read and come back with questions.

In groups, I educate members regularly about the effects of war trauma. For example, the 11 September 2001 terrorist attack on the World Trade Center in New York created a need for such education. For weeks after the incident, many members in our Drop-in Centre underwent a wide range of reactions, including panic, fear, irritability, nervousness, nightmares, and a sense of insecurity and hopelessness. When I explained that these reactions are a normal response to traumatic events, many felt relieved. This type of approach breaks down any self-perceived notion of being 'crazy' because they react this way. Many survivors feel embarrassed to discuss their reactions with family members or friends. Consequently, they often tend to suffer in silence.

During such discussions I use a collaborative approach to help participants gain relief from their symptoms. I encourage them to share their thoughts and feelings with each other and to identify support systems they rely on, apart from the group. In this situation, members were also advised to limit the information they took in through the media. Survivors were invited to share their own coping strategies, which included: praying for the victims and their families; turning to their friends and family for support; and distraction techniques such as going for a walk, doing some type of exercise, meeting friends, reading a magazine or book, and going to a movie. This discussion and collaborative approach created an opportunity for members to help each other, which left them feeling empowered.

Other forms of group education include teaching survivors leadership and public-speaking skills. For example, we help members overcome their fear of public speaking by teaching them to pay attention to their body language and projecting their voices into a microphone. Whenever a group member speaks, the staff and volunteers either sit down or move aside to encourage the group to focus its undivided attention on the person holding the floor. This validates and reinforces the member's importance to the group.

We also teach coping skills that enhance the quality of their lives. Our programs focus on managing stress, building healthy self-esteem, teaching assertiveness techniques, reframing negative thought patterns, fostering communication skills, controlling worry, managing anger, resolving conflicts, and dealing with depression, anxiety, and sleep disorders.

As our members' physical and cognitive health deteriorates, we also empower them to improve their situations by providing educational programs and articles that address their current health status and teach prevention and protection strategies. For example, we explain to them how to improve memory and balance, prevent falls, and protect themselves against crime; we advise them on the value of visual and hearing aids to improve sensory losses; we educate them about the health benefits of organic foods; and we share information about nutrition and diseases. Our members tell us they attend the Drop-to Centre to learn new ways to enhance their well-being and many integrate this information into their everyday life.

Another key strategy that empowers survivors consists of informing them about available community resources such as restitution payments and other related ·funds. We educate them about social-service and health-care resources, and ways to access them. During an interview, I sometimes learn that survivors' health and psychological functioning has deteriorated. If these survivors are receiving a monthly BEG pension from the German government, I inform them they may be eligible for an increase in their pension. For example, they may be eligible for an increase if they experience deterioration in the physical and / or psychiatric conditions that were originally assessed for their restitution eligibility. To apply for this increase they must fill out an application form and be examined by a medical practitioner approved by the German government. It is important that we are knowledgeable about the different resources available so we can refer survivors to them.

When I attend conferences and describe this education process to my colleagues, some service providers are surprised that survivors are capable of learning new skills. This is an example of an ageist perception that is based on myth rather than reality. Many older adults are highly motivated well into their nineties to enhance their well-being and to work on personal growth and development. They welcome new strategies and interventions. Survivors are no different. When we believe in them and encourage their capabilities and competencies, they reflect these strengths back to us. Mrs B. is a case in point. At age eighty-five she learned to use the Internet so she could send e-mails to her friends and grandchildren. Mr S., at age ninety-five, continues to attend community lectures and shares his vast historical knowledge with peers, staff, and volunteers.

Mutual-Exchange Educational Processes

Ochberg (1993) explains that the educational process is one of mutual exchange. I have always believed that survivors should be provided with opportunities to share their knowledge and expertise with staff, each other, and the community. For example, survivors sit on Holocaust Advisory Committees at CJCS where they advise staff on issues relevant to the survivor community. They review and approve requests from survivors who meet eligibility criteria for emergency-assistance funds. Members of the Drop-in Centre function as resource persons for artists in the community. One author turned to members for insight into a survivor character for his fictional work. A stimulating group discussion helped him develop a better understanding of the character he was writing about. Artists solicit volunteers for their visual-arts projects, and documentary filmmakers consult with our members as part of their research for their projects. In return, these opportunities imbue survivors with confidence and self-respect when they realize they have an important contribution to make.

Survivors share their creative interests within the group and lead discussions on such topics as life in pre-war Europe, the experiences of survivors who fled to Russia, their lives after liberation, the attitudes that greeted survivors when they immigrated to Montreal, their postwar lives and professions, current events, and stories about their trips to Israel and countries of origin. Sometimes survivors read inspirational poetry and prose, provide an overview of Jewish holidays, or lead discussions about the political situation in Israel.

Survivors also share special mementos with the group. They bring in articles about their European hometowns, certificates acknowledging their volunteer work in the community, information about organizations they support, and European identity cards. Many bring in pictures of their grandchildren and great-grandchildren, which they share with great pride. The members express joy every time a member shares news about a new great-grandchild.

Incorporating Empowerment Strategies in Programs and Services

My underlying objective in designing programs and services is creating structures that support survivors' empowerment and help them see themselves in a positive light. The following discussion illustrates some ways in which empowerment practices are incorporated into the programs and services I develop.

Examples of Outreach

Expecting all survivors-in-need to initiate contact for services is not realistic. Some must be contacted directly by actively reaching out to them and informing them about available resources. Outreach to them is an effective way to link these individuals with community services. As a frontline worker, I started a community-outreach program to unaffiliated and socially isolated survivors in the early 1990s. I began by identifying residential areas of the over-sixty-five Jewish population using census data. I discovered that some survivors in Montreal, mainly singles, did not migrate westward to these areas during the 1960s and 1970s when the rest of the survivor community did. They chose to remain in the 'old neighbourhood,' living as boarders in people's homes, renting apartments, or living in rooming houses. Their reasons for remaining were varied. Some had settled in these communities after the war and did not want to relocate. Others wanted to distance themselves from their Jewish identities. Montreal's trend towards gentrification in the 1980s, however, displaced these survivors from the old neighbourhoods and they ended up living in diverse parts of the city.

As a result, I established links with community centres, agencies, homeless shelters, and synagogues that referred socially isolated individuals. As referrals came in, I met with each individual, sometimes in their homes, sometimes in homeless shelters, and other times in the streets. I spent several nights on a Catholic community bus searching the streets for homeless people who might be Jewish. Each time I met with individuals I informed them about resources in the Jewish community and sometimes linked them with community services. When they were uninterested, I left them a folder of information about resources. Active outreach provided isolated survivors with knowledge about alternatives available to them, which empowered them to make informed choices.

For example, a local women's centre referred a physically frail survivor who was the sole Jewish tenant in a Hungarian low-cost housing development where she was subjected to anti-Semitic provocations. I referred her in turn to supervised housing in the Jewish community where, for the first time since immigrating to Montreal, she was able to live in a Jewish milieu. Another referral came from Sister F., a nun at a downtown homeless shelter. She was concerned about Mrs S., a seventy-four-year-old survivor with dementia symptoms. Many years ago, Mrs S. had fled from an abusive husband and the Grey Nuns Order provided her with shelter. The nun who supported her had died and Sister F. wanted to ensure that Mrs S. was connected with the Jewish community. I linked her with Jewish Family Services.

Consider, too, the following case study.

* * *

One of the most memorable individuals I came across through outreach was Mr D. He was born in Warsaw, Poland, and survived the Warsaw Ghetto, Mauthausen, and Auschwitz. His entire family, including his wife and two small children, were murdered in the Holocaust. After liberation Mr D. went to Israel where he proudly served in the army. In 1952 he immigrated to Montreal and worked as a finisher in a fur factory. He never remarried.

I first met Mr D. in 1991 when the late Sara Rosenfeld, director of the Yiddish Committee at Canadian Jewish Congress, referred him. He responded to an advertisement in the local Jewish press soliciting old Yiddish books. He donated several Yiddish texts. Sara was concerned because Mr D., in his eighties, lived alone on the third floor of an apartment building in the east end of the city, far away from the Jewish community. I decided to conduct an outreach visit. Mr D. suffered from severe angina and had not seen a medical doctor since the 1960s. It was becoming increasingly more difficult for him to climb the stairs to his third-floor apartment. He had no Jewish neighbours. When asked, however, he refused to move from the building he had lived in since coming to Montreal in the late 1940s.

I was struck by Mr D.'s tenacity and determination to maintain control over his disease and his environment. I was also moved by his commitment to the Jewish people and his love of Israel. He showed me articles he had collected over the years and donations he had made to local organizations.

On several occasions I accompanied Mr D. to the emergency room of a local hospital. As we waited for him to be examined by the doctor, Mr D. was convinced he would die if admitted. After he was hospitalized, the repressed memories of his Auschwitz experiences surfaced. His coping mechanisms were reactivated each time he was medically stabilized and allowed to return home. Eventually he accepted a referral for a visiting nurse who monitored his medication. Until his death, he was maintained in the community with nursing and meal assistance.

Mr D. was a private man who, for the most part, kept to himself. When the Drop-in Centre for Holocaust Survivors opened, however, he was one of the first survivors to respond to our advertisement. He quickly became a regular weekly member. Attending this group gave meaning and purpose to his life. He made several close friends and rarely missed attending. When he did, it was because he was in the hospital. Just before his death Mr D. spent two weeks in the hospital. He was supported and visited by Drop-in members who lifted his spirits. When he died, arrangements were made to fly his body to Israel because it was his wish to be buried there.

We held a memorial service for him in the Drop-in Centre. He died surrounded by people who cared about him even though he had no family.

* * *

Example of Group Self-Determination: The Drop-in Centre

By believing and respecting that survivors know what they need, I learned about an unmet need in the community. Survivors often told me they wanted to meet, within a community setting, other survivors who would understand them. Recognizing and acknowledging this gap in service led to development of the Drop-in Centre for Holocaust Survivors at CJCS.

Beginning in the late 1980s, when I started working in this area, many survivors told me about the central role of the *landsmanschaften* in their lives. However, as time passed, these organizations were shrinking in number and size. Consequently, remaining members, who were dependent on these organizations, began to feel lonely and isolated, and some became depressed. I believed there was a need for an organized centre for Holocaust survivors to replace the disappearing *landsmanschaften*. This need became even more evident in the 1990s when I contacted isolated survivors with no family or social support. Some were experiencing loneliness and depression. Others were dwelling on their Holocaust memories or becoming preoccupied with physical ailments.

As I considered establishing a drop-in centre, I researched existing group programs around the world (Dasberg, 1995; Fried & Waxman, 1988; Guttmann, 1995; Hassan, 1995, 1997). I discovered that these groups improve the quality of life for isolated survivors by creating new relationship networks and providing physical, mental, emotional, spiritual, and social stimulation. They also address survivors' needs to socialize with peers and to feel a sense of community and belonging. The Holocaust Survivor Centre (HSC) in London, England, conformed to my vision for a drop-in centre because of its empowerment philosophy (Hassan, 1995, 1997). In this mutual-aid model created by Judith Hassan, survivors are involved in all aspects of the program, from social activities to public speaking about their experiences. They celebrate holidays together, grieve their losses at commemorative events, and warn others about the rise of fascism.

I wanted to create a drop-in centre incorporating an empowerment practice model where survivors would take an active role in self-healing and self-determination, so I proposed the program with two goals in mind – providing a safe environment where survivors could socialize with peers and where information could be provided to them about community resources and services. I knew the importance of involving members in developing goals rather than imposing my own and I trusted that the members would be able to determine what other roles the centre could perform. Some colleagues questioned the absence of a structured group-program plan. I believed, however, that the program would evolve successfully by using an empowerment approach and developing a vision collaboratively with members. Eventually the timing was right and the Drop-in Centre opened with fifteen survivors.

From the beginning, we operated on the premise that individuals are knowledgeable about their needs. Survivors were encouraged to bring their issues and concerns to the group. I included an ongoing needs-assessment component in the program that tracked gaps in services. Each time survivors identified an area of concern, we searched for solutions together and devised a plan to incorporate the new service. For example, this process identified a need for a service to help survivors with compensation claims.

After two months of meetings with little structure, however, members became bored and requested more formal activities. We decided to identify and plan activities and programs that would be incorporated into the meetings. To this day, members act as the Drop-in Centre's Board of Management and we refer to them as such. They are consulted about all aspects of the program and participate in program planning every three months. Giving members a voice and supporting group self-determination continues to be an empowering principle in the Drop-in Centre. It is consistent with enhancing self-esteem and encouraging members to be actively involved, and it helps create other specialized services within the Holocaust survivor program.

Here are interventions and principles that enhance group empowerment and support:

• Treat the relationship between staff and members as a partnership.
• View members as historians who have lived a unique history and have much to teach. Encourage their roles as historians, consultants, and advisers.
• Ensure that professional staff, volunteers, and students are aware of, and sensitive to, the historical context of members' lives and their psycho-social issues.
• View members as competent, adaptive, resourceful, and resilient individuals. Use language that reinforces this view.

- Trust that members are knowledgeable about their needs and, if not, then help them identify and explore them.
- Share power. Involve members in decision making and problem solving.
- Use a collaborative approach to plan programming.
- Provide opportunities for involvement in activities that offer meaning and purpose, for example: volunteering (chapter 6); commemorative activities (chapter 10); and intergenerational programming (chapter 12).

Example of Peer-to-Peer Support: The Survivor Assistance Office

The absence of a centralized location to assist survivors with survivor-specific issues is an example of a gap in services identified by survivors. To address this need, we began by setting up an Information Line at CJCS to answer questions about issues pertaining to restitution and social-security payments. Through an empowerment approach, opportunities were created for Holocaust survivors and second-generation descendants to volunteer as staff. We trained them to provide information about restitution and social security to callers.

The Information Line quickly became a lifeline for many survivors who resisted turning to a community agency for assistance. This peer-to-peer model, where they received information and support from their fellow survivors, generated trust quickly and callers opened up about other problems concerning their daily living. Apart from sharing general information, the service referred callers to the appropriate service both within and outside CJCS.

This service grew rapidly into a full-fledged Survivor Assistance Office (SAO) supported by the Claims Conference (chapter 9). Other SAOs, being piloted in the United States at the time, were staffed with professional workers and paralegals. I believed and advocated that our volunteers could be trained to offer the same service. Today this office provides, at no charge, help with restitution, compensation, and social-security programs; translates foreign documents; and stamps (validates) annual Life Certificates (survivors who receive restitution payments from the German government must have life certificates validated annually to prove they are still alive). The Information Line still responds to all issues pertaining to the survivor community. Using survivors to staff this program is a wonderful example of creating opportunities for survivors to help each other. Who better understands a survivor than another survivor? These volunteers also find meaning and purpose in their own lives by being of service to their peers.

Examples of Supporting Group Advocacy on Political and Social Issues

Survivors feel empowered when they advocate on issues of significance to them. Advocacy also has a beneficial effect on their self-concept. For example, members of the Drop-in Centre wrote to the 'special master' of the Swiss Bank Settlement. Members circulated a petition advocating that the $22.5 million of 'looted assets' be paid directly to individual survivors instead of to organizations that provide them with support. Members also speak up and condemn the mass atrocities that are committed against other people such as in the Darfur region of Sudan. The group wrote a series of letters to local newspapers and Canadian government officials calling for a more aggressive approach in protecting these African civilians. Survivors identify with other mass atrocity victims and feel it is their duty to speak up against such brutalities. We also encourage and support individual survivor initiatives for advocacy. For example, we supported a child survivor who lobbied the Israeli government to release the names of survivors who were put into institutions immediately after the war and still remained there. The group sent parcels to them at Chanukah.

We collaborated with the Canadian Jewish Congress, the former political arm of the Jewish community, to ensure that survivors' voices were heard and that issues of concern to them were recognized and taken seriously. The members actively participate in both local and national issues. For instance, when there was a violent anti-Israel riot at a local university, the group wrote a letter to the chancellor condemning these acts. When the Israeli consulate in Montreal was on the verge of closing for financial reasons, they invited the regional chairperson of the Canadian Jewish Congress to a group meeting to talk about the situation. He suggested they write a letter of protest to the Israeli government, which they did.

Reframing Self-Concept through Intergenerational Programs

We also organize intergenerational programs (discussed in chapter 12). Our members transcend their victim self-concept when they assume roles as 'witnesses to history' and 'educators' in the community. Exchanges with students instil survivors with confidence and self-respect when they realize they have important contributions to make. Teaching younger people has a therapeutic healing effect that brings hope, meaning, and purpose into their lives. Knowing their experiences will not be forgotten after they are gone also brings them peace of mind.

Institutional Adaptation

Ensuring that health-care and social-service systems are responsive to survivors' unique needs is a critical strategy that supports survivor empowerment. As service providers, we need to address the following issues and ensure that policy makers do so as well:

- What gaps in services need to be filled to deal effectively with this population?
- Are there barriers that impede access to service delivery, decision making, and culturally appropriate services?
- Are institutions adapting their environments and services to accommodate Holocaust survivors?
- How well educated are service providers about the unique needs of Holocaust survivors such as their psycho-social functioning, their diversity, and the resources available to them?

Examples of Institutional Barriers Faced by Survivors

ATTITUDES
Some service providers avoid working with survivors because their attitudes and emotional reactions about the Holocaust may overwhelm them and cause vicarious trauma (discussed in chapter 16). Also, survivors are sometimes labelled paranoid, delusional, and / or depressed, which may cause referrals to an inappropriate service. Social problems may also be overlooked because of this labelling. For example, two survivors who were referred to a survivor discussion group had to be redirected to a more appropriate resource. One woman was being harassed by a tenant in her building and was afraid to leave her apartment. She was referred to a storefront organization that deals with tenants' rights. Another woman was being emotionally abused by her husband and was referred to an elder-abuse centre.

ACCESSIBILITY
Technology and language barriers may impede survivors' ability to access social services. Some are intimidated and / or frustrated when

encountering automated telephone answering systems rather than a human voice. Older survivors, who speak their mother tongues and lack proficiency in the local language, may not understand automated instructions to press the required sequence of numbers to reach a worker or department. These factors hamper their ability to access social services. There are also issues around culturally appropriate services (such as gender issues in the Haredi community) and the importance of having workers who speak the survivor's mother tongue. For instance, survivors living in rural areas of Quebec, where the majority of the population is French-speaking, often have difficulty obtaining the services they need in a language they understand.

In chapter 17, I make other recommendations for institutional change and share my thoughts about creating a national resource to streamline and improve services to survivors.

9 Creating a Specialized Program

Listen to survivors, listen to them well. They have more to teach you than you them!

– E. Wiesel (1982)

LISTENING, LEARNING, AND RESPONDING

Mass atrocity survivors have unique needs that are addressed best through specialized services. Creating such services requires considerable knowledge and understanding of the survivor community. While traditional study and work experience is necessary, listening directly to survivors provides me with my most inspirational and insightful lessons. I use empowerment principles, which restore power and control to survivors, and encourage their involvement in developing new services. Recognizing their strengths and reinforcing a belief in survivorship – rather than seeing them as fragile victims – helps me create service models that promote healing and growth.

My knowledge and understanding of service needs for Holocaust survivors in the Montreal community is gleaned from a variety of personal and professional experiences in different settings. I will share the lessons learned along my path and associated milestones. In so doing, I hope to inspire other service providers to seek out the resources and support needed to develop specialized services for their own survivor communities. My approach and service models are applicable to survivors of other mass atrocities. The particulars, however, are unique for each community.

A Daughter of Holocaust Survivors: Exploring Roots

I grew up with survivor parents. My father always talked about his family history and ordeals during the war. My mother, however, rarely spoke about her family of origin and her past. I began to realize I was missing a large part of my family history.

In 1979 I became a member of a support and discussion group for offspring of Holocaust survivors – the first of its kind in Montreal. This group helped me to understand the impact of the Holocaust on my own life. With its support, I found the courage to face my mother's tears and ask about her family. It was as if she had waited all these years for me to ask. She wanted to share her past but was afraid to impose it on me. However, once I showed an interest, she opened up and, soon afterwards, showed me photographs I had never seen before. They were pictures of her family that she had buried in the dirt of the Łódź Ghetto when it was liquidated, and then retrieved after the war. She continued to hide these pictures in a brown envelope for all those years since. In our discussions she brought them out and introduced me to her parents (my grandparents), her brothers and sisters (my aunts and uncles), and her grandparents (my great-grandparents).

Thus began our journey of healing, each of us grieving our losses. Her family pictures, so long hidden, finally found a place to rest. I had them restored and mounted copies in a family tree on a wall in our family room. My mother put the originals into an album and introduced my children to their deceased great-grandparents, aunts, and uncles. The process of sharing the Holocaust legacy and exploring my roots brought my mother and me closer together. I was able to develop a sense of continuity between my ancestors who were murdered and those who survived and pass on their legacy.

Encouraging my late mother to share her past showed me first-hand the healing power of disclosure. Before her death, my mother went on to write her memoirs and provided audiovisual testimony at the Montreal Holocaust Memorial Centre. In the years after she opened up, her sadness and grief lessened, and her life took on new meaning and purpose. She became active in the Łódźer Society, where her leadership skills surfaced when she assumed the role of Ladies Auxiliary chairperson. At that time, the auxiliary initiated important projects in Israel and Montreal. In retrospect, my role as witness to the atrocities my mother endured allowed her to release repressed memories. This, in turn, enabled her to alleviate her grieving and achieve some peace of mind.

These conversations with my mother also taught me lessons about forming a relationship with a survivor. The most important is that serving as an empathetic, active listener and validating the survivor's experience in a non-judgmental manner supports and encourages a survivor to heal.

Volunteering in the Community

During my volunteer work at the Canadian Jewish Congress, I discovered that survivors institutionalized Holocaust education and remembrance activities, spoke out against anti-Semitism, founded an Association of Survivors of Nazi Oppression, created a speakers' bureau, honoured 'righteous Gentiles' (non-Jews who saved Jews during the war), and helped establish the Montreal Holocaust Memorial Centre and the Holocaust Remembrance Committee of the Canadian Jewish Congress. I learned that survivors had an ongoing mission to remember and honour memories of their murdered families, friends, and extinguished communities. They did this by organizing educational programs and commemorative events that bear witness to the atrocities they endured. I also learned about their commitment to fight racism and social injustices (discussed in chapter 4).

Studying as a Social-Work Intern

As an intern at Jewish Family Services in the mid-1980s, I was exposed to Holocaust survivors living in the community. My caseload consisted of socially isolated older adults, some of whom were survivors. When visiting their homes to conduct bio-psycho-social assessments in response to their requests for social services such as home-care assistance, meals-on-wheels, and transportation, I found that survivors wanted to talk about their war experiences. It was difficult to shift their attention back to the assessment and, most of the time, I was unable to complete a service plan. Most thanked me for listening to them and said they felt some relief from their pain as a result.

I brought these observations to my supervisor, who suggested I speak with other workers to see if they were witnessing the same behaviour. As it turned out, they were, but they usually directed the discussion back to the assessment. They also told me that many Holocaust survivors came to the agency with issues of loneliness and assorted difficulties with activities of daily living. They quickly realized, however, that these survivors wanted to talk about their wartime past. In my own case, I found this need most pronounced among socially isolated survivors who lacked cognitive, emotional, and social stimulation. I was amazed that, forty years after the end of the Holocaust, many survivors living in the community were still preoccupied with their wartime experiences. I began to understand that they needed to be heard and validated, and the system was not responsive. I also learned that, while some survivors did not want to talk about the Holocaust under any circumstances, many did not talk because when they had done so in the past they encountered avoidance and indifference.

Masters Research Project

In interviews with Montreal survivors during my master's research study at McGill University, I learned about the importance of their *landsmanschaften*, which fostered a camaraderie based on shared traumas. Survivors repeatedly said they felt acceptance, recognition, and security in the company of those who had seen each other in the most degrading situations but had managed to survive with dignity. In these organizations many found sympathetic people who could understand their ordeals. Members comforted each other as they mourned their losses and fulfilled their commitment to remember by participating in commemorative rituals, often at the site of monuments erected to memorialize their martyrs and obliterated communities. These organizations also served as a vehicle to transmit the history and culture of their pre-war *heim* to their new environment and families. I discovered the importance of support groups to fulfil survivors' needs for socialization with peers and foster a sense of community and belonging. During this research I recognized the need for a drop-in centre for survivors whose *landsmanschaften* activities were diminishing.

Survivors also taught me about the importance of memorialization. Commemoration of family members was an urgent concern for survivors who formed or joined organizations. Survivors were able to grieve their losses at annual memorial services, *hazkarahs*, and *yizkors*, as these services are called. To this day, survivors view their participation in commemorative activities as sacred duties and obligations. Eva Fogelman (1988) and Yael Danieli (1999) discuss the healing value of memorialization and ritualization in communal commemorative activities that provide opportunities for shared grieving.

Commemorative activities have been integrated into all group programs I create. For example, the survivors in the Drop-in Centre organize and participate in the agency's annual Holocaust Commemoration Service. The last session of each of the survivor discussion and support groups (discussed in chapter 10) includes a commemorative service with candle-lighting ceremony and recitation of the *kaddish*. Survivors also fill out *Pages of Testimony*, distributed by the Yad Vashem Museum in Israel, which memorializes, in printed form, family members who were killed in the Holocaust.

In addition, while conducting interviews with survivors, I picked up important clues about how they wish to be treated. I subsequently integrated these observations in all my programs and interactions. Interventions include: viewing survivors as individuals who have lived a unique history and have much to teach; listening in an empathetic, nonjudgmental way; treating them with dignity and respect; validating their experiences; and acknowledging their competency, accomplishments, and coping skills. These interventions are discussed in more detail in chapters 8 and 13.

Professional Social Worker

In 1988, when funds from the Claims Conference became available to community agencies providing services to survivors, I was asked to write a proposal for the implementation of specialized services in Montreal at Jewish Support Services for the Elderly (JSSE). In July 1989 JSSE received a three-year allocation to implement an outreach and transportation program to assist isolated and frail Holocaust survivors. It was the first agency in Canada to receive such funds. I was hired in September 1989 to coordinate the outreach program. While doing outreach, I identified survivors' unique needs and implemented a few programs and services to meet those needs: actively searching for isolated survivors and informing them about community services; providing information, referrals, and advocacy; creating support and discussion groups in collaboration with the psychogeriatric clinic of the Jewish General Hospital; and co-founding, with the Jewish Nursing Home Day Centre and the Young Men / Women's Hebrew Association (YM-YWHA), a psycho-social group where half the participants were survivors. I also initiated staff-training workshops for my peers.

During my time at JSSE I learned about survivors' reluctance to receive help, their vulnerabilities in the community, the impact of isolation, activities that trigger wartime memories, their fear and mistrust of government bureaucracy, and the importance of group services. I also recognized the importance of outreach to isolated and unaffiliated survivors. I began to identify services unique to survivors' special needs, such as a drop-in centre for their exclusive use, an intergenerational oral-history program, and a centralized office to deal with compensation and restitution issues. However, when I proposed new services along these lines, I found myself at odds with senior management, who believed that survivors' needs were no different from those of the rest of the older adult population. I had reached an impasse.

Private Practice

I left JSSE in 1995 and opened a private practice specializing in therapeutic and educational services for Holocaust survivors and their families, and the individuals and agencies that supported them. Within individual therapy sessions, I helped survivors work through their losses and feelings of guilt, rage, and shame. Some were able to integrate their Holocaust experience into their present lives and went on to write memoirs and educate others. They divulged secrets they had never told anyone. Some were able to achieve some peace of mind, a task not easily accomplished.

I also organized educational workshops that helped survivors understand the impact of their traumatic experiences on their personal lives, and those of their sons and daughters. For their children, I facilitated time-limited psycho-educational second- generation awareness groups. In addition, I conducted educational workshops for health and service providers to sensitize them to the unique needs of Holocaust survivors and to share practical interventions.

The most significant lesson I learned in private practice is that survivors are able to engage in a trusting relationship with a therapist. This was contrary to the literature. (See chapter 13 where I discuss the techniques and interventions I use to build a therapeutic alliance.)

The need for a drop-in centre for Holocaust survivors also became increasingly evident to me while I was in private practice. I found that many survivors had little or no family and were living in isolation without social-support systems. Many of their friends had died or moved out of town. Some had previously been members of *landsmanschaften*, but when these organizations disbanded, they did not join others. I often heard about their desire to belong to a group of peers who had shared similar life events and who would understand them.

CREATING A SPECIALIZED PROGRAM WITHIN THE COMMUNITY

In 1996 I submitted a proposal to the Jewish Community Foundation of Montreal to establish a specialized drop-in centre. The Community Planning Department of Federation CJA (Combined Jewish Appeal) conducted consultations with the executive directors of community organizations and a long-term-care facility serving older adults in the Montreal Jewish community. The department also convened a meeting to discuss the feasibility of such a project. The agenda included discussion about an appropriate location for a drop-in centre. I wanted a community-based setting that promoted positive ageing and wellness, and that would also provide opportunities for involvement in a variety of social, recreational, and educational activities. I was concerned that locating a centre within an institutional environment would reinforce perceptions of survivors as weak, vulnerable, and ill. The former Golden Age Association (now merged into CJCS) came closest to my vision.

After deliberation, the Community Planning Department recommended that funds be allocated to the Golden Age Association to create a half-day drop-in centre that would be open to survivors as a once-a-week program. The Jewish Community Foundation of Montreal provided seed money for the first year of operation and I was retained under contract for seven hours a week to establish and coordinate the program. Planning and development began in August 1997 and the Drop-in Centre opened on 31 October. The centre was well received and membership grew. I decided to leave private practice in May 2000 to join CJCS where I could focus on developing, coordinating, and supervising an expanded service. The program evolved into the present-day Services for Holocaust Survivors and Their Families at CJCS, which continues to run the Drop-in Centre along with other specialized services that are developed when additional needs are identified.

Organizational Context for Survivor Services

In 1998, shortly after the Drop-in Centre began, CJCS was formed by amalgamating two constituent agencies of Federation CJA that delivered overlapping services to older adults in the Montreal area. The former Jewish Support Services for the Elderly offered a wide range of social services to frail seniors; the former Golden Age Association was a community centre providing social, recreational, and educational programs along with some social services. The merger reduced bureaucracy, improved accessibility, and eliminated duplicate services. The merger also created an opportunity for the community to offer a broader range of programs and services for all older adults in a more cost-efficient manner. Today this large non-profit community agency provides a continuum of social, recreational, educational, and psycho-social services to address the needs of adults over fifty years of age. It strives to maintain an atmosphere that promotes positive attitudes on ageing and acknowledges the dignity and self-worth of all individuals regardless of whether they are functioning autonomously or not.

CJCS's Department of Social Services includes a centralized intake system – not exclusive to survivors – that serves as the entry point to the agency's social services. There is no waiting list. Skilled intake workers provide older adults and their families with information, referrals, advocacy, and crisis intervention. They conduct needs assessments by telephone or in person. Through home visits they determine individuals' level of functioning and identify risk factors in their living environments. In addition, they usually work in collaboration with other workers in the public sector and other agencies. These intake and assessment services are free, are designed to be user-friendly, and provide easy access to health-care workers, programs, and services. Individuals refer to the system as 'one-stop shopping.'

Intake workers also function as case managers for people who require ongoing supervision and care. They develop individual care plans with older adults that often include family involvement. They may serve as a liaison with family members who live out of town. These case managers monitor the individual's situation, collaborate with health professionals, and coordinate services such as:

- Home care: for older adults who need assistance with personal hygiene and care (bathing, dressing, grooming, incontinence issues); accompaniment for errands (shopping, banking, medical appointments); assistance with routine household tasks (meal preparation, laundry, light housekeeping); and respite.
- Assisted transportation and accompaniment: for older adults who cannot travel on their own to medical and other essential appointments.
- Meals-on-wheels: provides fresh or frozen kosher meals to older adults who have difficulty preparing their own meals.

These services empower older adults to maintain control over their environment and prolong their autonomy in the community.

Services for Holocaust Survivors and Their Families fall within the Department of Social Services at CJCS. The programs offered by the department include: Comprehensive Care Management; Homecare; Kosher Meals-on-Wheels, Assisted Transportation and Accompaniment Service (ATASE); a Community Mental Health program for older adults with mental illness; and Day Programs for older adults with varying degrees of memory loss. Having specialized services for survivors within an agency that offers a wide range of services provides faster service referrals, less bureaucracy, diverse programs, and progressive care.

Specialized Program for Holocaust Survivors and Their Families

The following specialized services were developed and are offered within the survivor program. Most were created in response to survivors' needs. The program started with the Drop-in Centre and expanded to include the other components. These services are provided in addition to the regular services available at CJCS.

Drop-in Centre for Holocaust Survivors

Detailed information about the evolution of this long-term group service is discussed in chapter 11.

Intergenerational Programming

A variety of intergenerational programs are discussed in chapter 12.

Survivor Assistance Office

Initially, many survivors came to the Drop-in Centre with questions pertaining to restitution and social-security payments. Some had received letters written in German, which they did not understand. Others were frustrated and confused by the application process for new compensation and funding programs. When they approached outside individuals and organizations, they often got the run-around and had difficulty obtaining accurate information.

The number of survivors needing assistance increased significantly in the fall of 2000 when the German government, along with certain German industries, announced a $5.2-billion fund to compensate survivors for wartime slave labour. Shortly thereafter, the Swiss Banks Settlement, which dealt with dormant Swiss accounts owned by deceased family members, was created. In response to the growing need for assistance with these programs, I established an Information Line, mentioned in the previous chapter. We set up a direct phone number that bypassed the CJCS receptionist. Using an empowerment model, I trained survivor and second-generation volunteers to provide information about these programs to callers. This approach streamlined and simplified an otherwise complicated process.

By January 2001, CJCS had become the central agency in Quebec for the distribution of slave-labour forms. Many survivors were unable to complete these forms and required help. We set up a satellite office in an area where a large number of survivors lived. The Claims Conference sent staff people who trained our volunteers to complete these forms. This 'local office' approach attracted many survivors with whom we had not worked before and we were able to empower them with information and referrals to other agency services and programs.

In 2002, after negotiating funding from the Claims Conference, CJCS opened a local Survivor Assistance Office. Igor Epshtein coordinates the service. He is one of the most knowledgeable people in Canada regarding compensation, restitution, and social-security pensions. Our SAO is internationally recognized as a state-of-the-art service used not only by our community but by callers from around the world. It provides 'one stop shopping' for survivors seeking information and assistance in all areas of their lives. In the early years we held public community forums to provide survivors and their families with information. Today, staff and volunteers reach out to community agencies and survivor groups with updates about compensation programs. The Information Line also continues to be an integral part of this service. It provides answers to questions about all issues pertaining to the survivor community.

Emergency Assistance Program and Home Care Services Program

Many survivors need financial assistance for special situations. Such assistance is available for eligible survivors to address immediate needs such as medication, medical equipment and treatment not paid for by government-funded programs, rent, utility payments (heat, hot water, electricity), food, dental care, home equipment and repair, and other contingencies. The Claims Conference allocates funds to social-service agencies and organizations, such as CJCS, which administer the Emergency Assistance Program (EAP) and assist survivors with requests. In Montreal, Federation CJA contributes funds to the EAP as well. In 2010 the Home Care Services Program also became available for eligible survivors who need home-care and cleaning services. Funding for this program is the result of Claims Conference negotiations with the German government to enable survivors to remain in their own homes for as long as possible. Both the EAP and the Home Care Services Program require an assessment and qualification process.

Stamping Survivors' Life Certificates

Listening to survivors, and taking their concerns seriously, sometimes requires advocacy. For example, survivors in the Drop-in Centre described the difficulties they had travelling downtown to have their annual Life Certificates stamped at the German Consulate. Chava Respitz, a long-time volunteer at the Drop-in Centre, and I met with the German consul general to discuss this issue. Shortly thereafter, CJCS was authorized to validate survivor Life Certificates. Several staff members applied for commissioner of oath status allowing them to stamp certificates. On behalf of these survivors, we also send these certificates to the German Consulate in Toronto (previously they were sent to the German Embassy in Ottawa).

Local Health Resort Cure (Kur)

Survivors in the Drop-in Centre also alerted us that Quebec did not have any health-resort facilities for survivors. For survivors who receive monthly BEG payments in compensation for damage to their health caused by the Holocaust, the German government pays the costs of such treatment. Some were going to facilities in the Catskill Mountains in New York. However, it was becoming increasingly difficult for many to make these trips because of physical fraility. Others were precluded from travelling to New York either because they lacked the financial means or because they were unable to obtain traveller's health insurance owing to their pre-existing medical conditions.

Chava Respitz and I began to lobby the German Consulate to approve an already-existing health-resort facility in the Laurentian Mountains, north of Montreal. We specifically wanted to include Camp B'nai B'rith, a kosher community camp with a seniors' village. It took several years, and a series of meetings and letters, but eventually the German government approved several facilities in the Laurentians, including Camp B'nai B'rith.

During this advocacy process, we also established a collaborative relationship with the German Consulate enabling the latter to refer survivors who require assistance to our agency. The Consulate is an important resource for reaching out to isolated, lonely, and sometimes cognitively impaired survivors who may not know where to go for help in the community.

Holocaust Survivors' Tracing Centre

In November 2007 I received a Red Cross Tracing Request Form from a survivor who attended a presentation at the Montreal Holocaust Memorial Centre. This form was distributed at the presentation to encourage attendees to initiate tracing requests to locate lost family and friends or determine the circumstances of death. I noticed, however, that the address on the form was far away from the Jewish community. I was curious if survivors availed themselves of the Red Cross Tracing Service and followed up with a telephone call. I learned that few survivors used the service. At this time the Red Cross was looking for a way to make its tracing service more accessible to the Jewish community.

I believed it made sense to locate a tracing service within an agency that already provides centralized services unique to the survivor community. We began discussions with the Red Cross and launched a joint project between CJCS and the Canadian Red Cross to establish a Tracing Centre at CJCS. The centre opened in February 2009, with initial funding by the Red Cross. This innovative service was the first time the Red Cross had opened a satellite site in a community setting to address the unique needs of Holocaust survivors.

Mara Schneiderman, a social worker at CJCS at the time, and I coordinated the program's development. She trained and supervised six volunteers to help survivors fill out tracing requests and oversaw the day-to-day operation of this service. Volunteers met with survivors privately and completed tracing requests which were sent to the Red Cross and subsequently forwarded to the International Tracing Service (ITS) in Arolsen, Germany, where the largest collection of digitized Holocaust-era records are housed. Designing the new service was easy because we already had a successful model – our Survivor Assistance Office. In its first year of operation, the Tracing Centre generated over sixteen times as many new requests as were received during the previous year by the Red Cross. The centre also attracted a new group of survivors and their families to our agency who did not know about the other services available to them. Unfortunately, this important service was shut down after its first year of operation because of a lack of continued funding.

Educating Social-Service Providers about Survivor Issues

Over the years service providers have often told me that they do not know how to interact with survivors. Many survivors, for their part, tell me that service providers don't understand them or may interact with them in ways that trigger traumatic memories. It is important to provide training programs to health and social-service professionals, para-professionals, religious leaders, and volunteers so they are aware of, and responsive to, survivors' needs. The programs I provide include the following components which are adapted to meet the needs of each setting: a historical overview of the Holocaust; survivors' psycho-social functioning: vulnerability and resilience; theoretical practice frameworks; trauma and ageing; clinical interventions; psycho-educational / social-service models; resources; and vicarious trauma. Health-care and social-service providers need easy access to this information and associated interventions on an ongoing basis.

The Wish Project: An Unrealized Service

Survivors often tell me of 'wishes' they have not been able to achieve in their lives. These wishes might include accomplishing life-long dreams, reuniting with family members, or completing projects. For example, some survivors would like to visit siblings and other family members who live far away but they cannot afford the price of an airplane ticket. One survivor in our Drop-in Centre has several great-grandchildren living in Israel whom she has never seen. Others are writing memoirs and need help to edit and publish them. Still others would like to complete a special project such as holding an art exhibition or writing a book.

A 'wish project' would make survivors' dreams a reality. Helping them to realize their wishes would enhance the quality of their lives by giving them something meaningful to look forward to. In addition, such a program would enrich their lives with hope, happiness, and cherished memories. Fulfilling their wishes could bring peace of mind at the end of their lives, and help families celebrate precious moments together.

A project like this, however, requires funding – perhaps from a benefactor. It also requires establishment of selection criteria and financial parameters, and a structure to review individual requests, make selections, grant the wishes, provide follow-up, and evaluate results. But the benefits would be considerable: generating tremendous goodwill and publicity around the community, bringing happiness to many, and providing meaning and purpose for sponsors.

A PIONEERING JOURNEY

Attitudes towards providing specialized services for Holocaust survivors began to change in the late 1980s when the Claims Conference started giving funding to agencies and organizations around the world. For example, in 2010 the Claims Conference allocated more than $208 million to organizations and institutions in seventy-five countries to assist and care for Holocaust survivors (Claims Conference, 2010). These allocations derive from a number of sources and in 2010 included the German, Austrian, and Hungarian governments; the Swiss Banks Settlement Looted Assets Class; the International Commission on Holocaust Era Insurance Claims (ICHEC); and the Harry and Jeanette Weinberg Holocaust Survivor Emergency Assistance Fund.

In the mid-1990s the Federation CJA's Commission of Services to Seniors identified Holocaust survivors as a priority population requiring special attention. Existing services for this population were inconsistent and fragmented. Somewhere along the line survivors fell through the cracks of community responsibility. Even though their unique needs had been identified by front-line workers, documented in books and journals, and discussed at international conferences, there was resistance in the community to funding specialized services for them.

Although it takes someone with passion and a vision to act as a catalyst when creating something new, it also takes a window of opportunity. Circumstances were changing and, in 1997, the timing was right to propose specialized services for survivors to the community.

In my first meeting with Herb Finkelberg, the executive director of the former Golden Age Association, he asked me: 'If you had a magic wand, what would Services for Holocaust Survivors and Their Families look like five years from now?' Herb encouraged me to think in broad strokes. I outlined the gaps in services I had identified. He replied that he, the management team, and the staff would support my vision. He also told me that there were a number of survivors who came to the agency and sat in the cafeteria all day. His staff was unsure how to respond to them. I realized the window was open and I was willing to return to work in a community agency to take advantage of this opportunity. It appeared that community resistance was shifting and now there was openness and readiness to begin a service tailored to survivors' needs.

In hindsight, I could not have predicted the sequence of events that resulted in developing services for Holocaust survivors. Although I began with a vision and some guiding assumptions, there were challenges along the way that required flexibility, open-mindedness, and the courage to stand up to criticism. Writing this book provided me with an opportunity to reflect on the major milestones in my journey.

Here are those milestones, which may help to inspire others to create services in their own areas of interest.

Creating a Vision around My Passion

I knew that working with Holocaust survivors was my life's calling ever since the time I was a social-work intern and first recognized survivors' unique needs. My early childhood also influenced me in choosing a career. As a young child I saw myself as an agent of change. This self-perception emanated from my birth, which transformed my parents' lives because I symbolized their survival and hope for the future. So, when I began to realize that there were no organized social services for survivors in Montreal, I wanted to change things. I developed a vision, reached an understanding of what was needed, and began a process to make it happen. Working with survivors helped me find fulfillment in a career that I care deeply about. Having a positive influence on others fuelled my passion, which continues today.

Identifying Gaps in Service by Listening and Learning

From the beginning I documented the issues that survivors brought to my attention. I listened and took their concerns seriously. I conducted my own research by consulting with other survivors and my colleagues. This led to my developing a plan of action. Most of the services discussed in this book evolved from listening directly to survivors. My varied personal, professional, and volunteer experiences within the survivor community were an asset, inspiring me to advocate and create services responsive to survivors' needs.

Securing Funding

This can be a challenge. I had the good fortune to work with individuals who believed in the importance and necessity of the service I was proposing. They connected me with community funding sources that had the power to make it happen. The community provided a venue for the Drop-in Centre and initial funding. Once the centre was operational and successful, other funding sources became available.

Changing Attitudes and Overcoming Traditional Approaches

When I first started as a social-work intern in the mid-1980s, the clinical literature predominantly focused on pathology. This tended to stigmatize and stereotype survivors. Even today, when I speak at conferences about my empowerment approach, most specifically the Drop-in Centre and its educational programming, sometimes I am asked if survivors are capable of learning new skills, participating in intellectual pursuits, and leading discussions. It seems that many programs focus exclusively on social activities such as Yiddish sing-a-longs, parties, and bingo.

I challenged prevailing attitudes and traditional approaches to practice by developing programs that focused on survivors' strengths and coping abilities. I believe that providing intellectual and physical programs, along with social ones, enhances the quality of life for survivors. They welcome the diversity and stimulation.

Being Creative, Thinking outside the Box, and Finding Ways to Test New Ideas

In the late 1990s I learned that the Claims Conference was initiating Survivor Assistance Offices in four United States cities that would help survivors with compensation and restitution issues. These offices were staffed by retired lawyers and paralegals who helped survivors with their compensation and restitution claims. Canada had no such office so I began to advocate for one at CJCS. However, I believed that it should be staffed by survivor volunteers who would provide peer-to-peer information and support to the survivor community. I was asked if survivors were capable of learning the vast amount of information about the different pensions and compensation programs. My immediate response was 'yes' because survivors were already providing this service on a centralized Information Line within the Montreal community. Today this successful service is an alternative entry point to the agency for survivors who call about a variety of issues.

Having the Courage to Face Criticism
and Being Open-Minded and Flexible

The establishment resists change. In the beginning, the directors of most agencies that provided services to older adults were against the idea of a drop-in centre exclusively for survivors. However, once I presented the rationale, and gave them an opportunity to discuss it, most wanted a drop-in centre within their setting.

Some colleagues also criticized me when I started the Drop-in Centre. As noted earlier, they questioned my lack of a structured group-program plan. Although I was well versed in group-work practice, I started the centre with only two goals. Using an empowerment practice approach, I trusted that new goals would emerge from the members as they developed a group vision. This approach worked and, to this day, members feel a sense of group ownership and a strong commitment to the program.

Dealing with Oppressive Situations and Growing in the Process

Working in an agency that did not support my vision of specialized services for survivors spurred me to become resourceful and creative. When senior management told me that survivors did not require specialized support and discussion groups, I found allies in the community who helped me make the case to provide these services.

Having the Courage and Willingness
to Change When It's Not Working

At some point we may realize that things are not working and change is imperative. I decided in 1995 to start a private practice so that I could specialize in services for survivors of genocide and war. Eventually attitudes in the community began to change and resources became available. Once this happened, I left private practice and returned to an agency setting so I could provide a more comprehensive service.

10 Short-Term Group Services

In this group I do not have to put on my I'm fine smile.
– Survivor in a Group Program

Group programs are an effective way to develop a mutual-aid process. I learned about the effectiveness of group work during my studies at university and, more notably, from survivors who described their *landsmanschaften*. Organizational activities included opportunities for socializing, educating members, sharing experiences, and giving meaning to survivors' lives. All groups I organize and develop include components of mutual aid. Belonging to a mutual-aid group is already a familiar experience for many survivors.

Task-oriented and support-oriented groups are discussed below. Although the models are different, the underlying assumption is the same for all these types of groups: a group of individuals, with common concerns, can be brought together to help each other.

GROUP COMPOSITION: HOMOGENEOUS OR HETEROGENEOUS

I am sometimes asked if it is better to create groups that have a homogeneous rather than heterogeneous membership. In other words, how alike or different should people be? In homogeneous groups, members have a common purpose for being in the group and share some personal characteristics (Toseland & Rivas, 2009). Heterogeneous groups may consist of members from different cultures and / or life experiences.

Early in my career I recommended forming a homogeneous psycho-social group that brought together survivors who were living in the community and were lonely and isolated. My recommendation was based on the findings of an outreach report I had completed and the research literature at the time, which identified survivors' unique needs. Management did not support the creation of a homogeneous group. Since I had no control over their decision, I consented to help organize and facilitate a psycho-social day program for older adults who were in a similar situation. Half of the members turned out to be Holocaust survivors.

This group program worked well in some areas and not so well in others. It worked well in common interest areas such as ageing, politics, healthy living, health care, and the celebration of Jewish holidays. But it did not work well in areas where members' experiences differed. Professional staff must be aware of, and sensitive to, survivor-related issues in a mixed group because occasionally disagreements arise that need to be diffused. For example, in the case of my group, non-survivor members did not understand why survivors' conversations were frequently interwoven with references to their wartime past. In one situation, several members who lived in Canada during the war described their own hardships, such as rationed food. This led to heated arguments comparing the suffering each had endured.

These conflicts can be resolved by organizing group programs where members inform each other about their experiences during the war years. Staff should create ground rules for these potentially conflictual discussions. For instance, participants should agree to listen to each other's experiences and respect each other's right to communicate them within the group. I also sensitized the group to current events that can trigger a survivor's traumatic memory, and the relief some feel when they talk about these memories with people who listen. After participants told their stories, the non-survivors concluded that there could be no comparisons between their experiences and those of the survivors. Both groups were able to share common concerns and the survivors felt heard and validated. As a result, this approach fostered understanding between the two factions rather than resentment.

I believe that heterogeneous groups have a limited benefit for many survivors, especially those who experienced negative reactions and hostility from their fellow Jews when they arrived in Canada. Yet mixed groups do work for some individuals and can lead to a better understanding between survivors and non-survivors who live together in the community. However, I had taken the idea of heterogeneity as far as I could in dealing with survivor issues and I continued to advocate for homogeneous groups.

After being involved with different types of groups, I can conclude that homogeneous ones deal more effectively with survivors' recovery and healing efforts, especially for survivors who were greeted with negative attitudes and societal taboos about the Holocaust when they immigrated to Canada. These attitudes created a chasm between survivors and the rest of the Jewish community that continues to this day. It is unrealistic to expect survivors who did not integrate into the general community to find a place of belonging in heterogeneous groups. They found a supportive environment within the *landsmanschaften* they created or resuscitated in the post-war years. These homogeneous group structures served as a model for the Drop-in Centre for Holocaust Survivors. The centre provides a safe environment for healing and recovery within a community setting that inspires survivors with hope, meaning, and purpose. The next chapter describes this environment.

So, in answer to the question about homogeneity or heterogeneity, the organizer must assess individuals' needs and the main purpose for the group. For example, I facilitated discussion and support groups (discussed later in this chapter) exclusively for survivors who were in distress because of a resurgence of painful traumatic memories. Group participation was limited to survivors with common symptoms and similar goals. These groups, which brought survivors together in a supportive environment to share their feelings, thoughts, and concerns pertaining to the past and present, were an effective venue in which to meet their unique needs. It would not have served any purpose to integrate non-survivors in a group of this nature.

HOMOGENEOUS TASK GROUPS

Toseland and Rivas (2009) define task groups as follows: 'Task group members create a common bond by working together to accomplish a task, carry out a mandate, or produce a product' (14).

The following discussion describes a task group for Holocaust survivors that I brought together and oversaw when I was a social-work intern. It is an example of strengths-based practice and empowerment intervention. Over time, the focus changed from therapeutic discussion

and support to a task group that organized a program for agency service providers.

Context: Identifying the Need for a Group

I noticed that some older adults at the Jewish Family Services Social
Service Centre were survivors who needed to talk about the Holocaust.
When I suggested forming a group, the idea was overwhelmingly supported by both Helena Sonin, coordinator of the Community Services
to the Elderly Unit (CSE), and the late David August, the senior caseworker who handled the majority of Holocaust survivors at the agency.
In fact, agency workers confirmed that many isolated survivors seeking
social contact were coming to the agency with loneliness as their presenting problem. During conversations with them, it soon became evident that they needed to talk about their war experiences.

Changing Staff Perceptions

After introducing the group concept and its objectives to the caseworkers, I sent a memo requesting referrals. I also conducted individual interviews with the coordinator of the intake unit as well as twelve case
managers and crisis workers. My purpose was to:

- develop a personal relationship with each worker;
- solicit support for this project;
- learn about their impressions and perceptions of survivors in their
  caseloads;
- familiarize myself with their clinical interventions with this
  population; and
- create a profile of the survivors they intended to refer to my group.

It came as no surprise that the profiles of the survivors in the workers' and managers' caseloads corroborated the clinical literature at the
time: traumatized individuals having difficulty coping with life. Here
are some of their comments:

- The Holocaust weighs heavily on them. When they come in, the first
  thing they talk about are their war experiences.
- Their coping mechanisms have been adversely affected by the war.
  They suffer from paranoia and are suspicious and mistrustful.

- They feel tremendous guilt at having survived.
- Their mourning is excessive and prolonged.
- They live in the past.
- They are mistrustful of doctors.
- They are very needy emotionally. They need the total involvement of the worker.
- There is a tremendous remorse about the past, a void as a result of the loss of a childhood and family.
- Many lost their self-esteem when they immigrated to Canada and their social status declined, an experience especially common among people from aristocratic pre-war families.
- They are hoarders and cling to things, such as newspapers and money.
- They have been uprooted from a completely different way of life and did not acculturate to life here. The older the person, the more difficult their adjustment.

Although I asked my colleagues for general impressions and perceptions of survivors, they presented profiles of psychopathology and victimization. Subsequently I asked them to describe some positive characteristics, assets, and coping strategies of these same individuals. The following list emerged:

- Generous with money; gives to charity.
- Enjoys living well; is a spender and not a hoarder.
- Very motivated.
- Tremendous drive to accomplish. He built a successful business.
- Made supreme sacrifices for his children.
- General acceptance of present circumstances no matter how difficult.

Coping mechanisms of this clinical population included:

- refusing to give up – even those in the worst physical states focus their energies on survival;
- recognizing the preciousness of life, having 'a thirst for living' even when severely ill;
- going on with life in spite of periodic breakdowns;
- withstanding pain no matter how severe;
- making a determined attempt to be released when hospitalized;
- living on a day-to-day basis, always with a smile and a joke;

- not dwelling on incapacities, but focusing instead on what can be done to change things; and
- accepting the present situation and circumstances, regardless of how bad these may be.

This process is an example of using interventions that focus on individuals' positive attributes to change perceptions about them. Taking this approach has direct implications for practice because our perception has an impact on our work. Hence, forming a pathological profile implies that individuals are incapable of determining their needs and organizing their own lives. As Saleebey (2006) states: 'Accentuating the problems of clients creates a wave of pessimistic expectations of, and predictions about, the client, the client's environment, and the client's capacity to cope with that environment' (4).

Group Formation

I conducted individual interviews with the survivors referred to the group by workers of the CSE unit. I began each interview with a positive statement such as 'many survivors are well-functioning, compassionate individuals, who, in spite of tremendous pain and suffering, rebuilt their lives and became productive members of the community.' The survivors responded by exhibiting their strengths. For example, my opening statement elicited responses such as the following:

- Mr G., a Yiddish writer, urged me to accompany him to the Jewish Public Library where he showed me a chapter he had written in one of the *yizkor bicher* (memorial books written by survivors at the end of the war). In addition, I learned about the autobiography he was writing.
- Mr D., a former Hungarian reporter, showed me newspaper articles he had written for the *Canadian Jewish Digest* as well as the *Montreal Star*, a now-defunct newspaper. He showed me a dossier he prepared for the Canadian Jewish Congress on the topic of Hungarian Nazis residing in Montreal. I also learned that he attended the 1938 Evian Conference in France where delegates from thirty-two countries discussed easing immigration restrictions for German-Jewish refugees.
- Mrs S. explained that she was the first Jew and woman to serve in the Polish government after the war. During the war, which she spent in Russia, she was responsible for saving many lives in the course of an epidemic.

- Mr S. recounted that he had served with the Hungarian storm troopers during the war. For the past twelve years he had been actively volunteering with different organizations in the Jewish community. He spent seven days a week in chronic-care hospitals visiting people who had no one else to comfort them.

The list of accomplishments and contributions made by this clinical population was long.

The approach I intended to employ, before I conducted the individual pre-group interviews, was therapeutic discussion where people would feel free to share their pre-war, wartime, and post-war experiences. I hoped that an atmosphere of camaraderie would eventually develop and that the group would function along the lines of a self-help or mutual-aid model.

I shared my goal for this group during the interviews and asked about the participants' expectations. Several individuals said they had a different vision. They told me they had talked considerably about their war experiences and did not feel the need to do so again in this group setting. Instead, they wanted to organize a committee to plan Holocaust-related activities for agency caseworkers. I noted that they preferred to call themselves a 'committee' rather than a group. Faced. with this kind of response, I revised my plan. The process taught me the importance of putting aside my own goals and respecting the needs and interests of the group members.

Once the group focus changed from therapeutic discussion to a planning committee, the criteria for membership changed. I explored the skills that potential members brought to the group and that would enable them to plan and participate in an effective program. For example, Mr G., a writer, had excellent writing skills; Mr D., a former journalist and broadcaster, possessed both written and verbal skills; and Mrs C. was both articulate and assertive, and had good organizational skills. The final group consisted of five survivors who met weekly for two and a half hours from November through April.

Group Process

At the initial meeting, after stating the group's purpose of planning Holocaust-related programming for agency practitioners, I outlined the importance of what we were doing. I spoke of the strengths of survivors and their resilience. This set a tone of pride and well-being as individual members introduced themselves, told their stories, and spoke of their achievements. Camaraderie and cohesiveness developed quickly, especially after the sharing of personal war losses. As each member relayed his or her war experience, there was genuine attentive listening and caring.

After this first meeting I realized how heavily the war still affected their lives and suggested that future meetings include a discussion, lasting about three-quarters of an hour, of their pre-war and wartime experiences as well as present-day challenges. They agreed.

Maintaining Flexibility

It is important to be flexible when planning and developing a weekly agenda for a group because it may need to be modified. Additional interventions may be necessary to address needs not fully identified during the pre-group process. In this case, while pre-group meetings identified a purpose geared towards tasks related to programming, an ongoing assessment highlighted additional needs and concerns. Hence, even though the primary objective during weekly meetings was program planning, sessions also included discussion of issues related to the Holocaust and present-day challenges.

The Task: Yom Hashoah (Holocaust) Commemoration Service

Throughout the initial phases of group development, different programming ideas were discussed and ranked according to priority. However, since some committee members expected to be in Florida during the winter months, it was decided to concentrate on one program: a Holocaust commemoration service for agency staff. Members came up with the following theme for the commemoration: to remember and mourn the six million Jewish people who perished during the Holocaust, with special emphasis on transmitting the legacy of the Holocaust to successive generations of Jews. As the weeks passed and the program structure solidified, the commemoration service assumed monumental importance in the group members' lives. They paid attention to every detail of the program as it developed. In fact, when two members left for Florida, they requested that I mail them the weekly minutes, which they responded to promptly with comments.

The commemoration service consisted of a candle-lighting ceremony with two generations participating; poetry and prose written and read by committee members in English, Yiddish, and French; recitation of the memorial prayer for the dead; and the singing of the Partisan Hymn and *Hatikvah* (Israeli anthem). Everyone was moved by the service. After the commemoration, comments made to the group members by the coordinator of the unit capture the moment: 'The commemoration was the most successful Jewish Dimensions Program ever held at Jewish Family Services. The complete management team was there. You touched the roots of who we are and for this we thank you.'

Benefits

This task-oriented group process provided the following benefits to its members and the community:

1. Members had an opportunity to grieve the loss of beloved family members in a public forum and receive public acknowledgment and support. Only one group member had attended a communal commemoration before.
2. When survivors saw members of the audience both Jewish and non-Jewish, crying, they felt that their Holocaust experiences had been validated. It gave meaning to their lives because they were able to pass on the legacy of remembrance to subsequent generations.
3. This group program and resulting commemoration service changed agency workers' perceptions about survivors in a unique way. Previously these survivors were seen as users of agency services. This program allowed survivors to give back by delivering a unique service to the agency. Their caseworkers began to see them as capable, empowered, and articulate individuals who had organized a memorable and meaningful event.
4. The experience enhanced participants' self-esteem and, for most group members, was a stepping stone to further community involvement. The writer became an active member of a literary group at the local seniors' centre. One member volunteered in the Jewish foster-home network and another helped to organize a Montreal chapter of the Simon Weisenthal Centre by reaching out and calling people.

HOMOGENEOUS THERAPEUTIC DISCUSSION AND SUPPORT GROUPS

I organized and helped to facilitate a number of homogeneous thera-peutic discussion and support groups for Holocaust survivors in the early 1990s. The following description is a composite of all these groups. Jewish Support Services for the Elderly and the Psychogeriatric Clinic of the Jewish General Hospital sponsored them jointly. My co-facilitators in each group were medical residents who had little expo-sure to Holocaust survivors. Dr Harry Grauer, former director of the Psychogeriatric Clinic, supervised the program and solicited the resi-dents. Doctors played an important role because they were often the entry point into the system during a crisis and needed training in un-derstanding Holocaust survivors.

These time-limited groups met participants' socio-emotional needs for verbalizing thoughts and feelings about similar experiences, learn-ing coping strategies, grieving losses, and socializing with peers. Par-ticipants decided to close these groups to new members after the second session because, as they shared confidential information with each other, a relationship of trust was developing.

Context: Identifying the Need for Discussion and Support Groups

During the Persian Gulf War in 1991, and shortly thereafter, a number of survivors were referred to me. The referrals came from a variety of sources including social-service agencies, psychogeriatric clinics of hospitals, doctors, and family members. Current events were triggering survivors' repressed traumatic memories and most of them felt vulner-able. Their beloved state of Israel was under attack by Scud missiles from Iraq. In addition, the spectacle of defenceless Jewish people sitting in sealed rooms and wearing gas masks to guard against potential poi-son-gas emissions from Scud missiles reminded them of their own Holocaust experiences.

I met with each person individually. Most were reliving their own wartime memories. They described themselves as feeling helpless and frustrated. Their body language was rigid. Many said they thought something was wrong with them because of these recent surges of mem-ory. All benefited from crisis-intervention statements such as 'What you are experiencing are normal reactions for survivors of war.' For some, telling their story and realizing they had been understood and heard provided instant relief. All wanted to communicate with others who were experiencing the same emotions.

Group Formation: Membership Criteria and Intake Procedure

The JSSE and the JGH used their extensive professional referral networks to advertise this program. The definition of a Holocaust survivor, described in chapter 3, was the one used. Individuals were admitted to the program only by referral, which initiated a thirty-minute pregroup telephone interview process to screen out people with memory impairment and psychotic behaviour. We also assessed survivors' ego strength and state of readiness to talk about the Holocaust. But, in spite of our screening efforts, one man who was unsuitable for this type of therapeutic process was assigned to a group. His somatic symptoms became more severe after two sessions and he dropped out. The average age of participants was seventy-two. Approximately seven survivors attended each group.

Group Process

The meetings consisted of twelve two-and-a-half hour weekly sessions. Transportation was provided because the sessions took place in the evening. The first two sessions were designed to help group members become acquainted with each other and provided an opportunity for some to vent their fears and frustrations or recount their wartime experiences. Problems around everyday coping, loneliness, difficult family relationships, and sleeplessness quickly became discussion topics. During the initial process, group members were invited to identify and rank discussion topics from which a weekly agenda was created. Here are some of the tasks that were identified as important:

- discuss Holocaust experiences in a supportive environment;
- explore ways to cope with everyday living;
- communicate with their children about the Holocaust and find ways to have them listen to their stories;
- deal with present losses such as death of family members and friends;
- discuss Jewish identity and faith during and after the war;

- share how people have coped and continued with their lives;
- find some peace of mind;
- explore differences between survivors and non-survivors, for example, lack of family and fear of uncertainty;
- reaffirm the vow 'never to forget or forgive';
- learn ways to deal with anti-Semitism and the resurgence of Nazism; and
- obtain information about restitution, social-security benefits, and community resources.

The first half-hour of each session, beginning with the third session, dealt with issues related to the survivors' present-day lives. For example, several of the participants were caregivers. One man's spouse was institutionalized in a long-term-care facility with advanced Alzheimer's. Another woman's spouse was terminally ill with cancer. Others were dealing with the death of their spouses and their own physical illnesses. Their discussions about their current losses were interwoven with the past.

The last half-hour of each session focused on positive aspects of ageing and reinforced survivors' resiliency and resourcefulness. In the words of one member: 'In my opinion, it is the eighth wonder of the world how survivors have coped mentally with their experiences and rebuilt their lives.' The session also concluded with relaxation exercises such as progressive muscular-relaxation techniques, breathing exercises, recorded music, and the use of guided visual imagery, for instance, using a calm scene to reinforce a relaxed state. Subliminal messages were introduced suggesting that participants would continue to be relaxed and sleep better. These exercises proved effective in closing wounds that had opened during the sessions. Most members looked forward to these exercises. However, a few had difficulty closing their eyes and relaxing because this meant being exposed to negative visual images. The last few minutes were spent in casual conversation focused on the present to ensure that participants left the group oriented to the here and now.

The rest of the group discussion focused on the topics raised by the group and scheduled in the weekly agenda.

Determining Group Focus

We used an eclectic group modality, its components including therapeutic ventilation in a supportive environment; normalizing statements;

interpretation of behaviour; teaching coping skills; education about restitution, social-security, and community resources; and participation in meaningful projects and activities that perpetuated the Holocaust legacy. Program media included pre- and post-group evaluation forms; forms from the Yad Vashem *Pages of Testimony* project; Survivor Registry questionnaires – a project of the American Gathering / Federation of Jewish Holocaust Survivors; and information about the International Red Cross Tracing Service.

All members benefited from the freedom to express thoughts and feelings pertaining both to their Holocaust experiences and to current issues in their lives. As one member said, 'In this group I do not have to put on my I'm fine smile.' Sharing experiences helped members bond quickly during the first session. Members listened to each other recall painful events. When one woman complained that her children had little time for her, two members quickly gave her their telephone numbers and volunteered to accompany her to the local seniors' centre.

Over time, the participants' mourning processes became increasingly apparent. Their discussions focused on their unresolved grief. One woman mentioned that, during her incarceration in the Łódź Ghetto, death was a common everyday occurrence and was not considered a tragedy. She said that in those days her emotions were numbed and, for many, hunger and the lack of food was the greatest preoccupation. Another woman's grief was triggered during her rabbi's sermon about the Holocaust. All said that right after the war they did not have the opportunity to grieve the loss of family members, because they were busy rebuilding their lives. We explained that their comments, especially those describing the numbing of emotions, reflected coping mechanisms that enabled them to go on with their daily lives under horrendous conditions.

Participants were encouraged to grieve their losses within the group. In one of the groups, once it was discovered that some members had pictures, the decision was made to devote a session to 'Life before the War.' Members brought in photographs and mementoes from their prewar lives which they had hidden for years and which they now shared with each other. They were also encouraged to participate in remembrance rituals outside the group. Several members attended, as a group, the community-wide Holocaust memorial service. The majority of members had perpetuated the memory of their parents by erecting plaques in their memory at synagogues and / or Holocaust monuments at cemeteries. As part of this grieving process we distributed *Pages of Testimony*, which many participants completed.

Since the ability to deal with losses was a significant concern for the group, the last session – which was also the formal termination of the group – took the form of a memorial service. Each person lit a memorial candle in the name of one or more people who were killed in the Holocaust and said a few words about them. We played a tape recording of *El Mole Rachamin*, the memorial prayer for the dead, that one of the members brought. Everyone shed tears and shared their sadness, and we comforted each other. This last session was also a celebration of survival and of having shared a unique experience. Members brought in homemade baked goods and everyone left feeling satisfied and grounded in the present. Some members continued to meet informally in each other's homes after their group concluded.

Common Themes That Emerged

Difficulty Sleeping

Most group members had sleep difficulties. Some slept only two to three hours a night. Others had recurring nightmares. Mrs B. dreamt about her parents, who were murdered in Auschwitz, family life before the war, her concentration-camp experiences, dogs, bread, and her brother who had escaped to Russia and was never heard from again. In her dreams she heard him knocking on a window and then woke up screaming. Another woman, a twin who had medical experiments conducted on her, dreamt of snakes being cut up into pieces and put into a glass jar. One sixty-six-year-old woman, who survived by hiding, was afraid to close her eyes for fear of being caught. When she looked over her shoulder she saw Nazis chasing her. Another member, who survived the Mauthausen death camp, often woke up screaming after dreaming about an intruder he was unable to recognize.

To help those with chronic nightmares, we used rehearsal techniques to restructure their dreams to be less threatening (Kellner et al., 1992). Members described in writing a recent nightmare, changed its content, and wrote down the revised version. Then, using imagery in a relaxed state, group members rehearsed the changed nightmare. For example, Mrs H, who dreamt of being chased by Nazis, was successful in changing her nightmare to a dream where good people behind her were helping her. We also provided suggestions for sleep improvement.

Difficulty Sharing War Experiences with Adult Children

In one of the groups, members shared their reservations about speaking to their children about the Holocaust. One woman said she did not want to pass on her hatred to her daughter. Another did not want to burden her children. In some instances, communication had bypassed an entire generation, but they were able to share their stories with grandchildren. We distributed articles about the Holocaust that we encouraged them to share with their families in the hope of stimulating discussion. Some of the group members shared these articles with their adult children and grandchildren.

Difficulty Dealing with the Resurgence of Nazis in Germany
and Anti-Semitic Events in Montreal

During the meetings of one of the groups there was an increase of violence in Germany perpetrated by neo-Nazis. Group members watched and read reports in the media about numerous incidents of violence perpetuated against foreigners and attacks on Jewish sites including cemeteries and memorials. These incidences were followed by the defacement of local synagogues with swastikas and Nazi slogans. All the group members became distressed and feared another Holocaust. Some were unable to sleep. One woman reported heart palpitations so severe that she believed she was having a heart attack. Another survivor recalled repressed memories of her family's murder for the first time. They had been forcibly removed from their home and made to dig their own graves where they were buried alive. One woman described her distress, when she saw or heard of such events in Germany, as a 'small burning panic on a low flame which gets ignited.'

All the participants were also afraid that these incidents would result in harm befalling their children. Two sessions were devoted to encouraging members to give a voice to their fears and anxieties. At the same time, we used two interventions to reframe their thoughts. First, group members were asked to identify ways in which the situation for Jews was different today than in the 1930s, that is, ways that demonstrate that Jews are no longer powerless. This cognitive reframing exercise appeased anxieties. The differences identified were typed up and distributed at the following meeting. Here is a partial list of what the members came up with:

- Young Jewish people are more vigilant than youth before the war.
- There is a democratic government in Canada with a strong Charter of Human Rights and Freedoms. Anti-hate legislation has been part of the Canadian Criminal Code since 1971.
- Some Jewish people hold influential government positions.
- Canada has a War Crimes Commission responsible for bringing Nazi war criminals to justice.
- Jewish people have the state of Israel to offer protection and sanctuary.
- Jewish people in the Diaspora are united, especially through their organizations.
- There are Holocaust-education courses in Jewish and non-Jewish schools.
- Inter-ethnic and inter-faith coalitions denounce acts of violence.
- In the aftermath of the desecrations of seven local synagogues, a broad section of Canadian society – including politicians, representatives of various organizations, and editorial writers in the French and English media – voiced their condemnation and outrage.
- There is a strong Jewish political advocacy by organizations such as Canadian Jewish Congress and B'nai B'rith Canada.

Then, as a group project, we asked members to cut headlines from newspapers expressing support for the Jewish community. The communications department of the Canadian Jewish Congress helped in this project by compiling articles from across Canada that documented the widespread revulsion over racist activities in Germany and Montreal. Participants glued these headlines on a piece of paper, which I photocopied and distributed to each member. Reviewing them, the group began to realize that survivors were not alone and indeed had allies in denouncing these events. We asked the group to post the headlines in a prominent location and to turn to them when they felt overwhelmed and distressed. Some of the headlines read as follows:

- 'Holocaust Survivor Speaks Out';
- 'Italians Demonstrate against Anti-Semitism';

- 'B'nai B'rith Calls for Royal Commission on Hate Groups';
- 'MPs Join Anti-Semitism Fight';
- 'Voices Must Rise against Racism';
- 'Conference tackles Anti-Semitism';
- 'Petition Denounces Rise in Neo-Nazism';
- 'NEVER AGAIN – Italy's Besieged Jews Fight Back';
- 'Holocaust Education in Poland';
- 'Germans Denounce Violence';
- 'German Newspaper Discredits Revisionist's Report';
- 'Canadian Jewish Congress Expresses Shock and Sadness over Violence in Germany – Calls for Strong Government Action'; and
- 'Israelis Denounce Violence in Germany.'

Maintaining Flexibility

Group facilitators must be flexible and design a program based on individual needs. Each group is different. For example, in the case of our program, one group was composed of survivors who had never spoken about the war; most of the sessions focused on sharing their experiences and venting feelings about their losses. In other groups, members chose to deal with present-day problems that needed to be addressed, such as difficulties in caregiver roles, loneliness, and widowhood. Here, the first part of the sessions began with a discussion of issues related to current problems in daily living. Each session started with a discussion of 'How was your week?' For the most part, however, current issues became interwoven with wartime experiences. For example, one survivor explained that widowhood released the feelings of emptiness she had felt at the end of the war when she realized she was the sole survivor of her large pre-war family. The diverse nature of support groups requires that facilitators be flexible and respond creatively to environmental stressors which may arise during group discussions.

Benefits and Adverse Effects

These small groups benefited the majority of survivors who attended them. All were grateful for the help provided and found a sense of relief and comfort. One participant started to write her memoirs and volunteered to be interviewed for a local documentation project. She also began to speak to schoolchildren about her experiences. Another was able to share with her daughter, for the first time, the letters her late spouse had written to relatives about his experiences in the war. All participants became more eager to participate in additional group activities and undertake new initiatives to perpetuate the Holocaust legacy. Their sense of isolation and loneliness diminished. Most reported that they were able to alleviate their distress symptoms by implementing the new coping skills they had learned.

We also learned that this type of group is not beneficial for some survivors. This became evident when Mr S.'s symptoms exacerbated after two sessions. Some survivors deal with their traumas and losses by avoiding and repressing them. His psychosomatic distress increased when he was in the presence of others who spoke about the war.

11 Long-Term Group Service:
An Incubator Environment

It's like a "family." We share good news and bad. We are learning and growing together. And we are the proof that people with different backgrounds and
nationalities can live together in harmony.

– Survivor in the Drop-in Centre

IDENTIFYING THE NEED FOR A LONG-TERM RECOVERY MODEL

Survivors' *landsmanschaften* had an important impact on their self-
concept. Members validated each other's experiences and acknowledged each other as capable people. Many felt a sense of pride and
accomplishment for the 'good work' their organizations performed.
Through educational, cultural, and social programs, they learned
about community issues and events, concentrated on self-improve-
ment, learned new skills, and participated in social get-togethers.
Some organizations published newsletters and books, and some were
politically active, especially on issues pertaining to Holocaust remembrance, Nazis residing in Canada, Holocaust denial, anti-Semitism,
and the survival of Israel.

As I listened to survivors describe their *landsmanschaften* with great
fondness, I began to realize that these mutual-aid organizations also
served as an environment that fostered healing and recovery. They often told me that belonging to their respective organizations enriched
their personal lives and gave them meaning and purpose. When I began conceiving of a drop-in centre for Holocaust survivors, I included
key elements of the *landsmanschaft* model. I felt that this type of organization and structure could work well because most survivors were
already familiar with its components. Even though not all survivors

were members of *landsmanschaften*, most had attended their functions, especially in their early years after arriving in Montreal.

DEVELOPING A GROUP TRAUMA-RECOVERY MODEL

My original objectives for developing a drop-in service model were to establish a safe environment for socializing and sharing; create an ongoing, open-ended group where survivors could find a sense of belonging with peers who lived similar traumas; facilitate grieving and remembrance by organizing commemorative activities; provide opportunities to participate in activities that give meaning and purpose; and teach skills to enhance coping strategies.

All my experience, training, and intuition came together in creating a group trauma-recovery model designed exclusively for Holocaust survivors. With input from survivors, professional staff, and volunteers, I developed a therapeutic service model that works. It continues to evolve and change as new needs are identified and integrated into programming. Members and their families frequently confirm that this long-term homogeneous group has become a lifeline for many survivors and is often the highlight or focal point of their week. The program nourishes them and improves their daily functioning when they are away from the centre. Members' consistency in attendance often surprises us: they find ways to get to the program in spite of inclement weather or changes to their transportation schedule. The only times they are absent is when they are ill, have a doctor's appointment, or are out of town.

This group not only helps survivors feel better, it empowers them to recognize and manage their reactions to disturbing events in their everyday lives. These reactions may, or may not, be related to war experiences. Sometimes they are triggered by events that occur outside the group such as anti-Semitic graffiti on buildings. Other times, the Drop-in Centre being a microcosm of the larger community in which they live, the survivors react with anger or distress to group discussions on topics such as members being required to wear name tags or establishing a fixed time to arrive at the centre. In this controlled environment, we deal with emotionally charged situations like these by encouraging survivors to 'give their feelings a voice' and talk about them. Depending on the issue, we may also enhance their coping skills by teaching interventions they can use away from the group. Here is an incident that illustrates this process.

One day a member pointed out that not everyone in the group wore name tags. She said it would be helpful if all members wore them so participants could remember each other's names. This led to a heated discussion. One survivor said it was important to wear the tags because no one had a name in the camps, only a number. This prompted another survivor to say she feels good wearing her name tag for all to see. Others said the tag reminded them of the yellow star they were forced to wear which identified them as Jews. The discussion also triggered a flashback in another survivor who began to relive standing in the freezing cold during a 4 a.m. roll call in a concentration camp. When questioned, she said these flashbacks are a 'part of who you are and are not limited to these group meetings.' Some members nodded in agreement. I asked if they wanted to learn a technique to manage these flashbacks. Some did, so I guided them through a grounding exercise to connect them with the present moment. I suggested they focus on their immediate environment, feel their body pressing against their chairs, and open their senses to the sights and sounds in the room. The technique worked for those having flashbacks. After they completed the exercise successfully, I suggested they use the same technique at the first sign of another flashback.

For this to approach to work, however, facilitators must understand their population and have insight into how a seemingly benign event or activity may evoke a response based on a traumatic experience. The triggering event may not always be apparent. Such was the case when we were forming the group and discussing an appropriate starting time. Some people became angry when I suggested starting the program at 9:30 a.m. I assumed that most members would be present by then. Much to my surprise, they did not want to be told they had to be present in the group at an exact time. They associated this with the roll calls in the camps when they were required to line up outside their barracks when the sirens went off. Those who were not fast enough were either beaten or shot. In an attempt to prevent fusion between past and present, I pointed out ways in which the present situation was different from the war. But my approach did not help. They refused to budge. Consequently, I decided to be flexible and not insist on a specific arrival time.

I would describe the Drop-in Centre as an incubator for personal growth and healing. We have created a safe environment where survivors interact with their peers in activities that provide opportunities for therapeutic interventions. It is important that social workers deal with emotionally charged issues and not avoid or deflect them. Some workers have a tendency to deal with survivors' sensitivities by avoiding incidents that may cause discomfort. The reverse is often a better approach. These situations can be opportunities for workers to intervene and teach coping skills that contribute to survivors' healing and recovery. Encouraging members to verbalize their feelings about distressing issues helps other group members gain insight into their own reactions and behaviours. With this awareness, healing becomes possible.

The key aspects of this recovery model are corroborated in the literature by Judith Herman (1992), who identifies the stages of individual trauma recovery as: establishing safety; remembering and mourning; and reconnecting with ordinary life. My trauma-recovery approach adapts Herman's by shifting from her focus on the treatment of individuals to a community-based mutual-aid group model for Holocaust survivors.

In the early years of the Drop-in Centre we concentrated on establishing a safe environment for survivors to socialize with their peers, similar to the *landsmanschaften*. It became a refuge where they felt free to talk about their pre-war, wartime, and post-war experiences as well as their present-day challenges. Today we perpetuate this feeling of safety by maintaining trust, providing stability, and keeping a consistent core group of staff and volunteers.

With safety and trust established, many of our programs focus on helping survivors work through the second stage of recovery – remembrance and mourning. In this stage survivors compose narratives that include their lives before the war as well as their traumatic war experiences. In so doing, they create 'continuity with the past' (Danieli cited in Herman, 1992:176). Some of the programs discussed in this chapter and the next help survivors construct such a narrative.

We also provide opportunities for shared grieving through our commemorative events. Members spend months planning the group's annual Holocaust Commemoration Service. They review its format and content, and we hold rehearsals. The entire group participates in these activities, which plunge some into profound grief. Members work through their intense feelings by supporting each other and speaking to staff and volunteers. Planning and participating in this program helps members work through their ongoing grief as they create rituals of mourning within a community setting.

We support the third stage of recovery by creating opportunities to help survivors find meaning and purpose in their lives. Teaching others about their experiences is a prime example of such an opportunity. In so doing, they transform their self-concept from a fragile victim to a survivor. Their roles as witnesses to history and educators in the community help facilitate this important shift. Some of these activities are also discussed in chapters 6 and 12.

These recovery stages are not a linear process in which one stage ends before another begins. Instead, they are a circular process that spirals towards recovery and healing. Supporting each stage also provides opportunities for empowerment practice, which is discussed in chapter 8. The overall goal is helping survivors attain mastery and control over responses triggered by their environment as they work through their losses. The structure of the Drop-in Centre serves as a long-term incubator where the survivors can work towards recovery and healing, tasks that they cannot easily perform on their own.

THE DROP-IN CENTRE FOR HOLOCAUST SURVIVORS

The Drop-in Centre for Holocaust Survivors operates as a weekly program for survivors living in the Montreal area. It serves a group of cognitively intact individuals who originate from a variety of European countries and who qualify as a survivor or a survivor's spouse. The centre operates on Tuesday mornings from 9:00 a.m. to noon and is housed at the Cummings Jewish Centre for Seniors, a constituent agency of Federation CJA.

The location provides survivors with a safe space for socialization with their peers and fosters a sense of community and belonging. It also serves as an entry point for survivors who have little or no contact with the organized Jewish community. This connection encourages some to become involved with other agency programs and services as well. The centre uses a strengths-based philosophy to empower members with a sense of capability and accomplishment, thus freeing them from seeing themselves as victims. A holistic approach to health and well-being gives members a sense of autonomy and control as they learn coping skills and wellness strategies to improve their quality of life. This program provides members with case management, eclectic programming, and activities that instil hope, meaning, and purpose.

In the beginning, an average of fifty survivors attended each week from a total membership of over seventy-five. Regular attendance has decreased today to an average of thirty-five because some members have died while others have become too frail and / or moved into a residence. It is important to note that a large number of men attend. Generally, social programs for older adults in the community attract primarily female participants.

Creating and Structuring the Group

Physical Setting

Physical setting is an important initial consideration when searching for an appropriate location to house a survivor drop-in centre. I believed that a community-based setting was more appropriate than an institutional one for several reasons. First, survivors should not be considered as separate from the rest of their community. Instead, they should be considered a part of it, in the same way as other people are. Second, a community setting – such as CJCS – promotes wellness and positive ageing rather than reinforcing perceptions of vulnerability and impairment. Third, in a community setting, survivors can easily participate in a variety of other educational, recreational, and social programs that help integrate them into the broader agency once they are ready.

Upon reflection, locating the Drop-in Centre at CJCS was the correct decision. Today most survivors feel at home there; many find themselves within a community setting for the first time since their *landsmanschaften* disbanded. After our members feel a sense of belonging in the Drop-in Centre, some go on to participate in other activities (such as social programs, meals with friends in the cafeteria, art and educational courses, lectures, exercise classes, and the like), thus increasing their sense of community participation and belonging.

Creating a Safe Environment

When I began developing the Drop-in Centre, I anticipated housing it in a dedicated location, which members could make their own by decorating it with sofas, small tables, wall pictures, and meaningful objects. I believed this approach would create a safe, informal, and comfortable environment for them. Consequently, I was disappointed when I found out that this would not be possible because space at the agency was limited. We would have to share the auditorium with other groups – which meant no permanent decorations. Surprisingly, this limitation had minimal effect on the members, though occasionally some people did say that it would be nice to put up pictures of Israel, newspaper articles, and group pictures taken at special events. Over the years the group location has changed several times and our members have adapted well. They realize that there is little we can do to control this situation and they accept it.

In retrospect, I realize that I placed too much emphasis on creating a safe physical space for the group. Gradually I learned that establishing a safe physical environment is secondary to the safety members feel in the company of caring and supportive people who understand them. Their primary concern is that everyone remains healthy and stays together. For me, this was an important lesson when planning groups in settings that have limited space.

Staffing

I planned and facilitated meetings alone when the centre began. Today I supervise the program and coordinate it with Vikki Brewster. Chava Respitz and Suzie Doupovec Schwartz are long-time volunteers who are dedicated and committed to the group members. They assist at group sessions and participate in team meetings with staff. Having a core of staff and volunteers who maintain a consistent presence with the group contributes to its stability and fosters a sense of safety for the members. It is important in a group of this nature that members can count on seeing familiar faces each week.

Having an adequate ratio of staff and volunteers to the members is a key consideration, especially as this population ages. As members become frailer they require more assistance such as helping them with their coats, guiding them to their seats, and serving food. There are also increased health and safety issues to contend with. For example, some of our members feel ill during the program or fall and require immediate intervention. In these situations, one staff person supports the individual while another focuses on the group to manage their reactions and any possible triggers. Volunteers provide support as needed.

This program also serves as a learning environment for university social-work students who do field placements in the Drop-in Centre. Some of these students are not Jewish. In the beginning, we thought this would have a negative impact on the members. However, as the group evolved and began to trust the staff and volunteers, the members accepted these students as well as other social workers and volunteers whose involvement is temporary. Our members love to engage in discussions with the students and visitors to teach them about the Holocaust. Outside professionals often visit this program as well to enhance their understanding of Holocaust survivors.

Recruiting Members

Half of our referrals initially came from CJCS and the other half from outside sources. In the beginning, the Drop-in Centre was advertised by sending flyers to social-service agencies, hospitals, community organizations, and synagogues. I made outreach visits to senior clubs and CJCS satellite centres, prepared press releases and articles, and placed ads in both Jewish and local newspapers. Social-service centres in outlying areas of the city were contacted by telephone to encourage them to refer isolated Holocaust survivors from their territories. I also established a collaborative process with the Canadian Jewish Congress and the Montreal Holocaust Memorial Centre for referrals and sharing information of relevance to survivors.

Today we continue to receive referrals from public- and private-sector agencies in the community and sister federation agencies. We also receive referrals from adult children and grandchildren of survivors. Frequently survivors will come in of their own accord as well.

Naming the Drop-in Centre

In the beginning I invited members' ideas for naming the Drop-in Centre. I was surprised when they said they wanted to retain the name I had been using: Drop-in Centre for Holocaust Survivors. They said it reflected the the message that this is an exclusive group for Holocaust survivors. Also, the words 'drop-in' imply they can come and go as they please. As noted, being told to show up at a certain time can be a triggering event for some survivors. To this day, staff members do not insist that participants arrive at a specific time. Although the structured part of the program begins at 9:30 a.m., some individuals arrive later for various reasons such as finding it challenging to get ready in the morning. The majority regularly attends the entire three-hour program while others turn up occasionally to connect with their peers or to inquire about resources and compensation programs. Both members and non-members are free to drop in for any part of the program and then leave. This easy-going approach gives them the freedom to determine their individual level of participation. Our only requirement is that they enter and leave the group quietly so as not to disturb the program taking place. Survivors also appreciate the ease with which they can enter this group. There is no formal assessment. The only criterion is their common identity as Holocaust survivors. And there is even flexibility with this. Several individuals, who are not survivors and / or not Jewish, have joined the group after their survivor spouse died. They feel a connection with other survivors and are accepted within the group.

Group Norms

In the Drop-in Centre's formative years we established a 'Code of Respectful Behaviours' within the group, which we periodically review for the benefit of new members. Members are encouraged to be courteous and respectful to each other and take responsibility for their actions. We inform members about our expectations and work to maintain harmonious interactions. In addition, we hold programs that focus on ways to enhance group cohesiveness and camaraderie as well as respect for each other's differences. The success of this approach is apparent when members refer to the *heimishe* (homey) atmosphere in this group. They feel a bond with their peers and some actually refer to the group as their family.

Ancillary Services

CASE MANAGEMENT
The Drop-in Centre has a case-management component. Although the number of survivors attending the centre has decreased, they have become a frailer population requiring more services and support. The majority of members are in their early to mid-eighties and some are in their nineties. Their physical deterioration becomes evident when we see increasingly more walkers lined up against the wall. Consequently, their need for individual case management is increasing. Social worker Vikki Brewster provides case management in response to members' psycho-social needs. Interventions include calling absent members, supportive counselling, crisis intervention, problem solving, and referrals to services and resources, both inside and outside the agency, such as emergency-assistance funds, meals-on-wheels, home care, transportation, medical care, and so on. Some members are followed by case mangers in the department who have a history with them. I provide

supportive counselling to individuals with whom I have long-standing relationships.

TRANSPORTATION AND FOOD

A number of our participants are unable to get to the program on their own because they have mobility challenges. Transportation is provided from several sources, including agency private taxis at a subsidized fee and the Quebec government's Paratransit service for persons with disabilities. Snacks are provided, and the Federation's food-services department prepares special food trays for the holidays and birthday celebrations. Although there is no charge for the program, most survivors voluntarily contribute $5 monthly to help defray costs.

Program Format

There is an eclectic mix of programming during each three-hour session. After a half-hour of socializing, there is a one-hour discussion period. This consists of welcoming members, providing an update about those members who are absent, and discussing current events and day-to-day challenges. Staff also informs them about agency and community services and programs and developments in compensation and restitution. This discussion period is followed by a half-hour exercise session with Hildy Silverman, a professional aerobics instructor, and ends with a refreshment break. The last hour of the session consists of a psycho-educational program, a lecture, an interactive social program, or some form of entertainment.

Program Components

Maintaining Community

The group fosters a sense of community and belonging. The program fulfils survivors' needs to establish surrogate families for friendship and support, especially when many of their peers are dying. Here they feel the freedom to talk about their pre-war, wartime, and post-war experiences, which are validated, shared, and understood. Many say that they have felt misunderstood by their Canadian peers in other groups they attended. In contrast, the Drop-in Centre has a *heimshe* atmosphere where they feel a bond with peers who speak common languages. For example, on any given Tuesday morning during the unstructured part of the program and break, survivors speak their mother tongues such as Yiddish and Hungarian. They also express their satisfaction at feeling understood by staff and volunteers.

Supporting Social Networking

Peer support is an important aspect of our program. We support developing relationships and maintaining friendships outside the group. Members also notice when someone is absent. They support each other when they are ill and call and / or visit members who are hospitalized. The entire group signs get-well cards, which are delivered or mailed to sick members. The centre provides up-to-date membership lists with contact information to facilitate this interaction and mutual support.

Providing Educational and Cultural Programs

Lectures, films, and discussions are an important part of our programming, which focuses on topics that include politics, hate propaganda, the place of God in the Holocaust, Israel-Diaspora relations, child survivors in Poland, anti-Semitism, wills and mandates, patients' rights in a hospital setting, how to access public social services, keeping the Yiddish language alive, and the history of Jews in Montreal.

Educational activities also empower survivors to improve and maintain control over their lives. We inform members about community resources and issues pertaining to restitution and social-security payments. We increase awareness and teach skills to help survivors improve their physical, mental, emotional, and spiritual well-being. We also invite guest speakers to address current medical concerns as our members' physical and cognitive health deteriorates.

Entertaining

In the centre's early years, some members had difficulty participating in joyful activities. Their unrelenting mourning processes prevented them from enjoying themselves and laughing. Today we notice a shift as our members request more 'light- hearted and fun programs.' During a workshop on laughter, members had fun as they learned to integrate humour into their lives. They look forward to enjoying themselves with their friends and celebrating special occasions. Some members sponsor group breakfasts on special birthdays and wedding anniversaries. We celebrate birthdays every month with entertainer Janie Respitz and organize parties on Jewish holidays. We also sponsor talent shows to feature members' creative abilities and skills. Frequently individual members lead the group in spontaneous singalongs from the 'old country.'

Memorializing and Grieving

Drop-in members plan, organize, and participate in the CJCS annual *Yom Hashoah* (Holocaust) commemoration service. Family members, friends and guests, volunteers, intergenerational program students, and staff from both the CJCS agency and Federation CJA attend. Memorialization is important for survivors and provides a forum for participating in rituals that help them to deal with their ongoing mourning. The program includes lighting six memorial candles with multiple generations, reading poetry and prose, reciting the *kaddish*, and singing the Partisan Hymn.

Creating Opportunities for Personal Growth and Development

Sometimes situations arise that provide staff with opportunities to help survivors move beyond limiting perceptions, judgments, beliefs, and fears. To do so, staff members must show sensitivity about subjects that may be emotionally charged for survivors, initiate group discussions where members are encouraged to express their views, and help in the mitigation of conflicting opinions. For example, when I consulted members about which schools to reach out to for our intergenerational programming, some insisted on approaching only Jewish schools. Others disagreed, emphasizing the importance of teaching the broader community about the Holocaust. Initially, I tried to have the group reach a consensus on the issue. But, with so many people present, this proved time-consuming and difficult. Eventually, through majority rule, the group decided to engage in programs with non-Jewish youth as well. Today we also hold programs with multiracial and multiethnic schools, some which have no Jewish students. The members of the group who initially resisted this idea now willingly participate, especially when non-Jewish students tell them they knew little about the Holocaust before the program.

Situations that push survivors' boundaries and gently guide them in new directions contribute to their personal growth and development. It helps them to see themselves and their world differently. Some members say that their fear of non-Jews has lessened since their involvement in these programs. Approaches such as this can be adopted because of the safety and stability that survivors feel in our group. Not all programs and interventions, however, encourage changes in perceptions, behaviour, and responses to triggers. Some increase self-awareness and encourage personal growth through discussions about self-love, the art of appreciation, accepting and giving compliments, expressing gratitude, and the effects of trauma and PTSD.

Creating Opportunities for Meaning and Purpose

We create opportunities and promote activities that bring meaning and purpose to survivors' lives. Our members serve as advisers and resource persons for university students, artists, and writers. Many speak to students on university campuses about their experiences at special events like Holocaust Education Week.

Activities within the program also provide a sense of accomplishment and recognition for our members. For example, an artist in the centre, Suzana Kohn, designed the logo for our membership pin as well as the cover of our book of memoirs: *Preserving Our Memories: Passing on the Legacy* (discussed in chapter 12). Over the years, at events organized by the Canadian Society for Yad Vashem, some of our members have been honoured by the federal government for their contributions to the country.

Our group newsletter, *Never Again*, provides recognition and visibility for our group both within the agency and the community. It is now published two times a year and reflects the spirit of the group. Readers tell us they look forward to each edition and share it with family and friends. Drop-in members contribute articles that reflect the group's activities and programs. They write about their pre-war, wartime, and post-war experiences, and submit their poetry, personal reflections, and short stories. The publication also includes a Yiddish corner; a congratulatory, birthday, and get-well section; and up-to-date information about restitution and compensation programs and agency services. Vikki Brewster, who compiles and edits the paper, solicits members' feedback and ideas, which result in new columns being added such as Israeli / Jewish news and health-information updates.

We create volunteer opportunities within the service and in other parts of the agency. For example, some members provide peer-to-peer support on the Information Line and sit on Holocaust advisory committees. Other members sit on various lay committees in the agency where they inform staff and volunteers about issues relevant to the survivor community. We work closely with external organizations to find volunteer opportunities as well. Some of our members provide the Montreal Holocaust Memorial Centre with documentary materials for its exhibits and participate as guest speakers in its programs or as candle lighters in its commemorative events.

Benefits

Members' Evaluation

On the Drop-in Centre's fifth anniversary, we distributed an evaluation form to our members. Fifty evaluations were completed and returned. Members gave the following reasons for attending the Drop-in Centre week after week:

> 'It's interesting. I like the program, discussions. I can participate.'
> 'It makes the week shorter. I enjoy it. I get out of the house. I learn new things. I have a place to go each week.'
> 'I greatly appreciate the staff persons for their knowledge and intelligence from which we all benefit.'
> 'It's like a "family." We share good news and bad. We are learning and growing together. And we are the proof that people with different backgrounds and nationalities can live together in harmony.'
> 'I get a sense of belonging as a Holocaust survivor.'
> 'I enjoy the friendship and the freedom to ask questions and to comment on any subjects concerning seniors and the general public.'
> 'I like the open discussion and various topics that touch the hearts of everyone.'
> 'I am happy. I look forward to coming to the Drop-in Centre. I don't want to miss any Tuesday. I come here and I don't feel like a stranger.'

Eighty-eight per cent (forty-four members) indicated they made friends in the group and 70 per cent (thirty-five) said their friendships extended outside it. This interaction ranged from telephone calls to social outings.

Forty-eight members responded affirmatively to the question: 'In general do you like the programs we have had?' Their suggestions for additional programs included: more outside speakers; involving youngsters during the holidays; museum exhibits; more current events and political discussions; programs on relaxation; a Christian person's perception of Jews; discussions with students; lectures on Ashkenazi and Sephardic history and literature; documentary movies; group luncheons; discussions on natural health and ageing; and movies.

The general well-being of the members who attended the program also improved. Of the fifty survivors who filled out the evaluation, 90 per cent (forty-five) indicated that their physical, emotional, and spiritual health had improved. Comments regarding their improvements included:

'I feel good. I feel happier. I sleep better. My appetite has improved.'
'I feel that I am no longer alone.'
'We understand life better in a more positive light.'
'I am more relaxed after the meetings.'
'I am learning to open up more.'
'Because of my problems, this helps me as an escape.'
'I was very depressed but now I have more energy. I am learning how to cope.'
'Because of contact with people it forces me to go out.'
'My feelings about the Holocaust lost the pathological pains I was suffering for years.'
'It's been an uplifting educational experience.'
'The staff pays attention to me.'
'I have adopted a positive mental attitude.'
'I'm learning to make more time for myself and how to "love" myself.'

Although the majority of respondents were known to CJCS, 22 per cent (eleven individuals) had never been involved with the agency before attending the centre. Thirty-four per cent (seventeen individuals) attended the Drop-in Centre only and did not partake in any other CJCS activities, programs, or services.

Special Considerations for Facilitators

Reframing Feelings of Isolation

Members in the group undergo multiple present-day challenges such as death of a spouse and / or friends; loss of autonomy; illness; lack of financial security; loss of social status; and alienation from their children. For some, these stressors activate feelings of loss, dependency, and vulnerability related to past traumatic events as well. Their severe victimization during the Holocaust may have an impact on their self-esteem, self-worth, and self-respect during these times, contributing to feelings of isolation, loneliness, and depression. We endeavour to reframe these feelings by

- viewing members as historians who teach as much as they are taught;
- soliciting members' opinions and advice about most aspects of the program;
- acknowledging and thanking members for their help;
- welcoming existing members and integrating new ones;
- reminding members of their resiliency on an ongoing basis; and
- regularly noting and praising members' achievements.

Adapting the Program to Accommodate Members' Increased Frailties

By necessity, the program evolves and changes as new needs are identified and integrated into the programming. We solicit the help of survivors, professional staff, and volunteers on a continual basis to identify and incorporate required improvements. For example, noticing that the group is becoming more important to our members as they grow frailer and their circle of friends diminishes through death or relocation to residences, we help members adapt to these changes by providing supportive counselling and organizing educational programs. Some, however, have difficulty accepting their physical limitations and resist using a cane or walker, thus placing themselves at risk of losing their balance and / or falling. In response, we enacted a policy that physically frail members must use their canes and walkers during the program, and we made clear that we would have zero tolerance on this issue. Policies like this can lead to some difficult decisions for staff. For example, a ninety-year-old man, who was unsteady on his feet, hung his cane on the coat rack and refused to use it during the program. He held on to the chairs to support himself. Eventually he fell, but still refused to use his cane. We asked his family to intervene. Unfortunately, he would not cooperate and was asked to leave because staff members were concerned that he would fall and hurt himself, and possibly endanger others.

We are also adapting the physical environment to work better for the members. We changed the room set-up to facilitate movement and relocated the amplifier so members could hear better. We also invite professionals from different disciplines to educate survivors about their health conditions and teach them to use their auxiliary devices or aids appropriately. Those who do use these aids encourage resistant members. Sometimes colleagues ask me how we deal with members who develop dementia because, for some, this program is their lifeline and the only one they attend in the community. In response, I note that I believe in a continuity-of-care model (Gulliford et al., 2006) whereby our cognitively and physically frailer members remain in the program as long as they are able to attend, do not get lost when leaving the room, and are not disruptive. Sometimes a caregiver accompanies them to the program. This model helps survivors maintain continuous caring relationships with their peers, staff, and volunteers and provides a stable environment that is responsive to their changing needs.

Dealing with Contentious Issues

There are some contentious issues that arise and must be dealt with to ensure continuation of the group. Staff must be sensitive to the anger that emerges from time to time and that can be detrimental to the group participants. Individuals who have been victimized may repress the anger or rage they feel towards their oppressor or situation. Once trust develops and they feel safe, this anger may surface and be displaced on staff and peers. Some survivors cannot contain their anger and lash out at fellow members and staff. In one incident, a survivor, who was angry with another group member, attempted to use the group setting to vent her feelings. I prevented her from doing this, emphasizing that individual problems between members need to be resolved outside the group. I attempted conflict resolution with the individuals involved as well as short-term counselling and anger management with the angry participant. Unfortunately, her outbursts persisted and continued to disrupt the group. Eventually, I asked this woman to leave the group. I left the door open for her to return, however, when she was ready to change her behaviour.

Over the years we have dealt with many other contentious matters. In the beginning, group membership was a divisive issue. European members tried to exclude individuals they did not recognize as 'real' survivors, such as Russians. We worked with the entire group and encouraged inclusion rather than exclusion. After sharing from both factions, the Russians were accepted. Deciding on the language of operation was also conflictual at times. The Yiddish-speaking members wanted a place where they could speak Yiddish with their peers. Interestingly, this included the Russian survivors who did not speak English. We emphasized the Yiddish language in the beginning but soon realized this was a mistake because our participants originate from diverse European countries and speak different languages; for example, many Hungarian survivors do not speak Yiddish. And so we had to establish our language of operation as English. The relationship between the religious and secular Jews in the group is another area of tension that surfaces periodically. Around the Jewish holidays, some observant survivors want a rabbi to speak to the group while some secular members object to this. The group came to a compromise solution by having members rather than a rabbi facilitate holiday discussions and arranging for a rabbi to deliver opening remarks at our annual Holocaust Commemoration Service.

Maintaining Balance: Perceptions of Professionals
Who Visit the Drop-in Centre

When professional service providers who have little experience with survivors visit the group, they expect to hear discussions that focus exclusively on the Holocaust. They are surprised to witness the eclectic range of topics, some having nothing to do with the Holocaust. They are also surprised to see our members dance and sing at birthday and holiday celebrations. We explain that war stories are sometimes interwoven into the discussions, and other times not. It depends on the individual survivor and the nature of the discussion. In fact, some survivors are unwilling to talk about their trauma histories at all. Others, who want to focus on them exclusively, cause some group members to become agitated and suffer nightmares. Situations like this create challenges for a facilitator to balance both needs.

I find that professionals tend to see survivors in one of two ways. Some see them as fragile victims and others see them as larger-than-life heroes. Both perceptions are gleaned from films and literature about the Holocaust that usually do not depict survivors accurately. There is no single perception that applies to all survivors. Many professionals are taken aback when they realize that survivors are ordinary people who have lived through extraordinary events and are coping with life as best they can.

12 Intergenerational Programs

When I first started to speak about my experiences, the words stopped in my throat and I couldn't get them out. I had to stop. Now I can talk about it without crying. I know it happened and it is a part of me.

– Survivor in the Drop-in Centre

SHARING THE PAST AND CREATING A LEGACY

Intergenerational programs empower Holocaust survivors to transcend their victim self-concept and assume roles as witnesses-to-history and educators in the community. The therapeutic goals of intergenerational programs are set out below.

Process Traumatic Memories into a Structured Narrative

Students use structured questionnaires in some of our programs to help survivors focus on pre-war, wartime, and post-war experiences. This tool helps both survivors and students as they work together to structure the story into a meaningful whole.

Integrate Traumatic Past into the Totality of Their Life Experience

Integrating and accepting that the traumatic experiences are a part of their lives is a challenge for many survivors. However, it becomes easier for some with repeated telling of their story. Mrs V. participates in programs with high school students and describes her involvement as follows: 'When I first started to speak about my experiences, the words stopped in my throat and I couldn't get them out. I had to stop. Now I can talk about it. I know it happened and it is a part of me.'

Change Self-Concept from a Fragile Victim to a Survivor Who Is a Witness to History and an Educator in the Community

Intergenerational exchanges imbue survivors with confidence and self-respect as they realize they have an important contribution to make to society as first-hand witnesses to mass atrocity. Sharing their stories with interested listeners also validates the survivor's experience.

Find Meaning in Survival through a Sense of Purpose and Mission

Teaching younger people about their extinguished European communities and their wartime ordeals has a therapeutic healing effect that generates hope, meaning, and purpose in survivors' lives. They also develop some peace of mind from knowing that their past will not be forgotten.

Benefits to Survivors

The benefits that intergenerational programs offer survivors are several. Such programs

- form bonds with younger generations to pass on survivors' legacy;
- heal survivors by allowing them to talk about their past, many for the first time;
- develop continuity between past and present by integrating pre-war, wartime, post-war, and present life experiences;
- enable surviviors to find some peace of mind through knowing that their experiences, deceased family members, and extinguished communities will not be forgotten;
- create hope, meaning, and purpose in survivors' current lives;
- increase survivors' confidence and self-respect as they recognize and acknowledge their important achievements and contributions in life; and
- strengthen survivors' self-image by helping them to view themselves as historians and teachers.

Our intergenerational programs help many survivors in the Drop-in Centre as they journey towards healing and recovery. Here are a few examples of intergenerational programs, appropriate for Holocaust survivors, with elementary, high school, and university students that we coordinate through the centre.

Celebrating Jewish Holidays with Children

We celebrate the Jewish holidays in intergenerational programs with elementary schools. These events focus on sharing the joy of the holidays, not recounting Holocaust experiences. Participants play games, sing, and have fun together. Survivors who believe that life is serious business, however, may find such events challenging.

For example, several survivors cried during a program with Grade 5 students from a Jewish day school. One woman said she felt two emotions: the joy of seeing so many young children in one place, which filled her with pride and attested to the rebirth of the Jewish people; and the pain of remembering children in her family who had been killed during the war.

It is difficult to predict situations that may trigger painful memories. Day-to-day occurrences, seemingly benign to us, may hold special meaning for some survivors and cause painful memories to surface. One survivor said: 'The students are precious. It's bittersweet because the students bring back memories from the war of what happened to Jewish children. At the same time it gives me strength to see the children.'

During one of the celebrations, I asked a survivor who was crying to join me at the back of the auditorium. She talked about her siblings and other children in her family who were deported to Auschwitz. My listening to her compassionately in this brief encounter was enough to help her work through her tears. She returned to the program composed and happily engaged with the children. Simple interventions – such as active, empathetic listening for a few minutes in a noisy auditorium – can bring comfort for individuals.

Yom Hashoah (Holocaust) Commemoration Service

The annual theme for the Drop-in Centre's Holocaust Commemoration Service is 'From Generation to Generation.' Members plan the program and participate in the service. Family members, friends, guests, CJCS agency members and staff, and Federation CJA staff attend. Students, who participated in intergenerational programs during the year, also attend – sometimes with their teachers, family members, and school principals. The intergenerational portion of the program consists of:

- A candle lighting ceremony performed with multiple generations to symbolize transmission of the Holocaust legacy from one generation to the next. Survivors light candles with their children, grandchildren, agency / Federation staff persons, or individuals from the community.
- A dialogue between survivors and younger generations in which the survivors set out their legacy and the recipients accept it and describe how they will integrate it in their lives and pass it on.
- A 'Lasting Impressions' segment in which selected individuals (students, social-work interns, teachers, artists, filmmakers, and so on) who are, or were, involved with the Drop-in Centre during the year share their personal reflections of working with survivors.
- A segment in which survivors, and occasionally younger generations, read poetry and prose in Hebrew, English, and French and sing the old ghetto songs.

In the early years of the program, all the participants were Jewish. As survivors began to understand and embrace their mission to educate the broader community, non-Jewish participants were invited. Today, the survivors are reaching out to the community in ways that could never have been predicted. For example, a Muslim student, visiting from Egypt, participated in one of the intergenerational programs and was invited to speak at a commemoration service. He told the audience how interviewing a Holocaust survivor, as part of learning about a historic period which he knew little, touched him deeply. In his words: 'My own heart has been softened towards people who are different than me because of my experience at this [Drop-in] Centre' (Never Again, Summer 2009:7).

Supporting March of the Living Participants

The March of the Living program takes students from around the world on a two-week trip to Poland and Israel to learn more about the Holocaust. In Poland, the students visit wartime concentration camps and sites where the vibrant pre-war Jewish community flourished before it was destroyed. In Israel, they travel to key sites in the Jewish homeland that encapsulate the re-emergence and survival of the Jewish people.

We hold intergenerational programs with March participants before the trip. Survivors and students engage in an open dialogue which helps the participants understand the historical events they are studying and the significance of the locations they are about to visit. The survivors, some from Poland, tell them about their pre-war lives in their European communities. They also describe their wartime experiences. One Auschwitz survivor asked a student to take a picture of the bunk where she had slept while interned there. After the trip, the students return to our program to share photos and describe the towns, villages, and camps they had visited.

Survivor-Memoir Project

Sometimes participants in the March of the Living program are inspired to translate their experience into something more concrete and permanent. For example, one student, Ian Tobman, wanted to counteract present-day anti-Semitism. After meeting with him, and wanting to support his enthusiasm, we devised a survivor-memoir project. Ian and a fellow student, Mara Schneiderman, solicited the involvement of fellow students. Over the course of four years, fourteen students, using a structured questionnaire, interviewed seventeen Holocaust survivors about their pre-war, wartime, and post-war experiences. They took notes, recorded their interviews, and made written transcripts. We preserved the manner of survivor expression, without perfecting the grammar, so each survivor's story is conveyed in his or her own voice. The participating survivors were consulted about all aspects of the project. They also had final approval over the presentation of their individual story. For example, when two survivors were not pleased with their edited interview, we assigned another interviewer and started their process again.

The students were also encouraged to include their personal reflections in the final product. Vikki Brewster, the project coordinator, and I did minor editing and volunteers verified spelling, historical locations, and other information where possible. The project culminated in 2006 with the publication of *Preserving Our Memories: Passing on the Legacy.* I was able to find private funding from two benefactors to cover the publishing costs.

This project provided an opportunity for survivors to write their memoirs and leave a legacy for future generations. Outside guests, media, and members of the Drop-in Centre were invited to the book launch. During the project, Raymond Barry took photographs of all the Drop-in members which we incorporated in a large display. Along with the photographs, which were selected and approved by each survivor, we included a brief biography of their individual experiences. Today we give the book to students in our intergenerational programs, make it available to educational institutions, and offer it for sale in the agency boutique.

Interactive Learning Program

This unique intergenerational program began in collaboration with the CJCS Programming Department. Holocaust survivors in the Drop-in Centre meet with elementary, high school, and university students who are learning about the history of the Second World War and / or the Holocaust.

Each survivor meets with one or more students to discuss their pre-war, wartime, and post-war experiences. The first-hand testimony of the survivors corroborates the history the students are learning in class. Staff and teachers work together to customize the program to meet the students' needs. Each program is different and is geared to the students' level of understanding. Most programs consist of one session, but others have comprised a four-part series. Some programs are incorporated into the core curriculum of the schools. Here is a summary of this program and its benefits to each generation.

Program Preparation

The program is carefully structured. Specifically:

- Students use a structured set of questions as a guideline for discussion. These questions focus on survivors' pre-war, wartime, and post-war experiences.
- Students and teachers adapt the questions to meet the learning objectives of their curriculum.
- The adapted questions are presented to the Drop-in members beforehand so they know what to expect.

Sensitization Session

A week or two before the program date, I hold a one-and-a-half-hour sensitization session with the students in their school environment to:

- provide an understanding of Holocaust survivors and their psycho-social functioning;
- teach interviewing skills; and

- explore students' thoughts and feelings about the program (for example, students are frequently concerned about asking questions that may trigger painful memories and cause the survivor to feel sad and cry); and
- teach interventions to help students respond to survivors' emotional reactions.

Program Format

The format is structured carefully as well:

- the program lasts approximately two and a half hours;
- students are paired with survivors;
- interviews last one hour;
- at the end of the session, students and survivors present a summary of their dialogue to the entire group; and
- at the end of the program, after the survivors have left, we conduct a debriefing session with the students to help them come to terms with the emotional impact of their interviews.

Student Presentations

Students process and record their experience in different ways after the program. Some schools return to the Drop-in Centre to share their completed projects. Project presentations have included a book of poetry and prose written by the students and teacher; three-dimensional artwork; and a scrapbook of poems, drawings, prose, and photos summarizing the student's personal reflections.

Benefits of the Program to Each Generation

STUDENTS
Students benefit in several ways from the program. They

- are provided with opportunities to personally interact with survivors;
- hear personal stories of first-hand witnesses who lived during historical events they are studying;
- learn personal lessons, which they integrate into their lives;
- relate the lessons of the Holocaust to their own lives (for example, bullying);

- learn about contemporary social issues such as racial intolerance and prejudice;
- learn about humanistic issues such as the ability of the human spirit to transcend traumatic life events; and
- discuss the program with their families, many of whom learn about the Holocaust for the first time.

Student comments about the program include the following:

'It made me appreciate my life and realize how lucky I am. I will share it with everyone, even my own kids one day.'

'She was left with nothing after the war … everyone can benefit from this example … I can apply it to my own life.'

'This was eye-opening. It showed me first hand what people went through.'

'I got some important tips on life. I can't let bad things take over. Be happy with what you have. Appreciate it.'

'She showed me the importance of perseverance and strength.'

'It doesn't matter what colour you are. We are all human.'

SURVIVORS
As for survivors, they also benefit in many ways. They

- feel heard and believed by an attentive younger generation;
- find healing and some peace of mind in knowing that their legacies live on in the hearts and minds of a younger generation;
- find meaning in their survival and purpose in their present lives;
- begin to see themselves as witnesses to history and educators in the community; and
- have an opportunity to warn students about the dangers of racial hatred.

Survivors' comments include:

'You should have seen her face. She listened to every word.'

'I was not prepared to talk about my story. By the end of the interview I was into it. Talking one-on-one makes a difference.'

'It is very good to explore our pain. I was happy to have someone to talk to. These students wanted to listen to us. We didn't have this when we came to Canada.'

'We don't do it because we want to ... we have to. It's a costly event for some people.'

'It is a very good idea to bring non-Jewish children. They know very little about the Holocaust.'

Effect on Teachers

Survivors' role as educators has also made an impact on the teachers involved with this program. Some are deeply moved by their students' experiences. Others are pursuing more meaningful ways to translate this sensitive information to their students.

For example, Elaine Lipstein, a Grade 6 teacher at United Talmud Torahs-Snowdon, wrote her impressions of this program in the foreword of a book of poetry and prose she helped her students compile after the program, thanking the survivor participants in these words:

> I could provide my class with the facts of this dark period of history; however, I could never do for them what you did. By opening up your hearts to these children, by bearing witness to them of what you lived through, what you suffered, what you endured, you became the supreme teachers. They heard your stories and felt your pain. They took your histories home with them and shared them with their families. Some of these children then learned for the first time about how their own families had been touched by the Holocaust. (Lipstein, 2005:1)

This program created a special opportunity for Deborah Dixon, a former teacher at Beurling Academy in Montreal. She was searching for a way to make these intergenerational exchanges more meaningful for her students so they could 'walk away with a resolve to make a positive difference in their interactions with each other and especially towards those who differed from them' (Never Again, Fall 2010:4). She was one of thirty-four teachers, eleven from Canada, who were chosen in the summer of 2010 to participate in a special program for educators at Yad Vashem's International School for Holocaust Studies in Israel.

Dialogue with Austrian Gedenkdienst Interns

In 2005 I learned that several *Gedenkdiener*, or volunteer interns, from the Austrian Holocaust Memorial Service (AHMS) were working at the Montreal Holocaust Memorial Centre. I thought it would be interesting to invite these interns to the Drop-in Centre to learn about their organization and hear their reasons for coming to Montreal. Before speaking to the members about such a program, I researched the organization. Andreas Maislinger, who had adopted the idea from the German Action Reconciliation Service for Peace, founded it in 1992. This independent and largely government-funded foundation provides assistance to Holocaust-related archives and museums around the world by sending Gedenkdiener interns to study and preserve Holocaust history in lieu of military service. The AHMS has been sending interns to the Montreal Holocaust Memorial Centre since 1998.

When I initially suggested this program and shared my research on it with the Drop-in Centre, there was dissension within the group. However, the members agreed to hold one session with these interns, and then decide if another meeting was advisable. In the course of the first session, a member asked the interns about their grandparents' involvement during the war years. One intern answered that his grandfather had served in the Austrian army during the Second World War. I knew immediately that his response angered many people. Although they sat silently, their body language reflected their emotional states. They were upset with the intern and with me for inviting them to their safe space. Some expressed their anger to me after the interns left.

I knew I had let them down. Sometimes, however, I struggle to separate my role as the daughter of survivors from that of a professional social worker. The more I thought about the exchange I also realized that there was an opportunity for healing here, both for them and for me.

As the daughter of Holocaust survivor parents, I too live with ambivalence about anything German, sometimes manifested by feelings of hatred, especially towards older Germans and Austrians. To this day, whenever I hear German spoken by an older person, I think to myself: 'What did you do during the Holocaust? Were you in the army, or perhaps a guard at a concentration or death camp? Did you try to help your Jewish neighbour(s)?' Nevertheless, several factors have helped me to change my attitude towards my German peer group.

One was the film *Dark Lullabies*, made by Irene Lilienheim Angelico and Abbey Jack Neidik in the mid-1980s. They explored, through a series of interviews, the impact of the Holocaust on Jews and Germans born after the war. The offspring of German perpetrators disclosed the pain and guilt they felt about their parents' and grandparents' roles in the Holocaust. There is one message from this film that had a significant impact on me. One of the individuals observed that, when second-generation Jewish offspring ask their parents about their Holocaust experiences, it brings them closer together. The opposite is true for the offspring of German Nazis. When they learn about their parents' roles in the Holocaust, it alienates them to the point of estrangement. This statement made me reflect upon my attitudes towards my German peers and I began to empathize with them.

Another reason for changing my attitude was meeting compassionate Germans who are working to redress the injustices of the past. I discovered that some work on *kibbutzim* in Israel, volunteer to help vulnerable Holocaust survivors with tasks in their homes, or belong to German groups that help out in nursing homes. I found one organization, the Action Reconciliation Service for Peace (ARSP), to be very eye-opening. A volunteer organization 'founded by Christians seeking to confront the era of National Socialism in German history' (Action Reconciliation Service for Peace [ARSP]), it performs 'good deeds' to promote reconciliation in the countries of all 'peoples who suffered violence at our [Germany's] hands.'

I decided to share my perceptions about my German peers with the Drop-in Centre members. I felt I had succeeded in stopping the perpetuation of my own hatred against a generation of Germans who had nothing to do with the war, and wanted to give the members an opportunity to do the same. I believed that increasing awareness and deflecting their hatred from subsequent generations could result in healing at some point. I was encouraged to do this when I read a statement by a Holocaust survivor, Elie Wiesel, who links hate with destruction: 'One can rage and protest but to hate serves no purpose other than the final destruction of humanity' (Wiesel cited in Lichtenberg & Shapard, 2000:9).

I anticipated that there would be conflict when I introduced the idea of a dialogue between the Drop-in members and the Austrian interns. And I was right. For the next two weeks we held gut-wrenching discussions about the feasibility of such a program. Many survivors said they would never have anything to do with someone of German or Austrian descent, no matter their age. Some said that to engage in such a program would dishonour the memory of their dead family members and friends, and demonstrate their disloyalty. Others felt it would negate their own horrendous experiences. Many were angry with me for suggesting such an idea.

We reached a stalemate. I continued to share my personal thoughts with the Drop-in members and they continued to say they would never forgive any German person, for generations to come. I felt I had taken the issue as far as I could, decided to accept their viewpoint, and was prepared to drop the idea. Much to my surprise, however, as the members struggled with the issues, ten of them volunteered to participate in an initial dialogue. Meticulous planning went into the preparation. Survivors and interns separately prepared a list of questions they wanted to explore with each other. I conducted an orientation session with the interns to prepare them for this dialogue. Eventually, we held two meetings.

The survivors' questions focused on the reasons the interns wanted to participate in a discussion with them; what their parents and grandparents had told them about the Holocaust; whether they were raised with hatred against Jews; whether they would pass on what they are learning about the Holocaust to their peers in Austria; and whether they would be willing to advocate for Holocaust education when they returned to Austria.

The interns, for their part, wanted to learn about survivors' experiences in their families of origin before the war, including if they encountered anti-Semitism and had non-Jewish friends; if some friends had turned into enemies and betrayed them; their experiences in the war and what had helped them to survive; whether any members of their families had survived; the reasons they chose to come to Montreal and the reception they received; how they are coping with their past; their feelings towards Germany and Austria today; whether they are afraid that another Holocaust will happen; and whether they have shared their stories with their children. They ended the session by asking the group members to tell them the most important message they wanted them to take back to Austria. In response, members asked them to ensure that the Holocaust is incorporated into the Austrian educational curriculum and to include in that curriculum information about anti-Semitism and hatred. The interns assured the survivors that, upon their return to Austria, they would pass on their stories of suffering to their families, peers, and colleagues, and work towards fighting anti-Semitism. In fact, one of the interns, a history teacher, said he would work towards incorporating Holocaust education into his curriculum.

The program was an important step towards reconciliation with Austrian youth born after the war. In the following weeks, survivors continued to talk about it and reflect on the impact it had on them. They were pleased to play a role in educating Austrian youth about the Holocaust, especially since Austria does not have mandatory Holocaust education in its school system. Survivor participants in this program felt they had planted seeds that would eventually grow.

This dialogue had a deeper significance for me. I believe that such initiatives contribute towards world healing and peace.

PART IV

Professional Interactions with Survivors

13 Therapeutic Responses

In the thicket of trauma, pain, and trouble you can see blooms of hope and transformation.

— D. Saleebey (2006)

Recovery from mass atrocity includes grieving losses, resolving internal conflict, alleviating psychic pain, rebuilding self-esteem, and finding meaning and purpose in survival. Here are common presenting issues I come across in both individual sessions and group programs along with therapeutic techniques and approaches used to respond. These techniques are derived from my social-work training, personal experiences, professional relationships, and clinical literature pertaining to trauma survivors.

CREATING A THERAPEUTIC ENVIRONMENT

Before one attempts to use interventions to address therapeutic goals, an appropriate therapeutic environment and relationship needs to be established. Professional therapeutic relationships are one type of relationship, from among many, in which survivors engage. Most Holocaust survivors, however, do not seek professional therapy to deal with the psychological impact of their traumatic experiences for several reasons:

• talk therapy is alien to most European survivors;

- speaking about one's problems to people outside the family is not part of their belief system;
- traumatic memories may be stored in their implicit memory system and survivors are unable to verbalize them; and
- some survivors refuse to pay for therapy.

The literature suggests that those survivors who do turn to health professionals for assistance are unable to enter into a trusting relationship (Brodsky Cohen, 1991; Cohen, 1977; Hass, 1990; Kren, 1989). While this may be true for some survivors, it is my experience that many survivors will engage in a therapeutic alliance. Perhaps it is we, the professional community, who are ill-equipped to provide assistance. Danieli (1988) states that therapists' personal emotional reactions and attitudes to the Holocaust cause difficulties in working with this population. In interviews with sixty-one mental-health providers, she documented forty-nine 'countertransference' themes that affect these therapists in their work with survivors and their families. Their emotional reactions included defence mechanisms used when listening to Holocaust experiences; bystanders' guilt, rage, shame, dread, and horror; and grief and mourning. The most common reactions reported by participants were defence mechanisms such as feeling overwhelmed and numbing themselves, and disbelieving and accusing survivors of exaggeration. Avoidance reactions included 'forgetting,' 'turning off,' 'tuning out,' and 'getting bored with the same story over and over again' (224). Danieli suggests that these reactions are in response to Holocaust stories rather than survivors' behaviours. She recommends that therapists acquire knowledge about the Holocaust to have a better frame of reference to determine the types of questions to ask survivors.

As discussed in chapter 4, it is essential that we examine our own attitudes towards survivors. If we accept the notion that all survivors are severely impaired by their past and are scarred victims, then our relationship with them is unlikely to succeed. Conversely, a trusting relationship is more likely to develop when we view the survivor as an individual who exhibits strength and resiliency on his / her road to recovery in spite of the presence of traumatic symptoms.

Establishing trust and forming an alliance is a crucial first step in creating a therapeutic relationship with an individual. Bussey (2007) suggests that caring social environments, such as 'the presence of a safe listening environment and the process of therapy itself,' fosters resilience after traumatic experiences (307). Skills and techniques that help create a caring therapeutic environment are set out below.

Establishing Trust

Trust often develops slowly and is dependent on many factors, such as the personalities involved; the therapeutic approaches used; attitudes and perceptions; openness and honesty; transference and countertransference issues; vicarious trauma; maintaining appropriate boundaries; and building rapport. I find that, with survivors, trust, rapport, and safety are generated more easily with workers who are from a survivor-family background and share this part of their identity. For the worker, then, saying a few words in a survivor's mother tongue generates trust and builds a connection faster. It is important to keep in mind, however, that not all Holocaust survivors speak Yiddish. For example, survivors originating from Hungary, Germany, Austria, or Russia may feel reassured if the worker converses briefly in an appropriate ethnic language from their country of origin.

Respecting the Survivor's Personal Space

The worker should position herself to face the survivor. Whether the two parties are standing or sitting, the survivor should be asked if the distance is comfortable. If not, the worker should be prepared to adjust it, encouraging the survivor to set the appropriate boundary. Also, the survivor's body language should be observed to see if he is at ease. This process allows survivors to control the physical environment and communicates respect for their personal space.

Communicating Empathy

The worker needs to pay attention to her facial expressions, posture, body language, and tone of voice. Individuals who have been tortured are keen observers and are acutely aware of non-verbal communication. The worker should impart messages of caring, warmth, and security, demonstrating that he has been touched by the survivor's story. Empathic workers create an environment in which individuals feel safe to explore their thoughts and feelings. As discussed in chapter 5, studies demonstrate that empathy is an important skill for effective therapeutic intervention.

Active and Respectful Listening

The worker must have patience, allowing the survivor to think, reflect, and feel at her own pace. The survivor should also be permitted to set the direction and content of the discussion. Painful recollections may occasion a pause. But the worker should remain patient and empathetic, which will serve to contain the survivors' memories. Non-verbal communication skills, such as nodding one's head, leaning forward, and maintaining eye contact, should be used. When traumatic memories emerge, being a compassionate witness is one of the most healing responses a worker can provide.

Non-Judgmental Attitude

As professionals, we must have a non-judgmental attitude. This is especially true when we hear descriptions of survival that may test our own values and beliefs. It is important for a worker to have a caring and supportive attitude and show that she has been touched by the survivor's experience. Providing messages of caring, warmth, and security builds trust and strengthens the therapeutic relationship.

Equalizing the Power Differential

Any therapeutic alliance may begin with a power differential, or power hierarchy. For example, some people view the act of asking for help as a sign of weakness, an admission that they are unable to manage their lives independently. Survivors may also perceive a social worker / therapist / service provider as an authority figure who has greater power. This is a natural assumption because our knowledge and training provides us with skills that we bring to the therapeutic relationship. However, we must not overlook the life skills and strengths of survivors. Recognizing that both parties bring strengths to the process facilitates the building of a respectful and collaborative working relationship.

Herman (1992) suggests guiding survivors to reframe their thoughts about asking for help. For example, a worker might point out that it requires courage to take charge and initiate an action to change one's immediate situation. When a service provider states this observation explicitly, it empowers survivors to reframe the act of asking for help as a sign of strength rather than a weakness.

Survivors may perceive service providers as authority figures and feel vulnerable or angry. This power differential can be equalized by consulting with survivors about their wishes, offering them choices, and including them in the formulation of an intervention plan. Survivors' ability to make their own decisions was a driving force in rebuilding their lives (Ehrlich, 1988). It remains important today as ageing, and its accompanying losses, lead many to lose control over various aspects of their lives. When we make recommendations, individuals must be given permission to disagree with our action plan. This empowers survivors and restores control to them. As Judith Herman (1992) points out: 'The guiding principle of recovery is to restore power and control to the survivor' (159).

Regarding survivors as historians and teachers, rather than as clients, is another technique that helps equalize the power differential. Helping survivors view themselves as historians who have lived a unique experience and have much to teach imparts a message of competence (Rosenbloom, 1983). I invite survivors to teach me about their past. Eventually they begin to see themselves as survivors rather than as victims. Instead of referring to survivors as clients, I prefer to view them as individuals who have lived a unique history.

I also encourage survivors to bring in resource materials pertaining to their past. Many survivors have a wide range of documentary material in their possession. Some have shown me their German passports and identity cards. Others have brought in their *yizker bicher*. These books, which are named after their pre-war communities, memorialize in print family members who were killed during the Holocaust as well as their obliterated communities. Many contain historical and personal accounts of Jewish life in Eastern European communities. Some recount the destruction of their communities, while others include a glimpse of communal adjustment in the post-war period. Most are written in Yiddish, but some contain English and Hebrew sections. In their role as historians, survivors review their memorial books with me, sometimes reading excerpts aloud. In this process they educate me about their country of origin, introduce me to their family members, and recount their war and post- war experiences. Providing survivors with an opportunity to share their resource materials in the therapeutic process helps to build a reciprocal relationship where each party contributes knowledge from their respective areas of expertise.

THEMES AND RESPONSES

Struggle between Remembering and Forgetting

Many survivors struggle with the push and pull forces of wanting to re-member and needing to forget. Remembering their war experiences and multiple losses often brings sleepless nights accompanied by nightmares. However, they fear that not remembering will relegate their beloved fami-lies and friends to oblivion. The following anecdotes illustrate this point.

* * *

In a group program, composed of survivors and non-survivors, one member suggested visiting the Montreal Holocaust Memorial Centre. Survivors in the group saw this activity as an opportunity to teach the others about their experiences. Some survivors participated even though they knew that they would have nightmares that night. They believed that participation was part of their responsibility to bear witness and to educate members, staff, and volunteers about the Holocaust. A week later, one of the survivors began to talk for the first time about his internment at the Mauthausen death camp in Austria. Afterwards, he created a scrapbook filled with prose and pictures, and began to write his memoirs.

* * *

Mrs B., in her mid-eighties, participates in intergenerational dialogues knowing she may experience post-traumatic symptoms such as being flooded by war memories. These memories cause her anxiety and sleep-lessness after the dialogue is over. Yet she views her involvement in these exchanges as an important mission to educate others, especially when students tell how their lives change after participating in the program. Because these dialogues provide meaning and purpose to her life, Mrs B has learned to manage her symptoms with relaxation exercises and other self-care practices and medication.

* * *

Wanting to Communicate Experiences

When survivors begin to recall incidents, it is often with acute clarity, as if the event is frozen in time. Some preface their remarks with state-ments such as: 'Please believe me.' Some say that, if they heard their story from someone else, they would think it was fabricated. Telling their story often occasions great pain, especially for those doing so for the first time. However, sharing their secrets has tremendous therapeutic benefit. For example, one man who was sexually abused by camp guards as a child was so relieved to tell his story for the first time that he was able to go on to write his memoirs.

I notice that Holocaust survivors approach the recounting of their experiences in different ways. Here are common approaches that they use to indicate they want to tell their story and the responses we should make to support them.

Some survivors, particularly those who have been isolated for a period of time, pour out their story in gruesome detail at the beginning of a session. It is important to listen to them and validate what they say in these instances. The listener serves as a compassionate container for the memories so they become less overwhelming and more manageable. Quite often the survivor responds, after telling their story, with 'Thank you for listening.'

Other survivors, during an interview, drop historical clues. For example, some make references to having been interned in specific ghettos, labour camps, and / or death camps. Having a historical knowledge of the Holocaust enables the practitioner to respond to these clues. There is sometimes a brief period of silence after the dropping of clues while the survivor observes the listener. It is important for the latter to validate what the survivor has said and ask questions such as: 'Are you willing to tell me where were you during the war?' 'Would you like to tell me about your experiences?' 'What helped you to survive?' The survivor needs to feel that they have been heard and believed. The worker should encourage expression of the cognitive and affective aspects of the experience. Visual aids may help them structure their story. For example, I use concentration-camp maps to help survivors describe the sequence of events during their incarceration (Krell, 1989). However, the survivor's pace must be tracked and respected. In other words, one must be careful not to probe too deeply. Some survivors become upset if they feel they are being interrogated.

There are survivors who test the therapeutic relationship in the first session by divulging some gruesome details. Many will not engage in a trusting relationship until they feel that the therapist is willing and able to listen to the details about their ordeals.

Refusing to Talk about Experiences

Some survivors refuse to talk about their traumatic past, even when asked about it (discussed in chapter 6). They avoid any situation that may trigger memories of it. These survivors cope by repressing their memories. We must respect their defences and not challenge their inability or unwillingness to recall traumatic events. Some survivors deteriorate psychologically when pushed to self-disclose and are left with distressing recollections they cannot suppress. They prefer to focus on their present-day challenges without references to the past.

Although, as a rule, I accept a survivor's desire to avoid talking about their traumatic experiences, there are times when I suspect that their resistance may be more about protecting me than themselves. For example, after they drop hints and I ask about their war experiences, some say: 'I do not want to burden you with my story.' These words indicate to me they want to protect me from their pain. I show interest by framing their experience within a historical context. For example: 'You have an important story to tell, and by telling it to me you are teaching me about the Holocaust, thus ensuring it will never be forgotten.' This technique reinforces the obligation they feel to transmit their Holocaust legacy to subsequent generations and encourages survivors to go on when they want to disclose but are hesitant to do so.

Regulating Emotional Arousal: Constructing a Narrative

Some survivors come to therapy when traumatic memories about their war experiences are triggered by current events. For example, on one occasion, a severe ice storm in Montreal forced many survivors to leave their homes. There was no heat and electricity for weeks and grocery-store shelves were empty. Most people relocated to emergency shelters, which caused some survivors to fall into states of despondency. For one child survivor, this event awakened frightening memory fragments of the sexual and physical abuse she had endured during her years of hiding in different locations. I helped her retrieve her fragmented memories, make sense of them, and structure them into a chronological narrative. As a result, she learned to recognize when a current event triggers memories of her past so she could manage her emotional reactions.

Sometimes I help survivors, who have never spoken about their experiences, prepare for video testimony. They may have done some soul-searching and feel ready to leave a legacy for their children. However, they are afraid of being overwhelmed with powerful emotions during the actual filming. I help them construct a narrative of their experiences. With some, the story is chaotic and filled with intense emotion when it first comes out. With repeated telling, however, it begins to take on the form of a chronological narrative that the survivor can talk about on camera without becoming emotionally overwhelmed.

Some survivors require emotional support after they are interviewed for a documentation project. Although most express a sense of relief and release when the interview is over, a small number decompensate. They may experience disturbed sleep and become preoccupied with traumatic memories that require clinical intervention. I became aware of this need for support in the mid-1990s when the Survivors of the Shoah Visual History Foundation, founded by Steven Spielberg, was interviewing survivors in Montreal. The foundation referred several survivors to me who decompensated after the interviews. I wish to add, however, that decompensation was an exception rather than the rule. With these survivors, I helped them calm their arousal levels by teaching deep diaphragmatic breathing techniques and safe-place meditation, which allowed them to imagine themselves in a safe place while focusing on the sensory perceptions of this place. One man discussed unresolved issues with a family member who did not survive the war.

Divulging Secrets

During therapy sessions I raise sensitive subjects with survivors, such as asking them to describe their most horrendous experience, one that they may not have told anyone about. Sometimes they divulge long-held secrets. For example, one man described fleeing to safety after he crawled out of a mass grave where many people from his town, including him and his family, had been shot and left for dead. He was the only survivor and lived with survivor's guilt. Others may recount, with hesitation, deeds they were forced to commit to survive. Mr R. described how he was assigned to the Sonderkommando in Auschwitz, where he transferred corpses from the gas chambers to the crematoria. He suffered from shame and guilt, and expressed remorse for having done this, even though he knew he had no choice if he wanted to live. Both women and men sometimes disclose sexual violence committed against them, usually rape.

Raising these sensitive subjects creates an opportunity to help survivors process their shame. It also helps them to verbalize feelings of guilt and to place responsibility for their actions on their persecutors. However, probing for secrets must be done carefully because some survivors' guilt may be due to actions committed to help themselves survive and may have endangered the lives of others, such as stealing a fellow inmate's bread or exposing fellow Jews to Nazi authorities. I notice that survivors rarely disclose these kinds of actions.

Some people recount recurring nightmares such as attacks by dogs, beatings, knocks on the door ordering them to move into ghettos, and the selection process at Auschwitz. Both men and women may disclose medical experiments that were conducted on them.

Issues with Identity

There are survivors dealing with issues specific to their Jewish identity, which they are reticent to disclose for fear of being judged by other survivors and / or the Jewish community. For example, one child survivor, who was hidden in a Catholic orphanage, finds comfort during stressful times by attending church services and listening to organ music. Both religions coexist for her because she also proudly identifies with Judaism. Survivors who were hidden in orphanages may also find comfort in Christian rituals and symbols. There are also families who hid their Jewish identity after the Holocaust and raised their children as Gentiles. However, as they grow older, they want to return to their Jewish roots.

Changing Negative Self-Perceptions

Often survivors berate themselves for their actions or inactions during the Holocaust. For example, some describe numbed emotions and their inability to cry when a close family member died. Others may have felt relief when a parent died because they are no longer a burden jeopardizing their own survival. The following anecdote illustrates this point.

* * *

Mrs T. felt guilty for displaying no sorrow when her mother died in the Łódź Ghetto. In fact, she was preoccupied with removing her mother's shoes and eating the remainder of her bread. Afterwards she remembered not wanting to throw her mother's body on the daily cart used to collect dead bodies. Instead, she undressed the body, washed it, and wrapped it in a shroud according to Jewish tradition. The following morning she placed the body on the cart. Throughout this procedure she did not cry or express any emotion. She had chastised herself ever since for being an uncaring person.

When I asked her why she had been unable to cry in the ghetto, she said she probably would not have been able to stop and may have gone crazy. I normalized her reaction by explaining that emotional numbing is a coping skill that enabled her to go on at that time. I explained that it happened to many people. I also pointed out that, by bathing the body according to Jewish tradition, she treated her mother with great dignity. She did the best she could under the circumstances. This cognitive restructuring technique helped ease her pain and allowed her to internalize a different view of herself.

* * *

Survivors' behaviours in their different environments must be understood within a normative context – their reactions were normal ones in abnormal and chaotic situations (Lifton, 1988). Their self-perception can be reframed by saying something such as: 'Your reactions were a normal response to an abnormal, horrific situation.'

Exploring ways in which survivors maintained their humanity is also a helpful intervention when survivors berate themselves for their behaviours during the war. This process reinforces their ability to remain human in spite of attempts to dehumanize, humiliate, degrade, and murder them. I often point this out when survivors describe ways they helped each other in the camps. For example, some shared food, encouraged each other to live and not give up, took care of the sick, stood in for each other on work duty, risked their lives by participating in secret holiday observances, fasted on Yom Kippur in spite of extreme hunger and starvation, and so on. This intervention helps survivors to conclude that they did the best they could at that particular time.

Enhancing Self-Esteem

To help survivors overcome their victimization and enhance their self-esteem, I adopt an approach that entails exploring tangible accomplishments which demonstrate the survivor's progress towards recovery, such as affirming religious, secular, and / or humane values; giving birth to a new generation to uphold life and continuity; putting down roots in a new country; learning a new language, trade, and / or profession; and becoming involved in organizational activities.

Sometimes I use an intervention that points out examples of survivor actions that have benefited all Canadians. For example, I say, 'We have survivors, like you, to thank for Canada's present day anti-hate legislation,' or, 'Survivors were instrumental in using the legal system to bring Nazi war criminals to justice.' Such statements convey gratitude for the actions that survivors took on behalf of all Canadian citizens and instils pride in their own achievements and accomplishments.

At other times I ask survivors to answer these questions: 'What are some of the successful things you have accomplished in your life?' and 'What are the relationships you are most proud of?' Their answers usually include:

- supporting each other during the war;
- surviving horrible conditions during the war;
- valuing commitments to their families, which continue to this day;
- becoming good citizens;
- placing an important value on education for their children and themselves;
- upgrading their standard of living;
- doing volunteer work to help others; and
- supporting and advocating on behalf of the state of Israel.

Survivors are also extremely proud of the relationships with their children, grandchildren, and great-grandchildren; their spouses; the friendships they developed in the concentration camps that continue to this day; and the new friends they made in Canada.

Internal Conflict: Survivor Guilt

Many survivors are haunted at one time or another by guilt for having survived when so many others did not. Gestalt reversal techniques may be helpful in resolving this guilt (Williams, 1988). For example Mrs N., a survivor of the Warsaw Ghetto, was consumed with guilt because her older sister, who helped her escape, didn't survive. Helpful interventions included statements like the following: 'You were not responsible for her death, the German Nazis were' and 'If your sister was sitting here instead of you, would you want her to live with the guilt you have lived with all these years?' or 'If you had died instead of her, would you blame her for your death?' This approach enabled Mrs N. to absolve herself of the guilt she was feeling.

Some survivors carry guilt feelings for having committed what they regard as an inappropriate action during the war, which they play repeatedly in their minds. For example, Mr S. described his experience at age eleven when he hid in a small space in a boiler room during a search by the Gestapo. The space was too small to accommodate both him and his older brother. His brother insisted that he hide there. He feels guilty for having listened to his brother because his brother was caught and he never saw him again. When I helped him explore what his options were as a child, he realized that he would have been killed also, and his brother did not want that to happen. In fact, his brother told him that a family member had to survive to tell others what happened to them. Mr S. decided to document his family's experiences, as his brother wanted him to, which helped appease his guilt. He also decided to write a letter to his brother explaining his actions during the boiler-room incident and his completed mission to document their family's pre-war and wartime experiences. He read his letter out loud in front of the cemetery monument that bore a memorial plaque with his brother's name. This process brought some peace and comfort to Mr S. because he felt his brother's presence there. Mr S. believed he had connected with his brother and carried out his last wishes.

Other survivors cope with generalized guilt by finding meaning and purpose in their lives and a reason for their existence. They believe their survival obligates them to give back to their community, peers, and God by performing good deeds and acts of kindness.

Psychic Pain

Some survivors believe that living with their painful memories, and associated pain, helps them remember their losses and honours their commitment to pass on their legacy. Consequently, many survivors resist letting their pain go and refuse to work through their grief, losses, and guilt for having survived. They believe that letting go of their pain and suffering betrays their family and friends. This responsibility is internalized and carried throughout their lives.

Hypnotherapy may help some of these survivors deal with their pain and guilt. During a workshop in Toronto, a hypnotherapist described helping one survivor compromise on the percentage of guilt she was willing to give up. Resistant to letting go of the hot pain in her body, the therapist asked her to consider localizing it to one hand. She agreed and the treatment worked.

Survivors can also discover how to fulfil their commitment in other ways that are less harmful to their well-being. For example, I find Yad Vashem's *Pages of Testimony* project to be an effective therapeutic tool. Survivors complete biographical information about each person killed in the Holocaust whom they wish to memorialize. Submitting this information enables them to externalize their pain and find some peace by knowing they have fulfilled their holy mission. Each page associates a name with a formerly anonymous victim and fulfils the survivor's responsibility to bear witness. These pages are placed in the Hall of Names at Yad Vashem – a paper cemetery that provides a final resting place for their loved one, thereby preserving their memory for future generations. In the words of one survivor: 'It lessens my pain.'

Occasionally this process leads to a surprising discovery. I helped a survivor complete a *Page of Testimony* in 1999 as part of his healing process. This led to the reunification of his siblings after his death. Heartwarming moments like these underscore the importance of this tool and inspire my ongoing work with Holocaust survivors (http://www1 .yadvashem.org/yv/en/remembrance/names/feedback.asp).

Another helpful technique to resolve psychic conflict linked with 'unfinished business' with a dead family member or friend is to have the survivor speak to the soul of the deceased, or write them a letter.

Helping Survivors with Their Traumatic Grief

Participating in Rituals of Grieving

Sometimes I work with adult offspring of survivors who do not include their surviving parent in funeral arrangements, or in selecting a gravestone, when their spouse dies. They want to spare their parent the pain of participating in these responsibilities. However, I encourage involving the surviving parent, if they are willing and able to do so, because it enables them to participate in a grieving ritual, something they were unable to do for their family members who were killed during the war.

Memorializing Dead Family Members

Survivors live with the ongoing mission of memorializing family members who were killed in the Holocaust. I help survivors explore ways in which they can honour their memories in meaningful ways. This intervention helps them with their ongoing grief process. While some have mounted plaques on memorials at cemeteries, others are buying memorial plaques at synagogues. In recent years, survivors have started adding the names of family members murdered in the Holocaust to existing headstones in cemeteries, thus ensuring they will never be forgotten. There seems to be an urgency for them to do so now because of their advanced age.

Participating in Community Commemorative Events

I also encourage survivors and their families to attend community Holocaust commemoration services. This makes the process of mourning a collective one that serves three functions. First, it comforts survivors by showing them they are no longer alone in remembering the past. Second, survivors witness that their legacy of remembrance is now transmitted to a new generation and the community at large. Third, they stand in solidarity with the community and affirm their own survival and that of the Jewish people, thus imbuing them with pride and hope for the future.

PTSD and Traumatic Flashback

As mentioned earlier, during the 1991 Persian Gulf War, many survivors had flashbacks of their war experiences, and felt agitated and anxious, as they saw their beloved state of Israel under siege on television. The spectacle of defenceless Jewish citizens wearing gas masks to protect against poisonous gas from Iraqi Scud missiles triggered repressed memories. Survivors began showing up in the health-care and social-service systems, and many were referred to me. Here is one such story.

* * *

Mrs N. was referred by the local Holocaust museum. As she sat in my office, she expressed fears about Israel's destruction and quickly switched to her personal war experiences. She said: 'You will understand because you are a daughter of survivors.' I am used to survivors opening up about their traumatic history, especially those who are socially isolated with little stimulation or diversion. It's like a faucet opening and the trauma story pours out in vivid detail. I listened because, in my experience, individuals felt calmer and expressed relief after I heard their story and validated them.

However, this incident was different. Mrs N. quickly became very agitated and began to panic, yelling, 'Bombs are dropping!' Suddenly, she jumped out of her seat and crawled under my desk screaming, 'We'll be killed! We'll be killed.' With hands over her head, her body language expressed intense panic, fear, panic, and anxiety. She was reliving a bomb attack in the war. This was the first time I came across someone experiencing a dissociative episode and going through such intense physical and emotional reactions.

I did not feel adequately trained to deal with the situation even though I had studied crisis intervention at university. Instinctively, I got down on my hands and knees and spoke to her in a calm voice, reassured her that she was safe, and explained that she was remembering an event that happened a long time ago. Then, I asked her to tell me her name and describe her surroundings. Soon she crawled from under my desk, a bit embarrassed. I continued the session by explaining her actions and helping her figure out the triggering event that caused her intense emotional reaction (describing Israel's vulnerability). She insisted on telling me about her war experiences and was eager to meet other survivors who were also reliving their wartime memories. She asked me questions to help her understand her behaviours both during and after the war, which I interpreted. I ended the session by ensuring she was oriented to the present before she left my office.

* * *

I was shaken by this experience. Although these interventions worked and Mrs N. left my office feeling calmer, the incident taught me to work differently with individuals, even though I never witnessed another survivor experiencing a flashback so vividly. For example, I help survivors to regulate their affective states before addressing their traumatic memories, especially those who enter my office in a state of hyperarousal. Social worker Babette Rothschild (2000) suggests employing the following somatic therapeutic interventions to help individuals modulate their reactions: self-soothing techniques such as imagining a safe place to use as an anchor during times of stress and anxiety; body-awareness techniques to regulate affective states; putting-on-the-brakes; and pacing trauma narratives.

Searching for Meaning and Purpose

Melendez, Maramaldi, and Naleppa (2008) state, 'As adults become older, they spend more time reviewing their life achievements and searching for personal meaning' (407). In gerontology, this developmental task is referred to as life review (Butler, cited in Melendez et al., 2008). The process of evaluating one's life and exploring unresolved conflicts can be difficult for Holocaust survivors. They may resist recalling painful memories from their war experiences, or pleasant memories of pre-war life in communities that were destroyed.

Bar-Tur and Levy-Shiff (1994) suggest that, instead of a life review, some survivors engage in a 'Holocaust review'which brings meaning and purpose to their lives. These survivors focus their energies on talking publicly about their experiences, writing books and poetry, and participating in educational projects and missions to fulfil their responsibility as witnesses to the Holocaust period. Unlike a life review, which covers the entire lifespan and elicits pleasant memories, Holocaust review never ends. The survivor assumes responsibility to preserve the memory of those who were murdered. In so doing, they find meaning and purpose, establish continuity with the past, and achieve partial integration.

I observe that survivors who participate in group programs with their peers, and are provided with opportunities to grieve their losses, do eventually talk about their pre-war hometowns. They read Yiddish articles about them and describe the way of life in their families of origin. As service providers, we can influence the life-review process by helping survivors write their memoirs. I help them structure the process by suggesting they begin with their pre-war lives, move on to the Holocaust and their post-war years, and end with their present-day life. I also suggest they include their achievements, things they are proud of, and an inspirational message to leave as a legacy for future generations. Other interventions to help survivors find meaning and purpose include:

- Encouraging survivors to write or record their memoirs – in their mother tongues if they prefer. Service providers can help structure the process.
- Encouraging survivors to participate in community documentation projects to leave a legacy for family and community.
- Facilitating survivors' roles as educators and historians. They can be encouraged to speak in educational settings. They can also be linked with high school and university students taking history courses about the Second World War to help them understand the Holocaust.
- Encouraging survivors to serve as docents and volunteers in Holocaust museums and organizations.
- Encouraging survivors to volunteer at social-service agencies. For example, survivors provide information on a variety of topics on the Information Line at CJCS. This important role provides them with meaning and purpose as they help fellow survivors and their families.

- Providing venues for intergenerational dialogues with younger individuals.
- Encouraging survivors to express their experiences and feelings through art, poetry, film, and song.

Survivors may also find meaning and purpose by serving as mentors to others who experience traumatic events. The following anecdote illustrates this point. In 1986, seven months after his wife and three children were killed by a terrorist bomb on an Air India plane, which caused the aircraft to crash off the coast of Ireland with the loss of everyone on board, Mr S., a Hindu, was referred to me. He had a specific request. He wanted to meet a Holocaust survivor who had endured similar losses and had gone on to lead a productive life. In his bereavement process, Mr S. employed several coping strategies to deal with the pain of his losses: he was in frequent telephone contact with two men who also lost their families; he was being treated by a psychiatrist; and he immersed himself in his work. However, he thought that a Holocaust survivor might help him to find 'a sense of hope' to offset his feelings of hopelessness and helplessness. I put him in contact with a Bergen-Belsen concentration-camp survivor who demonstrated by example that, eventually, life goes on. When a survivor helps another 'survivor,' they both benefit from this reciprocal process. The supporting survivor finds meaning and purpose by helping others.

Holocaust survivors need to know that communicating their experiences will inspire and help survivors of other traumatic events. They may never learn the impact they have on those who hear them speak or read their memoirs. For example, a student read the memoir of a survivor who had been raped during the war. After having the opportunity to hear this survivor speak about how she rebuilt her life and created a new family, the student became hopeful that she could also recover from her recent rape ordeal.

OTHER THERAPEUTIC RESPONSES

Complementary and Alternative Medicine

I believe that having an eclectic toolbox of conventional and non-conventional approaches available to help people heal from severe chronic trauma is important. I was exposed to alternative health in January 1991, during the first Persian Gulf War, when Israel was threatened by Scud missile attacks. As discussed in chapter 10, I decided to implement time-limited support groups. Fortunately, I co-facilitated one group with a family-practice medical resident who had worked with Vietnam War veterans. He introduced me to alternative interventions which included progressive muscular- relaxation exercises; breathing exercises; calming music; affirmations; and use of a calming scene through guided visualization to promote a relaxed state. Although some members had difficulty relaxing, others managed it and their body language reflected a letting go. As each session progressed, we noticed that the traumatic memories that had surfaced were gradually suppressed. Members left the group in a more relaxed state.

After witnessing these events, I decided that my traditional education needed to be augmented so I could offer a broader range of interventions. I registered for courses in natural health at the Natural Health Consultants (NHC) Institute, a leading private school in Montreal. This school introduced me to alternative approaches to well-being which I integrated into my practice. These include mind-body techniques, energy medicine, and medical practices of non-Western cultures. I learned that Eastern cultures do not separate the mind and body the way Western allopathic medicine does. In fact, their ancient medical science teaches that our minds and bodies are one. At the time I was studying these practices, many were considered esoteric and on the fringe by traditional mental-health professionals. The psychiatrist who supervised the groups discussed above asked if there was scientific proof of the mind-body techniques we used. Since this was the early 1990s, alternative treatments were just beginning to make their way into mainstream society. There was then little empirical evidence to support our practice. However, as we continued to use these interventions and group members integrated them into their lives, their feedback convinced us of their effectiveness in relieving post-traumatic symptoms. (Finger & Arnold [2002] provide a historical overview of mind-body interventions in the United States.)

The situation is different today because modern science is confirming the effectiveness of some of these practices. During the last decade there has been a mind-body revolution in the medical world as scientific research validates the mind's (thoughts and emotions) ability to heal the body and prevent disease (Benson & Proctor, 2010). Recent scientific breakthroughs in genetic research show that the mind can influence gene activity associated with health and disease (Benson & Proctor, 2010). Benson and Proctor (2010) explain these advances and benefits as follows: 'We now have scientific proof that the mind can heal the body. This means that *you* have the innate ability to self-heal diseases, prevent life-threatening conditions, and supplement established drug and surgical procedures with mind body techniques that can improve your physiology, biochemistry, brain functioning, and genetic activity. Furthermore, these benefits have the potential to reduce individual costs and the broader societal expenses of health care' (3).

The United States government supports research in mind-body medicine, one type of Complementary and Alternative Medicine (CAM) practice. In 1998 it established the National Center for Complementary and Alternative Medicine (NCCAM) in the Department of Health and Human Services. NCCAM funds research projects at scientific institutions around the word, trains researchers, and provides authoritative information to the public and health professionals.

NCCAM defines CAM as 'a group of diverse medical and health care systems, practices, and products that are not generally considered part of conventional medicine' (http://nccam.nih.gov/about/ataglance/). The term 'alternative medicine' refers to practices not commonly used in conventional Western or allopathic medicine. When an alternative practice, such as acupuncture, is used together with a conventional one, it is a called complementary treatment.

In recent years CAM has gained popularity in wellness-promoting treatments. Alternative treatments are making their way into mainstream society, especially when there is scientific evidence to support such practices. Integrative Medicine (IM) combines the best practices of conventional and alternative treatments. A number of well-known integrative medical centres exist, such as the Arizona Center for Integrative Medicine and the Complementary and Integrative Medicine program at the Mayo Clinic in Minnesota. Integrative practitioners focus on health and healing rather than disease and treatment and consider factors such as mind, body, spirit, community, and lifestyle that may influence an individual's health (http://integrativemedicine.arizona.edu/about/definition.html).

In 2011 NCCAM classified CAM practices as follows:

• herbal remedies and dietary supplements;

- mind-body practices that focus on the interaction between the mind and body, for example, meditation, yoga, deep-breathing exercises, hypnotherapy, progressive muscular relaxation, and tai chi;
- manipulative and body-based practices whereby practitioners use touch to massage, manipulate, and / or rub the bones and joints, soft tissues, and circulatory and lymphatic systems of the body to relieve pain, reduce stress, increase relaxation, and address anxiety and depression;
- movement therapies that promote physical, mental, emotional, and spiritual well-being, for example, the Feldenkrais Method, the Alexander Technique, Pilates, and Trager;
- practices of traditional healers who use methods based on indigenous theories, beliefs, and experiences handed down from one generation to the next;
- energy medicine, such as healing touch, qi gong, reiki, magnet therapy, and light therapy, which focuses on the body's invisible energy force, a force that, when blocked, may cause illness; and
- whole medical systems, which consist of practices and theories centred on both ancient and modern philosophies, such as India's Ayurvedic, traditional Chinese medicine, homeopathy, and naturopathy. (http://nccam.nih.gov/health/whatiscam#types)

Integrating conventional and non-conventional approaches enables me to be more creative and flexible in my work. It is important to note, however, that individuals must be consulted about these approaches and interventions must be applied in a manner that meets and respects their needs. Alternative interventions may be appropriate for some people but not for others. Survivors must be given the permission to say, 'I do not want to try this' or 'I do not believe in this.'

Here are some strategies I use that incorporate a mind, body, and soul approach to well-being. Although some techniques are not considered evidence-based practice derived from empirical research, they have produced beneficial and effective results for some individuals. Behrman and Tebb (2009) refer to these favourable outcomes as 'practice-based evidence' which is circulating among workers and their clients (131–2). Large numbers of people are using CAM interventions because they are experiencing desirable results which are improving their quality of life. Thus, it is important for service providers to read the CAM literature and research to learn more about these interventions, especially as more and more of our clients ask about them.

MIND

In my former private practice and now at our Drop-in Centre, I inform survivors about the mind-body connection. They are taught to release tension at the emotional level by getting in touch with their feelings and labelling them. They learn to develop an emotional vocabulary and express their feelings to a trusted friend, family member, or professional counsellor. Some write in a journal, often in their mother tongues.

Relaxation exercises, such as breathing techniques, and simple meditative exercises help survivors cope with their post-traumatic-stress reactions. For example, breath-counting meditation helps some people deal with their ruminative thoughts and allows their bodies to enter a state of relaxation. The method begins with deep diaphragmatic breathing, then breathing in and out while saying the number 'one' each time. They repeat this conscious breathing process to a count of four, and then repeat it once or twice more.

I also use guided imagery, such as visiting a special calming place, to promote relaxation and induce a serene state. Sometimes I integrate instrumental and environmental music into the process – while being careful not to select music that could trigger any adverse emotional reaction. If the survivors are open to it, I introduce them to aromatherapy, the ancient art of using concentrated oils from aromatic plants to promote physical, mental, and emotional well-being (Worwood, 1995). Some survivors find relief from anxiety and insomnia by using essential oils. For example, they might include lavender oil in their bath, or breathe it in by applying a few drops on a towel placed on their pillow. Others benefit from Bach Rescue Remedy flower essences. These liquid extracts are derived from flowers (Kaminsky and Katz, 1994) and sometimes work well in a crisis. Four drops added to a glass of water, or directly under the tongue, can induce a state of immediate calm. One survivor, suffering from long-standing anxiety, used Rescue Remedy to replace her dependency on tranquilizers. Some survivors drink herbal teas like chamomile, especially at bedtime, to induce sleep. During the summer I encourage survivors to spend time in a natural setting on a regular basis to activate the energy flow in their bodies. One woman put her recliner on her balcony and did her breathing exercises outdoors. She said it helped manage her chronic arthritic pain.

BODY

We explore an exercise routine with survivors and discuss healthy eating habits. Many survivor diets are the same as they were before the war and often include high amounts of fat and salt. Some of these foods may contribute to depression and anxiety. We teach members of the Drop-in Centre to integrate physical exercise into their lifestyles and to eat a healthy diet. The program includes a weekly half-hour aerobic exercise class taught by a professional instructor. Some members take these exercises seriously and practise them at home as well. Educational programs about nutrition focus on the benefits of whole foods (vegetables, fruits, grains); eating less red meat and more fish; decreasing fat intake; consulting with their doctors about vitamins and minerals; and reducing consumption of processed foods, caffeine, salt, and sugar.

During an educational workshop, a clinical psychologist at a large geriatric hospital told me about the positive affect of reflexology in calming an aggressive Alzheimer's patient. Energy treatments such as reflexology – the therapeutic art of applying pressure to the reflexes of the feet – benefit some survivors. These reflexes correspond to organs and glands in the body and, when pressed, release stiffness and tension to bring the body into a state of balance. Drop-in members were receptive to a lecture given by a reflexologist. Other survivors benefit from massage therapy to treat insomnia and pain. For example, one survivor said that, when she felt stressed, she broke out in a rash over most of her body that did not respond to medication. However, after two massage treatments, the rash and accompanying itchiness subsided.

SOUL

I have observed over the years that survivors differ in their spiritual beliefs. After the war, many devout survivors felt abandoned by God, causing some to lose their faith. In recent years, however, many are returning to their religious roots as they prepare for death. Other survivors continue to maintain strong religious beliefs while some have replaced religious values with other commitments such as family, involvement in communal organizations, support for Israel, fighting neo-Nazism and anti-Semitism, and / or involving themselves in Holocaust-related activities.

Discussion about spirituality sometimes occurs in my interactions with survivors. The spiritual dimension of our work is generally left to religious leaders. Some survivors, however, may refuse a referral to a religious leader. Therefore, spirituality needs to be addressed when it comes up. I remind survivors of their indomitable spirit, which helped them to survive and overcome adversity in the wartime and post-war years. Although most attribute their survival to luck or fate, when probed further, some recount specific actions they undertook to survive. I point out to them that their survival often required creativity and courage, and I encourage them to apply the same creative skills to their present challenges.

One spiritual intervention I employ with survivors who express feelings of helplessness, despondency, and despair deals with the concept of the soul. This intervention should be used only with survivors who believe in the *neshumah* or soul. When these survivors make statements such as 'I am feeling depressed,' 'I do not know why I am still here,' or 'I don't know how I can go on with my life,' I probe the ways in which they have been able to deal with life until now. I attempt to help the survivor recognize their strengths and coping skills. Then I suggest that their soul must feel that their work on this earth is not yet complete. I ask them what they feel they must still accomplish before they die. The intent of this intervention is to stimulate feelings of hopefulness and set goals to counter the despair. I also provide them with inspirational poetry and prose, and encourage them to turn to these materials for personal solace and enrichment. Many continue to collect material on their own.

Discussions that focus on spirituality involve:

- setting aside a quiet time for reflection;
- connecting to a higher meaning in life which provides an internal anchor, such as God, nature, or community;
- participating in activities which provide meaning and purpose;
- praying;
- telling jokes;
- exploring creativity;
- having a good time;
- practising daily acts of kindness; and
- expressing gratitude and appreciation.

Some survivors find themselves unable to celebrate happy occasions such as birthdays, weddings, and holidays. They are reminded of their absent family members during these family celebrations and their unrelenting grief prevents them from enjoying themselves and laughing. Some believe that life is serious business and they feel they will dishonour the memory of their family if they listen to music. This situation manifests in several ways. For example, when an entertainer sang songs in two different survivor social centres, some survivors left while others remained but cried throughout the program. When they were asked why they were crying, the answer usually was: 'I miss my family more during happy times.' When this happens, I sometimes make the following statement: 'If you could talk to your family member, would they forgive you for having a good time?' The answer is always: 'Yes, I know that they would not want me to feel sad for such a long time.' I respond with: 'Then why can't you forgive yourself and give yourself the permission to have a good time?'

Often this intervention leads to a discussion of their losses, a description of the last time they saw their family members, and their guilt feelings. Service providers should be aware of this outcome and ask these questions only if there is ample time available. This is not always the case in a group program. The process, however, can be very effective in empowering survivors to be happy during celebrations.

For example, one year during Chanukah – the Jewish festival of lights – I asked group members to share some past and present happy memories of this holiday. One survivor started to talk and then stopped, choking back his tears. He said there was too much pain. Members quickly identified with him and their sadness permeated the room. It was evident they were reliving the past. I intervened by suggesting they give themselves permission to enjoy themselves. One woman responded, 'I feel too guilty,' and other members nodded their heads. I asked them if they could speak with their families, would they want them to continue harbouring these feelings of guilt and grief? The majority said no. Then I asked them to reflect on the reason they couldn't give themselves the permission to be happy. This statement had an impact on some members and they began to share their happy Chanukah memories. Today, retrieving positive memories is an ongoing process and each time increasingly more people participate in the discussion.

Body-Centred Somatic Therapy

I have worked with individuals who are not able to put their memories into words, even though these memories are vivid in their minds. Instead, they relive their traumatic experiences as bodily states and sensations, resulting in a variety of symptoms, primarily depression and anxiety. Their unprocessed traumatic memories are stored in the body and 'encoded implicitly in the form of images, visceral and muscular sensations, movements and impulses, smells, sounds, feelings without words' (Fisher & Ogden, 2009:318). Body-centred somatic therapies help individuals to be more aware of their bodies and mindfully observe their internal sensations. This process can be combined with breath work and movement. Van der Kolk (2006) lists some approaches and techniques that have been extensively explored. These include focusing, sensory awareness, Feldenkrais, Rolfing, the Alexander Technique, body-mind centring, Somatic Experiencing, Pesso Boyden System Psychomotor Therapy, the Rubenfeld Synergy Method, and Hakomi Body-Centred Psycho-Therapy.

Another case of study is relevant here.

* * *

My experience with Mr G. allowed me to witness the somatic response first-hand. He was referred to a discussion group I was organizing. During my interviews, he described a long history of depression and anxiety managed with medication. He survived the war with his mother by hiding in an empty grave in the woods during the day and searching for food at night. He had never spoken about his ordeal. When I first met with him, he gave me some clues about his experiences during the Holocaust. When I asked about them, he tried to speak but only sounds came out. He put his hands on his belly and began to rock back and forth. The sounds started as a grunt emanating from his stomach and moved upwards in his body, becoming louder and louder. He began to cough and released a piercing noise that sounded like a wounded animal. His body heaved up and down and eventually he broke down and cried. After a while, he composed himself and said in Yiddish: 'I feel like a stone has been removed from my belly.' Then he insisted on telling me about his war experiences.

Throughout these sessions I acted as a witness, creating a safe space for Mr G.'s memories to unfold. This cathartic experience enabled him to discharge repressed emotions he felt localized in his belly; the back-and-forth rocking movement helped comfort him as he went through this process. He later wrote his memoirs, which he shared with his family. He also became a member of a writer's group that gave meaning and purpose to his life. His previous symptoms of depression and anxiety diminished.

* * *

Emotional Freedom Technique (EFT)

EFT is an energy psychology that was introduced by psychologist

Roger Callahan and expanded by Gary H. Craig (Craig, 2002; Feinstein et al., 2005). Energy psychology (EP), a derivative of energy medicine, combines Western psychotherapy practices with Eastern medicine (Feinstein, 2008, 2010a). EP 'postulates that mental disorders and other health conditions are related to disturbances in the body's electrical energies and energy fields' (Feinstein, 2008:199). An important corner-stone of Eastern medicine is the universal energy field that permeates the environment and is stored in energy centres within the body called chakras. This energy is distributed by a network of meridians. Medical science confirms the existence of these subtle energies. Researchers at the University of California, Los Angeles (UCLA) found that the area of the body associated with the chakras emit electrical oscillations of a higher frequency than the rest of the body (Feinstein, 2010b).

EFT is based on the principle that all negative emotions and behaviours, and many of the associated physical discomforts, are caused by disruptions to the body's energy system (Craig, 2002). This includes fears, phobias, anger, grief, anxiety, depression, traumatic memories, PTSD, worry, and guilt. EFT is an emotional version of acupuncture that does not require needles. Instead, release points in the body are stimulated by tapping on them with the fingertips. It combines exposure-based therapy and cognitive restructuring with manual stimulation of acupressure points on the upper body. Studies are currently under way to establish EFT as an evidence-based method beneficial in the treatment of post-traumatic-stress disorder and other conditions (Feinstein, 2008, 2010a).

I taught this technique in the Drop-in Centre. Some people were sceptical and refused to try it. Others, however, used it and shared success stories that included improved sleep, reduced anxiety levels, and pain management.

Imagery to Deal with Traumatic Memory

Some survivors continue to have flashbacks, which sometimes can be stopped through imagery (Naparstek, 2004). Mrs T., who survived the war by hiding her Jewish identity, had recurring flashbacks of being chased by German soldiers, which left her terrified. I helped her compose a visualization where she turned around assertively, faced the soldiers, and told them to leave her alone. When they asked her why they should, she replied in a loud voice, 'Because I am free now.' The soldiers turned and headed the other way. This particular flashback never came back.

Another survivor imagined herself inflating into a very large balloon, frightening her aggressors. Mrs K. used visualization to deal with a recurring image of seeing her mother shot before her eyes. She supplanted her traumatic memory with another image. Instead of seeing her mother lying on the ground with blood oozing from her neck, she superimposed a red rose, her mother's favourite flower, over the blood and imagined her sleeping peacefully. In all these instances the survivors chose visual imagery to overcome painful memories of their past.

Animal Assisted Therapy (AAT)

In the early 1990s I read about the benefits of pet therapy, known today as AAT, as a tool with older adults. This therapy uses trained animals to help individuals achieve physical, cognitive, and emotional well-being. I worked with survivors who spoke fondly about their pets, which provided companionship and helped them cope with loneliness. Consequently, I thought that members of the group would benefit from a visit by a therapist and her specially trained dogs. I soon learned how wrong I was to make this assumption. When the therapist entered the auditorium with her two dogs, two survivors, visibly agitated, ran out of the room.

I followed them, and one pointed to her neck to show me a large scar where a German shepherd had bitten her as she disembarked from a cattle car in Auschwitz. She yelled at me and pointed out my insensitivity for allowing the dogs into her safe space. She was right. The German Nazis used dogs, especially German shepherds, as guard dogs. These dogs often attacked people to scare them into submission, or killed them.

The other survivor, however, was open to exploring a way to control her lifelong fear of dogs. She told me that every time she saw a German shepherd on the street, she became anxious and afraid, and crossed the road. Using the behavioural process of systematic desensitization, I encouraged her to come back into the auditorium and look at the dogs from a distance. Slowly, she moved closer to the dog and eventually returned to the group circle. By the end of the session she was patting the dog. In a short time, her fear of dogs was overcome. The first survivor refused to come back into the auditorium and remained outside until the session ended. It took several weeks for me to regain her trust.

INTEGRATION OF DIFFERENT TREATMENT MODALITIES

There are a number of effective treatments in the trauma field. While some are evidence-based, others are not. At the beginning of this decade there was a 'huge debate' in the trauma field between the proponents of verbal-treatment modalities – such as prolonged exposure therapy – and body-centred somatic therapies (Sykes Wylie, 2004). Traditional psychotherapy addresses the cognitive and emotional elements of trauma. Somatic therapy focuses on the body's nervous system and muscular anatomy, and the relationship between these systems and the mind.

In my work, I notice that there is no single treatment approach that works with all people. Over the years, I completed training in cognitive-behavioural therapy for PTSD, eye-movement desensitization and reprocessing (EMDR), and mindfulness. I have also studied other trauma-treatment approaches such as Hakomi Body-Centred Psycho-Therapy and energy medicine such as Chakra Balancing and Emotional Freedom Technique. I believe that an eclectic mix of interventions is necessary. Some people are able to talk about their traumatic experiences and others are not. Those who are unable to do so may experience their memories as bodily states and sensations. Research and practice in the area of trauma continues to identify a variety of therapeutic approaches that help individuals recover. Examples include Cognitive-Behavioural Therapy (Foa et al., 2000); Eye Movement Desensitization and Reprocessing (EMDR) (Shapiro, 2001); Mindfulness-Based Stress Reduction (MBSR) (Kabat-Zinn, 1994; http://umassmed.edu/cfm/home/index.aspx); Sensorimotor Psychotherapy (Fisher & Ogden, 2009); Somatic Trauma Therapy (Rothschild, 2000, 2003); Somatic Experiencing (Levine, 1997); Energy Psychology (Feinstein, 2010a, 2010b); Hakomi Body-Centred Psycho-Therapy (Kurtz, 1990); Imagery Based Therapies (Naparstek, 2004); and yoga (van der Kolk, 2006; Behrman & Tebb, 2009).

14 Mitigating Responses
to Environmental Triggers

Specific circumstances have the potential to trigger painful memories for survivors of the Holocaust.

– P. David and S. Pelly (2003)

SITUATIONS OR EVENTS THAT MAY
TRIGGER MEMORIES OF PERSECUTION

Seemingly benign events, everyday sights and sounds, or certain comments may trigger painful Holocaust memories. Re-experiencing the original trauma in thought, emotion, behaviour, and physiology is a normal and natural response of individuals who suffer from PTS or PTSD. Survivors may react to these reminders with fear, sadness, suspicion, anxiety, anger, or withdrawal. This chapter lists some examples of triggers for Holocaust survivors, typical responses, and a brief explanation why the situation may cause a triggered response. Suggestions for possible interventions are also included. This information is gleaned from several sources, primarily the practice manual published by Baycrest Geriatric Health Care System, *Caring for Aging Holocaust Survivors: Practice Guide*, edited by Paula David and Sandi Pelly (2003); the video *Painful Memories*, and accompanying discussion guide produced by the Menorah Park Center for the Aging (known today as the Menorah Park Center for Senior Living) in Cleveland, Ohio (Gross, 1994); and articles by survivor Rita Hofrichter (1992) and social worker Ann Hartman-Luban (1999). In addition, I include triggers that I observe in survivors who attend community programs. It is important to point out that not all survivors are affected by these triggers, and those who do may not experience them in the same way.

* * *

ACTIVITIES OF DAILY LIVING

Routines and Schedules

REACTION:
> Non-compliance
> Anger
> Fear and anxiety about being late

REASON:
> The Nazis were efficient and orderly in their attempts to annihilate Jews. They were known for their efficiency and keeping on schedule. During a roll call survivors were required to line up with little prior notice. Those who were late were sometimes beaten or shot.

RESPONSE:
> Be flexible. Do not insist that survivors be prompt in attending group programs. For example, the program in the Drop-in Centre is structured so that members may come in anytime during the first hour. Some come in after the structured program has started.

Lining Up for Service

REACTION:
> Refusal to do so
> Anger
> Anxiety

REASON:
> In the camps, Jews lined up for food rations, toilets, roll call, deportations, and even to be killed. Sometimes they were awakened in the middle of the night and made to stand outside at attention for hours, regardless of the weather, until guards released them.

RESPONSE:
> As much as practical, avoid having people line up. In programs

where food is served, serve food to individuals in their seats rather than have them line up for it. Self-service for light snacks works if individuals can access it at their own pace.

Mealtime and Food Presentation

REACTION:
Refusal to eat
Overeating
Food hoarding
Chronic unhappiness with food

REASON:
Withholding of food, minimal portions, rough handling, and almost inedible foods were dished out to inmates after they waited in long lines in the camps. Many Jews starved to death. Thus, poor service (whether real or not), small portions, or new foods may be difficult for survivors to accept.

RESPONSE:
Meals should arrive as consistently, and be as personalized, as possible. When meals are delayed, explanations should be prompt, with clear time frames for when the food will be available. Accommodate residents in an institutional setting who feel a need to wrap up food to take with them. In community programs, wrap up leftovers and distribute to individuals when they leave.

Not Enough Food or Hunger Pangs

REACTION:
Hoarding or hiding food
Eating too fast

REASON:
During the war, food was scarce and people were always hungry. Many starved to death. When food was available, it was rationed to last longer. In the camps some ate their weekly rations quickly. Trading, stealing, or hoarding food could be punishable by death, so secrecy around food was common. Some survivors describe feeling hungry even on a full stomach. Leftover food is often comforting to survivors.

RESPONSE:

Establish an environment where food is available and it is safe for individuals to request it. Survivors should be allowed to take non-perishable foods with them.

Movies or Television Programs about the Holocaust or Other Genocides

REACTION:

Fear
Anxiety
Depression
Withdrawal
Nightmares

REASON:

These visual images remind survivors of their own experiences. Even though they may not want to, some feel obliged to watch in memory of their dead family members and friends.

RESPONSE:

Suggest that survivors turn off their television sets and radios when they feel upset. Explore other ways they can memorialize their dead family members.

Jewish Holidays

REACTION:

Sadness
Depression
Anticipatory fear
Not involved in festivities

REASON:

During the war, the Nazis often raided Jewish communities during the Jewish holidays. They knew their targets would be either at home or in the synagogue, which made it easier to round them up or kill them. Consequently, many Jews were murdered while observing a Jewish holiday. Deportations from the ghettos often took place around the Jewish holidays as well. This was the last time many survivors saw their families alive.

RESPONSE:

Staff should be aware of the Jewish calendar and upcoming holidays. Do not automatically assume there will be a negative effect. Explore how each survivor observes the holiday. If alone, ask if they would like to be linked with a community program, such as a Passover Seder. Provide understanding and support their wishes. Allow individuals to articulate their thoughts and feelings about the holidays in group programs.

Trains and Train Whistles

REACTION:

Anxiety
Fear
Adverse reactions
Refusal to board trains

REASON:

Overcrowded cattle cars transported individuals to the death camps. Many died of starvation and unsanitary conditions along the way.

RESPONSE:

Many survivors refuse to ride trains so other transportation alternatives would be more appropriate for them. Train whistles are often unavoidable sounds. Reassure survivors that what they are remembering happened a long time ago and they are safe now.

Music from the Ghettos and Camps

REACTION:

Anxiety
Fear
Pride

REASON:

Music served a number of functions in the concentration and death camps (Fackler, 2011). It was used to degrade, dominate, and discipline prisoners or to cover up the atrocities of their perpetrators. Detainees were ordered to sing Nazi songs during forced marches and German and classical music blared on loudspeakers. Musical ensembles and orchestras, composed of interned professional musicians, played during the selection process at death camps to deceive newly arriving prisoners. Detainees also participated in secret musical activities which were a form of spiritual resistance and cultural survival, as well as a necessary distraction from their abysmal daily lives.

RESPONSE:
Some survivors cry or become agitated at cultural events featuring classical music, which reminds them of the camps. They often get up and leave these programs and should be allowed to do so. Others feel a sense of pride when they hear songs from the ghettos because this music represented a form of spiritual resistance. In their case, listening to such songs may be encouraged.

Music from Pre-War Environments

REACTION:
Sadness
Joy

REASON:
Survivors' memories from their youth are tinged with sadness and joy. Songs from their counties of origin remind them of their pre-war lives with their families and friends in communities that are now extinct.

RESPONSE:
Some survivors cry when entertainers sing songs from their counties of origin. It is important to ask entertainers to vary their repertoire to include Hebrew songs that imbue survivors with pride about Israel. Ending concerts by singing *Hatikvah*, the Israeli national anthem, accomplishes this goal and also grounds them in the present.

* * *

HEALTH AND HYGIENE

Taking a Bath

REACTION:
Refusal
Unusual fear
Crying
Screaming

REASON:

Nazi doctors and researchers conducted horrific experiments with Jews while they were immersed in tubs of water. These experiments included freezing, scalding, and electrocution. In addition, many inmates were dipped into tubs of harsh chemicals for cleansing and delousing purposes.

RESPONSE:

When assisting a survivor, always identify yourself and explain the reason for your actions. Offer options of a shower or a bed sponge bath where appropriate. Be prepared to offer a flexible schedule. Check to see if a family member's presence would help. Do not force the issue.

_____

Taking a Shower

REACTION:

Refusal
Unusual fear
Crying
Screaming

REASON:

In the concentration camps, the Nazis herded Jews into the gas chambers, telling them they were going to take showers. They were stripped and pushed into rooms that looked like shower rooms. After they were crammed in for maximum efficiency, the doors were locked and poisonous gas released out of the showerheads. All were killed.

RESPONSE:

When assisting a survivor, reassure them that you are helping them to feel clean. Offer options of a bath or bed bath. Some survivors prefer a handheld showerhead they can control. Be patient and wet your arms and hands to prove that water is coming out of the showerhead. Check to see if a family member's presence can help. Do not force the issue. Always identify yourself and explain the reasons for your actions.

_____

Fear of Public or Strange Toilets / Smell of Urine or Feces

REACTION:

Refusal to use washrooms

Incontinence or withholding
Adverse reaction to strong smells

REASON:

The Jews were transported to concentration camps in cattle cars with no sanitary facilities, often for days at a time. People stood for hours with no food or bathrooms. Many died in transit. Strong smells were everywhere. In the camps there were makeshift waste facilities with no privacy. Sanitary conditions were atrocious. The smell of waste may easily trigger memories of those train rides.

RESPONSE:

Maintain a deodorized environment. In an institutionalized setting, make the washrooms as home-like as practical, for example, through pictures, coloured towels, familiar scents, and so on. Be respectful of nudity and inability to self-toilet.

Receiving Injections

REACTION:
Refusal
Fear
Anger

REASON:

Many survivors were tattooed with numbers for identification. These were done with needles without anesthetic. Once they were tattooed, only numbers identified them. An injection could symbolize a further loss of personal identity.

RESPONSE:

Explain all treatment options thoroughly. Provide a rationale for the need to give an injection and distinguish the present from their past. Normalize the procedure as part of the treatment plan. Try to have family, or a trusted friend, or a formal caregiver on hand for support.

Shaving, Haircuts, and Personal Grooming

REACTION:
Refusal
Anxiety
Extreme anxiety (for example, over baldness)

REASON:

Upon arrival at the concentration camps, the heads of both men and women were often shaved. This was another form of humiliation and dehumanization.

RESPONSE:

Spend time preparing the individual. Allow options regarding hair care, such as time preference, date, and style.

* * *

INTERPERSONAL INTERACTIONS

Service Providers Who Speak Foreign Languages or Have Heavy Accents

REACTION:

Mistrust and fear

REASON:

Many of the guards who persecuted survivors were of German, Polish, and Ukrainian descent.

RESPONSE:

Be sensitive to an individual's body language. If they appear fearful, try to establish a personal connection. Talk about your country of origin and the reason you moved. Allow the individual to ask you questions. Impart the message that they are safe. Be prepared to change home-care workers if the fear persists.

Directing People to the Left or Right

REACTION:

Refusal to do so
Anger
Fear

REASON:

Upon arrival at a concentration camp, Jews were selected to live or die and sent to the left or right. One direction led directly to the gas chambers and the other to slave barracks. These selections were often the last time that family members saw each other.

RESPONSE:
Accompany rather than direct individuals to a worker or another location.

Rough Handling or Speaking in a Loud, Harsh Manner; Loud Noises

REACTION:
Mistrust
Fear
Startle response

REASON:
The guards and soldiers in the ghettos and camps yelled at, shoved, and treated Jews roughly. Loudspeakers blared out demands for roll calls and lists of names for executions.

RESPONSE:
Speak calmly, softly, and reassuringly. Ask permission before touching survivors.

Word Associations

REACTION:
Fear
Anxiety

REASON:
Words that are benign to the ordinary person hold special meaning for survivors. *Experiment* recalls the feared medical experiments; *selections* determined who would live or die; *concentration* refers to the camps where people were herded together and used as slave laborers; *extermination* refers to the killing of millions of people.

RESPONSE:
Be aware that these words may hold a special meaning for some survivors and observe if their body language indicates they are reacting to a past memory. If they are, reassure them that they are safe now.

Discussion of Financial Matters

REACTION:
Overreaction to discussion of costs
Refuse to disclose financial matters

REASON:

Survivors were robbed of all their assets during the war and had to start over. Many are cautious about revealing their financial status today and want to ensure they have secured enough money, in case someone attempts to rob them again.

RESPONSE:

Survivors are sensitive to financial inquiries. It may be necessary to involve children or other family members to supplement costs if an individual refuses to pay the full fee, even if they can afford it. Always explain the rationale for the costs.

Uniforms: Police, Medical Personnel, Border Guards, Postal Workers, Etc.

REACTION:

Fear

Anxiety

REASON:

People in positions of power who mistreated survivors often wore uniforms. Medical personnel in white lab coats performed experiments that tortured or killed patients.

RESPONSE:

Reassure survivors that they are safe and the person in the uniform will not harm them.

Staff Vacations, Changes, and Temporary Student Placements

REACTION:

Inability to let go

Depressive reaction

Withdrawal

REASON:

Throughout the war, Jews saw their children, parents, relatives, and friends taken away or murdered in front of them. Most never saw each other again. After the war, survivors realized the enormity of their losses. Separation from significant people in their life may be difficult.

RESPONSE:

Staff consistency is important. Staff vacations and changes should be announced ahead of time with adequate time for farewells. Be cautious of promising ongoing relationships when they are not feasible (for example, students completing internship placements).

*　*　*

ENVIRONMENT

Small Spaces, Crowded Conditions, Lack of Personal Space

REACTION:

Anxiety

Fear

Withdrawal

REASON:

Jews were forced into ghettos or concentration camps or survived in hiding. All of these locations were cramped and overcrowded, with substandard living conditions. In the ghettos, several families were forced to share apartments or homes. In the camps, four to six individuals shared one wooden tiered shelf. Individuals who survived in hiding may feel cramped in a small space.

RESPONSE:

In institutional settings, allow for as much privacy as possible. In shared rooms, ensure a designated private space. Respect the individual's right not to join a group program.

Secure Areas, Locks on Doors, Physical Restraints, Limited Access

REACTION:

Frantic trying to escape

Feeling trapped

Panic

REASON:

Survivors were forced into walled ghettos, barbed-wire-enclosed concentration camps, prisons, and so on. All personal freedom was removed and escape was virtually impossible. Jews in hiding were rarely seen in public for fear of getting caught. Today, any sense of limited movement or restraint may be difficult.

RESPONSE:

Where possible avoid locked doors and accommodate wanderers with alternative options, for example, wandering alert bracelets. Where unavoidable, have internal wandering options available to give patients a sense of choice and control over their environment. Avoid the use of restraints.

Night-Time or Dark Rooms

REACTION:

Extreme fear

REASON:

Darkness brought fear of the unknown for survivors in the camps and in hiding.

RESPONSE:

Staff must identify residents who are at risk at night. Night-lights and well-lit rooms help ease fears.

Flashlights, Examining Lights, or Bright Lights

REACTION:

Fear
Anxiety
Refusal to cooperate

REASON:

Camps and ghettos were lit at night by bright searchlights to prevent escape. Guards used flashlights to find people in hiding and round them up for deportation.

RESPONSE:

Where possible avoid flashlights on rounds and bright examining lights. Night-lights in patient rooms and corridors are preferable. Strong overhead lighting in examination rooms should be avoided. If they are necessary the reasons should be explained.

Harsh, Strong, or Unpleasant Smells

REACTION:
Strong physical or emotional reactions

REASON:
Sanitation in the camp barracks and ghettos relied on the use of harsh chemicals and antiseptics such as chlorine and ammonia. People were often placed in lye prior to medical experimentation, so these smells may have horrible associations. Some survivors recall the smell of crematoria smoke, burning ghettos, and buildings where people were burned alive.

RESPONSE:
Where antiseptic smells are unavoidable, prepare individuals ahead of time and explain why it is necessary, for example, cleaning, maintenance, and so on.

Sounds of People Crying or Screaming

REACTION:
Fear or similar reaction

REASON:
Survivors lived through many different and painful horrors. The sounds of grief and tears are reminders of the past.

RESPONSE:
Spend time with people in pain and try to understand the nature of their pain. If this is ineffective, give them their privacy. Reassure other residents that the individual is being cared for.

Ambulance or Fire Sirens, Alarms, Bells, Whistles

REACTION:
Anxiety
Fear
Adverse reactions

REASON:
Sirens, whistles, and bells were often signals for people to be rounded up and deported. They were also used to communicate the time in the camps or preceded public announcements to prisoners.

RESPONSE:
These are unavoidable sounds. When they occur, staff should reassure survivors and explain what is happening and why.

Identity Cards, Membership Buttons

REACTION:
Suspicion
Fear
Refusal to have picture taken for membership card

REASON:
Survivors were dehumanized and their identities were taken away. Individuals in the camps were known by their numbers. Those who survived by hiding their Jewish identity and holding false identity papers were in a constant state of anxiety. Jews in the ghettos had to wear emblems, such as yellow cloth stars, to identify themselves as Jewish.

RESPONSE:
Explain the reason for taking a picture for an identity or membership card. Make the process as humane as practical. Give them a choice about wearing name tags and buttons.

Specific Clothing Items, including Colours

REACTION:
Fear or similar reaction

REASON:
A religious symbol like the Star of David, heels that resound on a hard floor, or even a certain colour may remind a survivor of a wartime incident. Different groups of internees were forced to wear different symbols, for example, Jews wore yellow stars.

RESPONSE:
If an individual exhibits fear and / or anxiety, remove the offending item. Shades of blue, particularly royal blue or the colours of the Israeli flag, are safe colours to use in publicity items such as brochures and flyers.

Christian Symbols

REACTION:

Adverse reaction to jewellery, holiday decorations, or seasonal music. Note: child survivors who were hidden with Christian families may feel comforted.

REASON:

Christian symbols, such as the cross or Christmas decorations, were part of the enemy's religion and holiday celebrations. Jewish children who were hidden in Christian orphanages participated in the rituals and holidays at a young age.

RESPONSE:

Be aware of the sensitivity some people may have to Christian symbols. It is impossible to generalize responses. Where there is an issue, remove the particular symbol. Validate the experiences of child survivors who disclose feeling comforted by participating in Christian rituals and holidays.

Dogs and Other Animals

REACTION:

Fear
Anxiety
Revulsion

REASON:

Dogs, especially German shepherds and Dobermans, were used as guard and attack dogs in rounding up Jews to imprison or intimidate them. SS guards with large dogs greeted survivors who arrived at the concentration camps. Dogs were also used to discover hidden Jews. Some were trained as attack dogs and killed people who tried to escape. Nazi pets were given more plentiful and better food than inmates.

RESPONSE:

Be cautious with pet therapy as a treatment modality. Always check if people are afraid of animals. Cognitive behavioural desensitization techniques may be helpful. Not all survivors fear dogs. Many benefit from owning pets.

Threats in the Environment such as Anti-Semitism, Holocaust Denial, Attacks against Israel, Reports of Nazi War Criminals, etc.

REACTION:

Anger
Fear
Anxiety
Withdrawal
Nightmares
Sleeplessness

REASON:

Survivors fear that atrocities committed against them may befall their children and grandchildren. Reports of anti-Semitism around the world may cause fear, anxiety, and sleepless nights.

RESPONSE:

Point out ways in which the situation is different today than it was in the 1930s. Focus on ways in which government bodies, inter-faith coalitions, community organizations, and political leaders are denouncing these incidents. Explain that the Jewish community has important allies.

15 Responding to Emotional Reactions

How do we respond to survivors who have reactions? With kindness, patience and understanding.

– B. Gross (1994)

This chapter sets out approaches that may be helpful when responding to emotional reactions of survivors in a social-service setting. Individuals may be coming to an agency for the first time. Their initial encounter with staff and volunteers may determine if they will have any further involvement with an agency or if they will be receptive to additional services.

EMOTIONAL REACTIONS

Preoccupation with Holocaust Memories during Telephone Conversations

Survivors may become preoccupied and want to talk about their Holocaust memories during routine procedures like a telephone-intake call. Their war memories and associated unresolved feelings are frequently triggered by conversation or questions which seem benign to a non-survivor but have special meaning for them; they may have the sense that they are being interrogated, perceive service providers as authority figures, feel vulnerable and powerless when asking for help, and so on. When this happens, a survivor may begin fusing past and present.

RESPONSE:
1. Listen for a very short while and then say, 'I am sorry to hear what happened to you and your family.' Then redirect the individual to the question you are asking.
2. Show empathy and understanding.
3. If necessary, be firm and consistent about focusing on the present. Note: it may be more difficult to refocus individuals on the present situation if they have dementia symptoms.
4. If appropriate, schedule a home visit.

Crying When Describing Experiences

Survivors may cry when describing their Holocaust experiences such as during a bio-psycho-social assessment. Some people, especially men who contained their emotions throughout their lives, may feel embarrassed when they break down and cry.

RESPONSE:
1. Crying is a natural response. It is a healing release of emotions.
2. Validate their reaction, for example: 'I can see this is difficult for you. It is painful to remember.'
3. Remain calm, empathetic, and respectful.
4. Have a non-judgmental, caring, and supportive attitude that conveys a message of caring, warmth, and security. It is important to show that their story has touched you.
5. Do not comfort survivors orally by saying, 'I understand' or 'It's all right' or 'I know how you feel.' Such comments tend to minimize their experience. Do not touch them, especially without asking, because some people do not like to be touched when they are upset.
6. Respect the sensitivity of the moment. Give survivors exhibiting such behaviour time to compose themselves. Sit quietly and have patience. Your empathetic presence will contain the memory. If you are unable to do this, then do some self-examination to explore what witnessing someone crying touches within you.
7. Pay attention to your body language. The concern you communicate with your posture and facial expressions demonstrates that you care.

Emotional Reactions When Completing Forms

Helping survivors fill out compensation and social-security forms may trigger traumatic memories, which can be accompanied by feelings of anxiety, fear, helplessness, sadness, and powerlessness. Many survivors become fearful and anxious when they receive letters from any government, and especially their annual Life Certificates from the German government. Understand that this event may be stressful for them and they may act somewhat compulsively. For example, they may call the agency repeatedly to schedule an appointment, or show up with their certificate in hand as soon as they receive it. They want these forms completed and mailed quickly.

RESPONSE:

1. Show kindness, patience, and understanding when answering questions.
2. If you are unable to provide assistance, refer the survivor to the appropriate service or community resource.
3. Survivors may disclose memories related to their war experiences that do not seem relevant to the question(s) at hand. When this happens, validate their recollections by saying, 'I am sorry to hear what happened to you and your family.' Then redirect them to the question. Show empathy and understanding. If you have the time, listen to the story. Unfortunately, most offices that help survivors fill out forms are busy places and staff may not have time to listen at length to individual stories.
4. If a survivor breaks down and cries during the conversation, validate this response: 'I can see this is difficult for you. It must be painful to remember.' Give survivors time to compose themselves. The concern you show is part of their healing process. It shows you care.
5. Some survivors project onto staff their anger and frustration regarding delays when waiting to have their forms completed. If a survivor becomes angry during the conversation, say, 'I can see you are angry and frustrated. I am trying my best to help you.' Try to avoid a confrontation. Speak softly, calmly, and reassuringly. However, if the anger persists and the survivor's voice elevates, assert yourself and set limits on this behaviour, for example: 'I see you are too angry right now to speak with me. Let's call a time out for a few minutes. When you have calmed down I will be happy to help you.'
6. To prevent the fusion of past and present, ensure that survivors are oriented to the present before they leave your office. Make small talk, for example, inform them about agency services; discuss the weather; if you know the person and they have grandchildren and great-grandchildren, ask about them.

Emotional Reactions When Medical Procedures Are Recommended

Survivors may experience anxiety when medical procedures are recommended.

RESPONSE:
1. Focus on the doctor's competence and reputation when making a referral. Generally, survivors prefer referrals to doctors who are department heads.
2. Explore the nature of survivors' traumatic experiences because it may provide a clue whether they will trust doctors, take medications, accept treatment, and so on.
3. Explain treatment options carefully. Be sensitive to survivors' history, the potential significance of their illness, and individual needs.
4. Explore survivors' thoughts and feelings about tests and procedures.
5. Explain the reasons for tests and describe procedures so survivors know what to expect.
6. Encourage them to ask questions and write them down along with the answers.
7. If possible, role-play a doctor's visit.
8. When there is no family available, arrange for accompaniment to the test procedures.
9. Respect the wishes of cognitively competent individuals who refuse treatment or referral to services, for example, transfer to a rehabilitation hospital after surgery.

Survivors Who Are Decompensating

Survivors who are reacting to a trigger or a traumatic memory may begin to deteriorate psychologically. They may become agitated, anxious, sad, and / or afraid.

RESPONSE:
1. Remain calm.
2. Validate and normalize their reaction.
3. Prevent fusion of past and present. Explain, in a reassuring manner, that what they are remembering happened a long time ago. Emphasize that they are safe now.
4. Show kindness, and understanding and have patience.
5. Speak softly, calmly, and reassuringly.

6. Convey a message of safety, warmth, and security.
7. If the stress response escalates, use the following calming techniques: deep diaphragmatic breathing and safe-place imagery. Ask questions that help ground survivors in the present moment, such as their name and where they are now, the date, or time, and / or ask them to focus on bodily sensations such as feeling the chair they are sitting on and their feet touching the floor.
8. Ensure that survivors leave your office oriented to the present and not wandering mentally and emotionally in the past. An orienting technique that I find useful for survivors who have grandchildren and great-grandchildren is asking them to talk about them, for example, their ages, favourite foods, hobbies, and so on.

Crying When Reference to the Holocaust Is Made in a Mixed Group

Sometimes references to the Holocaust in a mixed-group setting may cause a survivor to cry. If other group members do not respond to the individual, it is possible the Holocaust theme may be affecting them as well.

RESPONSE:
1. In this situation, the service provider must join with both the survivor(s) and other members. For example, when the service provider expresses empathy with the crying survivor, he must also join at the same time with the other group members who may not want to listen to the survivor's story. The service provider may say to the survivor: 'I'm so sorry to hear what happened to you / your family during the war.' Subsequently, the following statement can be made to the group: 'I know it's hard to listen to such a painful story.'
2. If the group is open to it, the survivor can be asked to tell her story briefly. Be prepared to intervene and set limits if the survivor gets carried away with the details. Some survivors do. If the group is not open to it, you can ask the survivor to meet with you privately after the group.
3. Non-survivors may question why survivors' remarks are so often interwoven with the past. The service provider can respond with: 'Present events often trigger past memories. It is important that these memories are expressed and validated, and that the person is made to feel safe and secure in her present setting.' This approach fosters understanding rather than resentment.

4. Sometimes people who lived in Canada during the war years make statements such as 'We also suffered.' Their experiences must also be validated. The service provider can say: 'Each of your suffering was different. However, no comparisons can be made with the suffering of Holocaust survivors.' Programming can include a discussion of each group's experiences during the war years. Emphasize the importance of communicating with each other, listening attentively, and respecting each other's right to share their experience.

Emotional Reactions When Israel Is Threatened

Many Holocaust survivors feel a strong bond with, and sense of commitment to, Israel. Visual images of wars or riots against Israel cause sadness, fear, anxiety, and anger for some survivors.

RESPONSE:

1. Give individuals time to share their thoughts and feelings. When they do, use normalizing statements such as: 'What you are feeling is a normal reaction and many people feel the same way.'
2. Encourage them to speak with their family, friends, and other interested individuals about their concerns. Giving a voice to their worries and / or fears helps diffuse them.
3. Encourage them to attend community rallies and lectures to show solidarity with their fellow Jews.
4. Many individuals feel a responsibility to remain vigilant and monitor the media. Some do this in the extreme, which affects their physical and psychological health. Give them permission to turn their radios and television sets off. If they are unwilling to do so completely, suggest that they limit their listening.
5. If people are open to it, suggest that they pray.
6. Reiterate Israel's strength. In spite of annihilation attempts over the years, Israel has survived and withstood adversity. Do this to instil a sense of hope, which counters feelings of hopelessness.
7. Encourage individuals to practise self-care, for example, proper diet, exercise, pleasurable activities.

Emotional Reactions to Threats in the Environment

Holocaust deniers, attacks on Jewish people, cemetery defacements, and anti-Semitic incidents – such as the 2008 terrorist attacks against

Jews in Mumbai, India, and most recently in Toulouse, France – may cause feelings of anger, fear, anxiety, withdrawal, nightmares, and sleeplessness. Some survivors view these incidents as the beginning of another Holocaust.

RESPONSE:
1. Listen as individuals share their thoughts and feelings. When they do, use normalizing statements such as 'What you are feeling are normal reactions and many people are feeling the same way.'
2. Point out ways in which the situation for Jews is different today than it was in the 1930s. Explain that Jews are no longer powerless.
3. Focus on ways in which government bodies, interfaith coalitions, community organizations, and prominent leaders are denouncing these incidents. Point out that the Jewish community has important allies.
4. Encourage these survivors to speak with their family, friends, and other interested individuals about their concerns. Giving a voice to their worries and / or fears helps diffuse them.
5. Encourage survivors to attend community rallies that demonstrate solidarity and express condolences to the families of these heinous crimes.

A Crisis Intervention Plan in Response to Synagogues Being Desecrated by Nazi Slogans

In the early 1990s, violent incidents against Jews took place in Germany, and in 1993 seven synagogues in the Montreal area were defaced with swastikas and graffiti containing the words *Juden raus* (Jews out), a Nazi slogan used during the Holocaust. In addition, a bullet was shot through a window at an eighth synagogue. In short, anti-Semitic incidents were now occurring in the very neighbourhoods and places of worship of the survivors with whom I was working.

These incidents in Montreal enraged both members of the Jewish community and society at large. There were public protests against them. Unfortunately, the incidents exacerbated anxieties and fears that were already heightened in some survivors by the events that were taking place in Germany. Many survivors interpreted these acts of hate as early signs of the kind of persecution against Jews that had occurred in Germany during the 1930s. As one woman said, 'Jews are never safe anywhere.'

During this time I was chair of the Holocaust Remembrance Committee, Quebec Region, at the Canadian Jewish Congress, and this organization was reporting an increase in calls from concerned survivors. Also, at JSSE, survivors in our programs were experiencing fear, nervousness, anger, helplessness, and anxiety. Some people reported sleep disturbances. One woman complained of severe heart palpitations. Several adult children of survivors requested assistance with parents who were greatly distressed. A rabbi described the shock of a survivor who broke down and cried uncontrollably when she saw the swastika on the wall of her synagogue. We became concerned that survivors, who were afraid, would begin to isolate themselves.

It became clear that a community response was needed. I obtained a list of the affected synagogues and recommended a community intervention plan with help from the rabbis of the defaced synagogues. Together with the rabbis and members of their congregations, we reached out to survivors who were afraid to attend services. We initiated discussions in the synagogues to help survivors reclaim their safe environments. The rabbis spoke about the defacements in their Saturday sermons. They validated survivors' fears and made distinctions between Germany in the 1930s and the present. This helped stabilize the survivor community and contain its fears.

Aggressive Behaviour

Survivors' anger may stem from their years of victimization and oppression during the Holocaust. Their anger may be suppressed and can be triggered in situations where they feel powerless and vulnerable, such as when they request help from social services. There are also other reasons for survivors' anger. Some felt betrayed by Jewish Canadians and assorted organizations during the Holocaust. Others encountered negative reactions from fellow Jews when they immigrated to Montreal, which created a chasm between survivors and the rest of the Jewish community. Some survivors may also be angry owing to circumstances in their present-day lives over which they have no control. Angry survivors may displace their anger onto staff and their peers. Some survivors use anger as a form of manipulation and control. Although it may be beneficial for survivors to express internalized rage in therapy, in an agency setting or a group program this expression can be frightening and detrimental.

Frequently, survivors' inappropriate behaviour is excused or tolerated because they suffered in the Holocaust. This is inadvisable. Staff must work with survivors to help them take responsibility for their behaviour and contain their angry feelings. Yelling and treating others in a disrespectful manner is not acceptable and service providers do not have to tolerate or bear the brunt of such behaviour. It is appropriate to set limits. My approach surprises some colleagues, but most were pleased when I addressed this issue in one of my publications (Giberovitch, 2006). If we allow survivors to project their anger onto us, we encourage and perpetuate their victimization. Adults take responsibility for their behaviour and actions. Survivors should be held accountable for their actions.

Angry Outbursts

Occasionally, I witness uncontrolled outbursts of anger from a few survivors. I even recall several times in my career when individuals lost control and tried to hit me. When we opened the Survivor Assistance Office, we were inundated with requests. A number of survivors refused to wait their turn, became hostile, and demanded to be seen by a service provider immediately. Sometimes they showed me their tattooed numbers to gain my sympathy. Apparently, environmental triggers – such as waiting in line, asking for help, filling out forms, and the like – were hindering them from behaving rationally. However, as much as we try to understand the origins of their behaviour and treat them with compassion, we must also set limits on aggressive and sometimes abusive conduct. Here is the approach I use, adapted from Lindenfield (1993):

1. Attempt to contain the anger:
   a. Validate the angry feelings, for example: 'I see this is upsetting you. I hear you are angry right now. I see / hear you are frustrated.'
   b. Give the individual the message that you are listening and are doing your best to understand the survivor's point of view, for example: 'I understand you are not satisfied with this service.'
   c. Express your wants and needs in a calm and persistent manner; feel free to share your own feelings; and use 'I' statements, such as 'I do not like being yelled at'; 'I feel frightened when you are so angry'; 'I do not deserve to be talked to this way'; 'I am doing my best to help you.'
   d. Try to avoid a confrontation. Avoid arguing, criticizing, or judging. Anger fuels and escalates the other person's anger.

2. Make a conciliatory gesture:
   a. State your regret about the issue, for example: 'I'm sorry you have to wait so long.'
   b. Accept responsibility for your share of the problem, using statements such as 'We did not expect such a large number of people'; 'We do not have enough staff persons to respond to the demand'; 'We are doing our best in these difficult circumstances.'
3. If the anger persists, set limits:
   a. State that abusive language and behaviour are not acceptable.
   b. Step away to regain composure, for example: 'I do not want to discuss this matter further until you have calmed down.'
   c. If the individual is in your office, ask her to leave. If the individual is in the hallway, walk away.
4. Find ways to manage your own emotions from the incident:
   a. Be aware if your buttons have been pushed and explore your personal reactions to an angry outburst, such as shock, feeling overwhelmed, shutting down, anger, aggressive behaviour, and so on.
   b. Talk to a colleague or supervisor about the experience.
   c. Find ways to relax and release physical tension in your body.
   d. Give yourself some positive self-talk.

RESOLVING GROUP CONFLICT

Service providers should not avoid dealing with contentious issues with Holocaust survivors. Sometimes I find that service providers tend to act like protectors trying to spare survivors from further pain and suffering, a dynamic with which I am familiar as the daughter of Holocaust survivors. We need to keep in mind that survivors are not fragile victims who fall apart with controversy. Conflict occasionally arises in group programs when members have different opinions about emotionally charged topics that polarize the group. When these topics are discussed openly, and we encourage respect for different viewpoints, we create opportunities for personal growth and development.

Our program with the Austrian interns, discussed in chapter 12, created significant controversy among our group of survivors. Various interventions, adapted from Atwater (1986) and Scott Boeckh (1995), were used to mitigate this controversy. I recommend them for other service providers. They are as follows.

Create an Environment Where People Feel Comfortable Expressing Ideas and Concerns

The Drop-in Centre provides a supportive environment where members are encouraged to speak freely and openly about any topic. They are welcome to voice both positive and negative viewpoints. We teach members interpersonal and communication skills that focus on sharing responsibility for group cohesiveness, camaraderie, and respect for differences of opinion. We attempt to make decisions by consensus; however, with so many people attending, we usually resolve issues by majority rule. Staff and volunteers also build a strong trust alliance with members. This trust enables members to engage in emotionally charged areas of contention.

Openly Recognize That Conflict May Arise When Individuals See Issues or Situations from Different Perspectives

Contentious issues polarize groups of individuals. The Drop-in members refer to their group as family and acknowledge that, as with families, conflicts sometimes arise. In this case, there were survivors who did not want to engage in any program with non-Jews, especially Germans and Austrians. There were others who saw this program as an educational opportunity for the Austrian youth to learn about the Holocaust first-hand. They believed that Holocaust education combats anti-Semitism and promotes tolerance and respect. Although both of these perspectives were respected in the group, there were incidents of name calling and insults.

Define the Conflict as a Mutual Problem to Be Solved

I positioned the Austrian student-intern program as an opportunity to work together as a family to resolve an issue that was dividing members and forcing them to take sides. We began with a discussion to explore and understand the different perspectives. The principles I followed were these:

1. Validate all perspectives and everyone's right to their opinions.
2. Focus on the person speaking: be fully present and pay attention.
3. Listen to what is being said and focus the group on understanding each point of view, for example: 'What you are saying is important and I want to make sure we understand it.'

4. Respect and address each individual's concerns and point of view. Use reflective listening techniques to clarify what has been said, for example: 'I hear you saying that ...'
5. Ask open-ended questions to better understand the situation or problem, that is, ones starting with 'how,' 'what,' when, 'where,' and 'who.' Avoid questions beginning with 'why.'
6. Encourage clear communication. Share personal thoughts and opinions openly and honestly through 'I' statements.
7. Pay attention to tone of voice and body language. Control personal emotions.

Search for Possible Solutions by Brainstorming and Looking for Common Ground

I encouraged all members to offer solutions to improve things. Emotions ran high. Some members vented angry feelings and refused to budge from their positions. Others were willing to set aside their opinions and compromise for the betterment of the group, and some focused their energies on encouraging respect for differences of opinion. They encouraged those who refused to budge to be open to new ideas. Eventually several members suggested that a subgroup meet with the students instead of the whole group. Most group members accepted this surprising suggestion.

Deal with Name Calling and Insults

Several people who opposed this program berated and insulted those who volunteered to participate. They demonized them and tried to change their minds. Staff met with each of the individuals privately, requesting they stop their negative behaviour. The inappropriate behaviour ceased during subsequent group sessions.

Implement a Plan of Action

We involved survivors in planning all aspects of this dialogue with the Austrian youth. They suggested starting with one meeting and evaluating the process before considering a second one. Two sessions took place. The group members composed a list of questions they wanted the Austrian interns to answer and they also wanted to know what questions the interns had for them so they could screen them ahead of time.

Evaluate the Program

After the program took place, we conducted a verbal evaluation. The survivors were impressed by the interest, attentiveness, and sincerity of the interns. One participant told the group that this had been 'a very emotional experience' for her. She was surprised that the interns were interested in their stories. Another said that she felt better when she heard them say they would fight anti-Semitism and hatred. The survivors referred to the interns as 'emissaries' who would further the cause of combating anti-Semitism back in their home country. Their last words to the interns were: 'Bring peace to the world and pass on our experiences to others.' The interns promised they would. This program helped the participating survivors change their perceptions about the new generation of Austrians.

16 Professional Considerations

Given the physical, psychological, spiritual, and emotional responses of our work, there isn't one of us who doesn't need to improve in some area of self-care.
– K.W. Saakvitne and L.A. Pearlman (1996)

PROFESSIONAL BOUNDARIES

I am frequently asked by colleagues and students to address issues around maintaining professional boundaries when working with survivors. Social workers and other service providers are required to maintain appropriate boundaries in professional interpersonal relationships. These boundaries are defined in the codes of conduct and ethics of our individual professions (Ordre professional des travailleurs sociaux et des thérapeutes conjugaux et familiaux du Québec [l'OTSTCFQ], 2012) or corporations (Canadian Association of Social Workers [CASW], 2005) in Canada. Unfortunately, some settings do not have policies around these issues and may offer little guidance to staff. This forces workers to rely on their own sense of what is appropriate.

Establishing and maintaining professional boundaries defines our relationship with survivors. Doing so helps us build safe and respectful alliances, place limits on our interpersonal relationships, clarify our responsibilities, and provide a model of professional behaviour and interaction.

Disclosing Personal Information

Staff and volunteers share selected personal information with Drop-in Centre members. For example, we tell them about births, marriages, graduations, and special anniversaries in our families. Occasionally we tell them about some of our activities and interests outside the agency. We also exchange information about our vacations. During group discussions I share my experiences and perceptions from my second-generation perspective when they are appropriate and contribute to specific group goals such as improving relationships with adult children or engaging in interactions with non-Jews. We keep our self-disclosures brief and are careful not to divert focus away from group members and the program. Survivors appreciate our willingness to be open, which encourages reciprocity, builds trust, and enhances mutual respect.

Dealing with Dual Relationships

Occasionally survivors whom I know personally from other settings come to the agency for assistance. They may be friends of my parents or I may have worked with them in another capacity such as when I did volunteer work. Frequently they ask personal questions about my family and me. Maintaining professional boundaries when a dual relationship exists can be challenging in these situations. It requires awareness and careful consideration to determine how much personal information I am willing to disclose. I try to keep my responses simple and focus on my children's careers and my father's health. I also share general news such as birth of a new grandchild.

Engaging in Social Interactions
Outside Professional Settings

Many survivors are lonely and want more social contact. Often they want to engage in social interactions with staff and volunteers outside our professional setting. For example, they may invite us to their homes for dinner or tea. At the beginning of my career, I gave out my home telephone number; however, I quickly learned to be selective in doing so to avoid inappropriate interactions. For example, one woman, who just returned from Florida, called me from the airport late at night and asked me to drive her home. Today staff, volunteers, and students limit their social contacts with survivors to the agency building. This may entail having a cup of tea or coffee together in the cafeteria, or dancing at a group program. We make exceptions such as visiting a group member in the hospital or, when one of them dies, visiting their family's home.

Responding to Survivors Who Tell Us They Love Us

Sometimes survivors tell us they love us. It is important to be aware of issues that may arise when survivors express their love for a staff person or volunteer in a group setting. Some members may think there is an exclusive relationship and feel left out. All members of a group should feel they are being treated equally. In the agency a few members say, 'I love you,' and wait for a response. Rather than reply with 'I love you, too,' which could be misinterpreted, I respond with 'I feel your love.'

Responding to Survivors Who Initiate Physical Contact

Some individuals crave touch and reach out frequently to hug and / or kiss us. Hugs and kisses on the cheek may be appropriate during special celebrations, crisis situations, or when members return to the group after a long absence. However, if we reciprocate automatically, they may confuse the professional relationship with a personal one. I teach survivors to respect my boundaries. For example, I encourage them to ask for a hug or permission to kiss me on the cheek to keep them aware of our professional relationship.

ISSUES WITH SURVIVORS

Crying with Survivors

Sometimes I supervise social-work students who are afraid they will break down and cry when listening to descriptions of atrocities. I had the same concern when I started in the field. This is a normal and natural reaction when working with survivors of catastrophic life events. There were times when I cried with individuals – especially at the beginning of my career. Shulman (2009) views crying with clients as an example of integrating our personal selves into our professional roles. In the case of my work, when we share survivors' pain and express our own sorrow, we give them the gift of our feelings. It allows them to see us as real people who care about them, and it helps build trust.

However, when I did break down and cry, I learned to compose myself quickly. Some survivors felt they had upset me and did not want to continue with their stories. Others felt they needed to take care of me. Eventually I learned to contain my feelings. It is helpful for service providers to explore their fear of reacting emotionally to determine if it is related to a personal traumatic memory or experience. Once they become aware of this, it can be addressed personally – with professional assistance if necessary. Other times crying is an empathic response to the survivor. I find deep diaphragmatic breathing useful to control my emotional reactions. After I compose myself I say: 'There is a lot to cry about. Your story has touched me.'

Difficulty Listening to Survivors' Description of Traumatic Experiences

Listening to survivors recount horrific incidents, such as torture and mass killings, is not easy. The person in front of us has experienced or witnessed the dark side of humanity they describe. Practitioners may find that their ability to concentrate diminishes, causing them to tune out the survivor's story. This is a natural defence mechanism. When I react to a survivor's story in such a way, I find it helpful to give myself a conscious message, such as a gentle pinch or poke, which helps me remain present. Sometimes I take a deep breath to ground myself. Then I consciously bring myself back to the present moment so I can continue to listen. There are times when I reach my limits and am unable to listen to another tragic story. This is a sign for me to seek support from colleagues or clinical supervision. Sometimes I need a break from trauma work, especially if there are stresses in my personal life that require attention.

Grieving a Survivor's Death

Service providers develop relationships with clients and, consequently, feel a loss when they die. Each person's grief is different. Sometimes I find it helpful to participate in mourning rituals such as attending funerals and / or paying respects to family members during *shiva*. Grieving our losses is important. I set aside time for reflection and find ways to express my thoughts and feelings about the death, through, for example, nature walks, peer support, journal writing, and so on. It is important to take care of our own health and well-being.

VICARIOUS TRAUMA

Working with survivors of mass atrocity can be challenging and causes many service providers to 'burn out' prematurely if they do not guard against vicarious trauma. Vicarious traumatization (VT) (Saakvitne & Pearlman, 1996), secondary traumatic stress (STS) (Stamm, 1995), and compassion fatigue (Figley, 1995) are terms used to describe the cumulative emotional reactions of service providers who listen empathetically and assist individuals who experienced traumatic life events. In the words of Judith Herman, 'trauma is contagious' (1992:140). Service providers may experience symptoms of post-traumatic-stress disorder (Herman, 1992). Herman (1992) discusses some reactions, which include intrusive mental imagery associated with the client's story; challenges to faith in humanity; heightened sense of personal vulnerability; identifying with the client's feelings of helplessness, rage, and grief; feelings of incompetence and underestimating personal knowledge and skills; assuming a rescuer role; boundary violations; doubting or denying the client's reality; and doubting or avoiding traumatic material.

Saakvitne and Pearlman (1996:40) describe signs and symptoms of vicarious trauma, including: 'no time or energy for oneself; disconnection from loved ones; social withdrawal; increased sensitivity to violence; cynicism; generalized despair and hopelessness; nightmares'; changes in core aspects of self (such as identity, beliefs, spirituality); and disrupted cognitive and psychological functioning (such as irritability, sleep disturbances, difficulty concentrating, intense fear, recollections, intrusive imagery, and startle responses).

Health-care professionals often resist working with Holocaust survivors for these reasons. Ongoing supervision, support, and a commitment to self-care strategies are necessary to help service providers deal with vicarious trauma. To cope with these reactions, Meichenbaum (1994) and Saakvitne and Pearlman (1996) recommend engaging in personal, professional, and organizational activities that prevent or lessen the impact of vicarious trauma.

Saakvitne and Pearlman (1996) discuss three central aspects of interventions to protect against vicarious trauma: awareness, balance, and connection. They recommend integrating these aspects into our personal, professional, and organizational lives. Awareness means paying attention to our inner states and disequilibrium. This requires quiet time for self-reflection. One way to achieve this is through mindfulness practice (Kabat-Zinn, 1994), a technique that brings our attention to what is happening in the present moment without changing or judging it. The second aspect is attaining and maintaining balance. Trauma service providers must maintain their inner balance as well as the balance between their personal and professional lives. Learning how to develop and maintain balance is an individual process of exploring techniques and approaches that work, such as time management, stress management, and healthy personal relationships. Finally, maintaining connections provides an antidote to the isolation many trauma service providers experience. This consists of establishing an inner connection attuned to our needs, seeking social support from colleagues and friends, and connecting to a higher meaning in life to provide an internal anchor (God, nature, the universe, humanity, and so on).

In her book *Help for the Helper*, Babette Rothschild (2006) provides screening instruments to help workers measure their quality of life and levels of stress and vicarious trauma. She recommends that they use these scales only as a guideline because the results may be skewed or have a bias. Throughout her book she emphasizes the importance of employing common sense coupled with body awareness and self-awareness to evaluate if one is experiencing vicarious trauma. Providers must be aware of personal stress levels and when individual limits are reached. She recommends taking seriously any feedback from colleagues, family, and friends if they say you look tired, are acting irritable, or seem depressed.

Personal Strategies

Colleagues sometimes ask how I have been able to continue doing this work for over twenty years without burning out, as many workers do. We cannot be effective in trauma work without consciously engaging in self-care practices. I was aware of the emotional impact of working with Holocaust survivors at the beginning of my career. I practised self-care techniques and integrated restorative habits into my personal lifestyle early on. For example, I now work part-time and set clear boundaries between my work and personal life. I have a support system with colleagues at work and engage in satisfying relationships with family and friends. I am also self-reflective, practise mindfulness, and am in touch with my physical body. I go to the country to relax and unwind in nature. I also engage in creative outlets such as playing with my grandchildren, gardening, jewellery making, and baking. Every service provider should develop self-care practices that address personal needs. The following personal strategies may be helpful:

1. Make personal life a priority.
2. Build a support system with people who are supportive, respectful, and kind.

3. Balance professional and personal life. Set limits on the workday and stick to them. Balance workday activities with leisure activities.
4. Pay attention to personal health. Eat a healthy diet filled with a variety of rich whole foods such as vegetables, fruits, grains, small amounts of lean meat and fish, beans, and nuts; and drink water. Limit consumption of sugar, unhealthy fats, salt, processed foods, and alcohol.
5. Stay home and rest when not feeling well.
6. Honour and respect personal needs and engage in restorative activities and practices that nourish your body, mind, and soul, such as rest, exercise, relaxation techniques, prayer, humour, interpersonal relationships, and creative expression.
7. Integrate mind-body self-care practices into your lifestyle:
   a. Exercise (walking, swimming, tai chi, yoga) enhances immune-system functioning; releases endorphins – the body's 'feel good' hormones and painkillers; and decreases depression and anxiety.
   b. Eat a healthy diet rich in foods that contain vitamins A, C, E, and B, which stimulate serotonin production – a brain chemical that calms and relaxes the body.
   c. Drink herbal remedies that calm the mind such as chamomile and lemon-balm teas.
   d. Practise relaxation exercises such as deep diaphragmatic breathing, visualization techniques, and progressive muscular relaxation.
   e. Listen to calming music: sounds of nature, or instrumental music with no emotional baggage.
   f. Spend time in a natural setting.
   g. Meditate using techniques like breath counting or mindfulness.
   h. Engage in tasks that require 'mindless' repetitive movements, such as washing dishes, cleaning, woodworking, gardening, and knitting.
   i. Have some form of body work done periodically, such as therapeutic touch or energy field work, for example, Reiki, reflexology, acupressure, shiatsu, deep tissue, or Swedish massage.
   j. Introduce essential oils into your environment such as lavender or rose. These aromas stimulate neurotransmitters and endorphins in the brain which reduce stress, relieve pain, and restore emotional equilibrium.
   k. Create a relaxation retreat or a personal sanctuary and decorate it with personal mementos, plants, and the like. Use soothing colours.

l. Explore inner thoughts and feelings through self-reflective writing or a daily journal.

8. Find a spiritual connection, for example: love, honour, and respect yourself and others; connect with and trust your inner intuitive voice; spend quiet time alone each day; search for a higher meaning in life to connect to an internal anchor; find meaning in and purpose for your existence; remember mystical experiences; and be in awe of something on a regular basis.

9. Surround yourself with objects that serve as metaphors for signs of life, such as flowers, plants, and inspirational pictures, and pursue activities that perform the same function, such as planting seeds and watching them grow.

10. Create rituals for purification and regeneration: breathing exercises, nature walks, swimming, basking in the sun.

11. Incorporate Daily Doses of Delight (DDD) into your everyday lifestyle (Pearsall, 1996). Ask yourself the question 'What makes me happy?' and follow through with action.

12. Think about or write down at least three things that you are grateful for each day. Remember to appreciate your body. Consider keeping a gratitude journal.

Professional Strategies

Here are a few professional strategies to consider:

1. Remember that vicarious trauma reactions are normal when providing services to trauma survivors.

2. Be aware if an individual's trauma story is reviving a personal traumatic experience. Find ways to deal with your own traumatic memories, such as expressing your feelings to a professional counsellor, trusted friend, or family member; writing in a journal; or having a good cry.

3. Service providers who work with survivors need ongoing supervision and consultation, when necessary, to maintain effectiveness. Peer-support groups are helpful.

4. If you have a choice, balance your caseload with individuals who do not have trauma-based issues.

5. Vary daily routines, through, example, contact with colleagues, breaks, and physical activity. Get fresh air periodically.

6. Attend professional trainings and conferences to network with colleagues and learn about new services and programs.

7. Recognize and focus on the rewards of this work. Herman (1992:153) points out the advantages of working with survivors of traumatic life events. These include acquiring an ability to appreciate life more fully and to take it more seriously; developing a better understanding of oneself and others; forming new friendships and deeper intimate relationships; feeling inspired by survivors' courage, determination, and hope; and gaining a sense of a higher purpose in life.

Organizational Strategies

There are many things an organization can do to support staff who provide services to trauma survivors:

1. Ensure that staff members have adequate supervision and consultation. Staff members can negotiate feedback mechanisms with their supervisors to ensure that reciprocal feedback is delivered effectively. Department team meetings can provide opportunities for staff to express feelings, debrief, and learn mind-body techniques. They can serve as a forum to elicit new and creative ideas. Hold these meetings away from the agency occasionally to provide staff with a change of environment.
2. Supervisors and managers can support their staff by offering positive feedback, showing appreciation for their contributions and accomplishments, and demonstrating that they are valued and respected. Staff need to be recognized for doing good work.
3. Ensure that service providers have personal physical space.
4. Support staff in decorating their space with personal objects which hold meaning for them.
5. Provide resources and support for continuing education so staff can acquire new skills in working with this population.
6. Provide staff with adequate time off. Service providers cannot continuously do this work well without time off for replenishment and self-care.

PART V

Going Forward

17 Recovery Milestones Applicable to Other Communities

If we better understood some of the long-term impacts of extreme, prolonged trauma, we might be able to provide interventions and help put social policies in place that could not only mitigate the negative effects of these horrific wars but also help foster more positive, long-term adaptations for the survivors.

B. Hollander-Goldfein et al. (2012)

The Holocaust officially ended more than sixty-five years ago. The majority of survivors were in their twenties and thirties when they were liberated. Now they are in their eighties. Traumatic Holocaust memories permeate the biological, psychological, and intellectual changes that occur during their ageing process. The coping skills survivors developed during the Holocaust serve them well in adapting to these changes. However, survivors never forget the horrors they endured and the losses they suffered. These experiences are etched in their memories and affect their lives as long as they live.

In my opinion, the cost of preventing mass atrocities is minimal when compared to the costs of perpetrating an atrocity and dealing with the aftermath. Damages inflicted on survivors of a mass atrocity usually include some combination of physical, mental, psychological, spiritual, and financial injury in addition to losses in property, friends, family, and community. Humanity also suffers monumental losses when entire religions, cultures, and knowledge bases of unique communities are lost forever and their terrains destroyed. The task of healing and recovery is enormous and, in some instances, insurmountable. There are regions of the world where people continue to commit atrocities against each other as they have for decades, even centuries. Healing and recovery has not happened in these areas. However, we must continue to pursue these goals because doing so, apart from assisting the victims, thwarts the perpetuation of the hatred and fear that leads to further mass atrocities.

My work with Holocaust survivors shows me that recovery from mass atrocity is possible. Recovering from genocidal trauma, however, is a long-term, and sometimes lifelong, process. While some survivors are able to recover on their own, most could benefit from some form of assistance to facilitate and accelerate the process. Mass atrocity induces trauma that may also span multiple generations (Danieli, 1998; Hass, 1990; Sigal & Weinfeld, 1989; Wardi, 1992). This makes recovery and healing a lengthy endeavour.

Holocaust survivors have discovered and traversed new paths for humanity towards understanding, and healing and recovering from, the effects of mass atrocity. Along the way, service providers have learned to minimize the psychological effects of trauma and facilitate survivors' innate recuperative abilities, even when they are advanced in age. We have discovered that the recovery process can be accelerated by implementing programs and services, such as those discussed in this book, which are responsive to survivors' unique needs. These recovery programs focus on embracing survivors and building supportive communities that understand them and reduce their social isolation. Group affiliations, like our Drop-in Centre, provide a safe place where survivors can grieve their losses by participating in commemorative events and creating mourning rituals. These groups also provide a place where survivors can engage in social activities with peers, learn new coping strategies, and leave memoirs as a cultural and historical legacy for the community.

Recovery and healing is a personal journey. Survivors cannot, and do not want to, forget what happened to them. We have learned that our role, as service providers, is to help survivors retain their memories in ways that are not harmful to themselves and that honour their murdered families, friends, and obliterated communities. Factors that help survivors to heal, and that they identify in discussions as key to their recovery, include:

- building a new family;
- talking about their Holocaust experiences;
- having a will to live;
- maintaining their Jewish religion;
- building Israel, a place of belonging and safety for Jews;

- being productive members of society;
- maintaining friendships with other survivors; and
- having a relationship with health-care and social-service professionals who understand them.

Supporting survivors on their individual journeys towards recovery and healing is the responsibility of both service providers and the community at large. Holocaust museums and related institutions are beginning to draw on experiences from that tragic chapter in history to teach society about genocide and its consequences (Article, 2010, Canadian Jewish News). In this vein, I will now discuss some of the lessons I have learned from Holocaust survivors as they struggle to heal and recover from their experiences. These factors can be applied to assist other populations who survived a mass atrocity. The major components that facilitate healing and recovery include acknowledgment, resources, and healing processes.

ACKNOWLEDGMENT

Acknowledging that an atrocity took place is the first step towards recovery. At the time of the Holocaust, the word *genocide* did not exist, and the word *holocaust* did not refer to the Jewish Holocaust. It is of Greek origin, meaning 'sacrifice by fire' (United States Holocaust Memorial Museum, 2012). Holocaust survivors describe the pain and suffering they endured in the post-war years when communities greeted them with ignorance, silence, and denial. They were told to forget and move on with their lives.

However, thanks to the efforts of Raphael Lemkin, a survivor, the term genocide was created and associated with the Holocaust experience. Today genocide is recognized as a crime against humanity. It forms the basis of international law that has evolved to recognize many similar crimes as mass atrocities. These atrocities are crimes subject to prosecution and punishment.

Holocaust survivors have also been instrumental in advocating for and developing national laws against mass atrocities. For example, Canada and other countries enacted legislation that criminalizes war crimes, crimes against humanity, and other atrocities. These crimes are not subject to any statute of limitations in Canada and are prosecutable regardless of when and where they occurred. The Office of Special

Investigation brings human-rights violators to justice in the United States. Such laws and governmental support form a basis for restitution claims and recovery services. Without these international and national laws, support for healing and recovery would be severely hampered. Holocaust survivors have demonstrated that acknowledging the suffering of victims and establishing that a crime was committed are important milestones in the healing and recovery process.

RESOURCES

Once society acknowledges that a mass atrocity was committed, resources can be assembled and mobilized to support the recovery and healing of its survivors. There are many aspects of recovery that are beyond the scope of this book to address, such as recovering stolen property. Also, some losses can never be recovered, such as murdered people and destroyed communities. My work, and this book, focuses primarily on the emotional, psychological, and spiritual healing of survivors in their attempt to rebuild their lives and restore their health and well-being. The types of resources needed for this journey include financial, community, and services.

Financial

Very little happens without financial resources. Funds must come from somewhere. Who is responsible ... the host communities, the perpetrators of the crime? Many communities around the world instituted programs and services for Holocaust survivors with funding from the Claims Conference. In some cases, the only services provided are those that the Claims Conference funds.

This raises a question of whether agencies are providing programs based on the needs of their local survivor population, or only providing programs the Claims Conference will fund. Roman Kent, a Holocaust survivor who is chairman of the American Gathering / Federation of Jewish Holocaust Survivors and treasurer of the Claims Conference, says that the latter is true. In his words: 'The organized Jewish community talks a great deal about the plight of needy survivors while they exploit the Holocaust to raise funds for themselves, yet most organizations only help survivors if they receive Claims Conference monies to do so. If they don't get money, the survivors don't get help' (The Jewish Week, 3 September 2010).

This underscores the importance of securing funding to support survivors of mass atrocities. Criminal prosecutions of perpetrators that lead to their incarceration or death is not enough. Mass atrocity leaves an aftermath that requires considerable time and resources to recover from. Holocaust survivors are fortunate to have organizations like the Claims Conference to advocate for them. This organization negotiates and oversees restitution and compensation payments from responsible governments. Survivors of other mass atrocities must find ways to finance their healing and recovery. Where does the responsibility lie? Does it lie with their own community or with the perpetrators of the crimes? What is the responsibility of host countries that offer refuge to survivors from a mass atrocity committed in another country? What are the consequences to a host country that does not support healing and recovery services for its immigrant survivors, and assimilation into its society? Funding healing and recovery programs is important because, in addition to helping survivors, they contribute towards preventing future mass atrocity crimes by promoting education, awareness, and reconciliation.

Community

Survivors need understanding and support for their healing and recovery process. Making them feel welcome within an understanding and supportive community is critical to their recovery. Establishing safety and security when perpetrators and victims continue to live together can be challenging and is beyond the scope of this book. However, rebuilding a congenial community must be accomplished when survivors remain in their communities and countries of origin. Sometimes this is not easily accomplished and survivors migrate to new countries, as happened with many Holocaust survivors. In this situation, survivors are faced with the challenges inherent in moving from one country to another as well as those involved in their own healing and recovery.

Services

Facilitating Assimilation in a New Country

On a number of occasions my father described his disappointment after immigrating to Canada. He said: 'When we arrived I thought they would lift us up in the air and carry us around considering the hardships we had gone through.' Instead, survivor immigrants were greeted with a housing shortage and negative attitudes. Survivors living in Canada were initially forced to create their own mutual-aid and support organizations.

When immigrants arrive in a new country, they are baffled by bureaucratic immigration procedures and face the difficult tasks of communicating in a foreign language and adjusting to strange surroundings and a different culture. Survivors are also dealing with their traumatic experiences and personal losses. The degree of shock on arrival can be mitigated by cordial reception from relatives, friends, and representatives of social-service agencies. Besides needing support for their healing and recovery process, most survivor immigrants need help with basic needs such as housing, food, language and cultural education, and employment, including the learning of new vocational skills, if necessary. Their new communities and host countries should be willing and prepared to address these issues.

Establishing Mutual-Aid Groups and Support Organizations

Many immigrant survivors in Canada quickly banded together to form new mutual-support organizations or joined pre-existing ones, which served to ground them in their new environment and helped them adapt to a new society. They thereby established a sense of community with people who shared similar backgrounds and interests, which effectively created new extended families for them. The various social, cultural, and philanthropic activities of these organizations reflected the values inherent in survivors' pre-war European life. The organizations also served as a vehicle to transmit the history and culture of survivors' pre-war lives to future generations. Combining the mutual-aid model created by these organizations with psycho-social services tailored to trauma survivors forms a basis for creating groups that accelerate healing and recovery.

Establishing long-term mutual-aid groups, like the Drop-in Centre, to address the needs of mass atrocity survivors should be included in community and governmental policy decisions. These groups, facilitated by knowledgeable professionals who understand survivor issues, provide a safe environment where trust is rebuilt, mutual bonds are established, and a culture of mutual aid is developed. They help their members to re-establish surrogate families, mourn their losses, and, to the extent possible, preserve their cultural heritage. Such an environment also accelerates healing and recovery by assisting individuals to adjust emotionally, spiritually, and psychologically as they deal with their trauma, losses, and assimilation. Survivors' traumatic experiences can be normalized and understood more easily within a community of peers. Healing and recovery are enhanced within a mutual-aid peer group.

RECOVERY AND HEALING PROCESSES

There are many important survivor recovery and healing processes that can be supported by the community, a social-service agency, or within a psycho-social mutual-aid group. Here are some examples:

Grieving and Commemoration

Participating in Commemorative Activities

Survivors around the world regard the organizing of commemorative services to mourn their losses as a sacred duty and obligation. In the years immediately after the Holocaust, survivors grieved privately with their fellow survivors, usually within the mutual-aid organizations they created. However, it is important that surrounding communities join with survivors to organize programs such as agency-wide commemorative services, community-wide memorial services, a national day of remembrance, and so on. These programs are important for several reasons. First, they provide an opportunity for shared grieving with peers who have suffered similar losses. Second, with the presence of community, survivors realize that they are not alone in reflecting on their past. They feel supported and comforted. Finally, providing survivors with a forum for memorialization and ritualization helps with their ongoing duties and obligations to mourn and remember their losses. Psycho-social support groups can facilitate the coordination of these services.

Institutionalizing Educational and Commemorative Activities

To honour their commitment to murdered families and friends that they would never allow the world to forget what happened to them, survivors established Holocaust remembrance committees in community organizations such as Canadian Jewish Congress and lobbied to have Holocaust education incorporated into courses and activities in schools. They also continue to found Holocaust museums and educational centres, publish memoirs and books, and participate in documentation projects. In 2005 the United Nations designated 27 January 1945, the date Auschwitz was liberated, as an International Day for Holocaust Commemoration (Article, 2010, Canadian Jewish News).

Similar commemorative events and educational initiatives may be appropriate for survivors of other mass atrocities. They must be conceived and conducted in a manner appropriate for each unique survivor community.

Finding Meaning and Purpose in Survival

Survivors of genocide carry an important message. Opportunities should be created for survivors to educate others about their experiences and the inherent dangers of racism. Many have a heightened sensitivity to human-rights violations and are among the first to detect abuse of those rights. Many insist on developing safeguards to prevent racism and genocide so that future generations can benefit from their ordeals.

Allowing survivors to bear witness helps them to transcend their victim self-concept and assume roles as 'witnesses to history' and 'educators' in the community. The process of educating others, especially younger persons, has a therapeutic effect which often brings hope, meaning, and purpose to their lives. It also brings them some peace of mind knowing that their history will not be forgotten.

Service providers can begin by listening to survivors and providing opportunities for them to speak publicly. Intergenerational dialogues are helpful here; so is allowing survivors to bear witness by acting as museums docents and speakers in educational settings.

Recovering from Psychological Trauma

The long-term complications from exposure to severe trauma were not well recognized or understood during the mid-1900s. Soldiers were considered to have conditions such as 'shell shock' or 'battle fatigue.' Holocaust survivors were believed to have 'concentration camp syndrome.' Today the effects of exposure to severe trauma are better understood and severe cases are diagnosed as post-traumatic-stress disorder. Extensive research has given rise to various treatment modalities. There is a wealth of information from different disciplines that informs our practice with trauma survivors. Fortunately, post-traumatic symptoms can be recognized and sufferers can be taught to manage and cope with their triggers and flashbacks. With awareness and conscious effort, survivors can learn to move their traumatic memories to the periphery and improve their quality of life. Recovery is possible and can be facilitated by specialized programs and services, such as those discussed in this book and elsewhere.

Restitution and Reparation

The cost of healing and recovery from a mass atrocity is immense. The financial burden should not have to be born entirely by communities who offer refuge and asylum to survivors; the perpetrators and governments responsible for the crimes should make reparations. That being said, the practicality of enforcing such responsibility is challenging. Today there are national and international laws making crimes against humanity punishable. The aftermath of the Holocaust has paved the way for determining responsibility and establishing precedents. Survivors of mass atrocity, and those choosing to support them, must find ways to fund recovery and healing. Holocaust survivors serve as role models in this area. They were instrumental in initiating and winning several large class-action law suits against institutions that persecuted them and others during the Third Reich's reign of terror, such as Swiss banks, Swiss businesses, and the Swiss government (Holocaust Victims Assets Litigation); European insurance companies for unpaid policies held before and during the war years (International Commission on Holocaust Era Insurance Claims [ICHEIC]); and German companies that used slave or forced labour (Foundation for Remembrance, Responsibility and the Future).

Many Holocaust survivors, however, struggle with issues related to applying for restitution payments from the German government. Some view restitution as 'blood money' and say that no amount of money would ever compensate them for their losses. Others view restitution as an admission of guilt and wrongdoing by the perpetrators. One man told me recently, 'I don't care how much money I get. It shows they've taken responsibility for their actions.' Danieli (1999) believes that economic compensation should be legislated and paid to the victims of governmental wrongdoing. If some individuals refuse to accept these payments, their respective allocation should be placed in a special fund dedicated to providing for their care and well-being as they age, educating society about the Holocaust, and preventing further atrocities.

Formal Apologies

Some survivors are comforted when governments take responsibility for their crimes and apologize publicly for their actions. A formal apology acknowledges and validates that a crime was committed against them. It is also a crucial step towards any possibility of reconciliation. Survivors can be supported to advocate and apply pressure on responsible parties to elicit an apology.

A NATIONAL RESOURCE FOR SURVIVOR SERVICES

Streamline and Improve Services to All Survivors

During my career I observed that services for Holocaust survivors across Canada were inconsistent from community to community. In 2008 I began envisioning a national resource within the Jewish community that could provide a focal point for the consolidation and coordination of services and information. The window of opportunity to create a national resource for Holocaust survivors may, unfortunately, have closed. However, mass atrocities continue to create a steady influx of survivors into the national, as well as world, community. Perhaps a national resource for all survivors of mass atrocities who are accepted into Canada might be appropriate.

Such an organization could serve as a liaison between survivors and their families, local communities, service providers, and funding sources. For example, a national resource could help communities identify, develop, and implement appropriate services for survivors as their demographics and circumstances change. It could also provide healthcare providers with practical information, skills development, and resources for working with survivor populations. The mandate for a national resource could include the following:

1. Develop and conduct needs assessments to identify national gaps in services and help communities find creative ways to meet them.
2. Make recommendations to improve and facilitate quality and consistency of services across local communities.
3. Develop qualitative and quantitative measures to evaluate the effectiveness and efficiency of existing programs and services. How do we know whether these programs address individual needs

(for example, adequate dissemination of information, easy access, level of satisfaction)?
4. Encourage communities to develop programs that empower survivors, facilitate their healing, and provide meaning and purpose to their lives (for example, intergenerational and commemorative programs, writing and publishing memoirs, oral-history projects, wish fulfillment, photographic exhibitions).
5. Disseminate information to the survivor community:
   a. Establish a central address for collecting and disseminating information pertinent to survivor communities (for example, efforts to restore Jewish cemeteries in Europe, survivor reunions around the world).
   b. Compile a national list of organizations and universities that record survivors' testimonies and inform survivors about them.
   c. Disseminate up-to-date information about restitution programs, assistance funds, and pensions to local survivor communities.
   d. Compile a list of organizations collecting survivors' memoirs and disseminate the names to regional communities so they can refer survivors to them.
   e. Facilitate survivors' searches for family members. Establish links with organizations such as:
      i. International Red Cross Tracing Service;
      ii. Yad Vashem: *Pages of Testimony* project; and
      iii. National Registry of Jewish Holocaust Survivors, a project of the American Gathering / Federation of Jewish Holocaust Survivors at the United States Holocaust Museum in Washington, D.C.
   f. Encourage communities to reach out to centres and agencies in outlying areas and establish a liaison and referral process to refer isolated and unaffiliated survivors to appropriate resources and services.
6. Provide program information and clinical support to social-service and health-care providers serving mass atrocity survivors. Specifically:
   a. consult about services and programs offered to survivors; and
   b. provide clinical supervision on understanding the unique needs of survivors, their psycho-social functioning, ageing and traumatic memory, clinical interventions, creative social programs, empowerment strategies, and holistic approaches to well-being and vicarious trauma.

7. Provide educational materials to service providers about survivors' unique needs, psycho-social functioning, environmental triggers, and activities that provide meaning and purpose. Function as a liaison between service providers. Specifically:
   a. compile a resource list of relevant articles and innovative international services and programs and make it available to local communities;
   b. encourage the sharing of information between service providers;
   c. encourage institutional adaptation to deal with environmental stressors that may trigger traumatic memories; and
   d. ensure culturally appropriate services to minimize triggers such as language or government bureaucracy.
8. Advocate on issues of concern or benefit to survivors such as negotiating special services or discounts (for example, asking local banks to waive service charges for depositing restitution payments). Other examples, related to Holocaust survivors, include:
   a. arrange meetings with German consulates / embassies to obtain authorization to stamp Life Certificates and to establish health-resort facilities in local communities for survivors who receive restitution and are eligible for a health cure; and
   b. coordinate dialogue with the Hungarian Justice Department and Hungarian Compensation Office regarding their request that survivors provide death certificates for family members killed in the Holocaust in order to meet eligibility criteria for their recent compensation program.
9. Promote working relationships with academic and international communities to encourage communication and information exchange.

Benefits of a National Resource

If such a national resource were created, it would have several benefits for survivor communities, service providers, and governmental and ethnic organizations alike.

Survivor Communities

For survivor communities, a national resource would

- ensure that all survivors across Canada have up-to-date information about issues that affect them;

- improve availability, consistency, and quality of services to survivors;
- establish communication between survivors and service providers to identify emerging needs and design programs to meet them;
- provide a national focal point for assistance with survivor issues; and
- promote new projects that facilitate healing and enhances survivors' quality of life.

The Service-Provider Community

For service providers, a national resource would

- facilitate information sharing: peer-to-peer communication;
- improve service delivery and ensure that emerging needs are met; and
- promote the sharing of best practices, cross-learning, and so on.

Concerned Governmental and Ethnic Organizations

For these organizations, finally, a national resource would

- establish creative programming to address the needs of vulnerable community populations;
- provide a focal point for benefactors and funding: allowing the setting up of a process to match benefactors with projects;
- encourage collaboration and working relationships with health, social-service, and academic organizations across the country;
- provide visibility and recognition at the community, national, and international levels;
- create a credible and influential voice in representing and working with the older adult population; and
- establish a state-of-the-art quality-care program for survivors, which can be shared with countries around the world and used as a model.

Afterword

After more than sixty years we have to enjoy ourselves. We punish ourselves if we don't. We cannot change what happened in the past. If we do not go on, then the Germans are still punishing us.

– Survivor in the Drop-in Centre

I am privileged to have accompanied and supported so many survivors as they progressed along their journey towards recovery and healing. Survivors in the Drop-in program who have been there since the beginning are not the same as they were fifteen years ago. Significant psychological and social changes have taken place. In the beginning, members told me that they ruminated about the Holocaust during most of the day, especially when alone. Today, although they are physically frailer, they are in many ways psychologically more fit. The intensity of their emotional pain has diminished. They are able to talk about their Holocaust experiences without getting choked up or crying. Many have been able to move their traumatic memories to the periphery and are no longer flooded by them on a daily basis. The wounds are still there but they are no longer open wounds that bleed and hurt. Now they are scars, often deep scars, which remind them of their experiences and losses.

Members have begun to realize how much they have changed since they joined the Drop-in Centre. For example, in 2009 Mrs E., one of the founding members, announced to the group that in a few weeks she would commemorate the anniversary of her family's deportation to Auschwitz from the Hungarian ghetto where they were interned. It was the last time she saw her parents. She asked for the group's support because this was a difficult time for her. However, she went on to say that, a few days after the anniversary of this event, she would be off to Israel. This was the first time since liberation that she set a limit on her grieving and allowed herself to anticipate joy of a trip to Israel. Listening to Mrs E.'s excitement as she described her upcoming trip brought tears to my eyes. I pointed out that twelve years ago she would not have given herself permission to experience such happiness. She agreed.

There are other ways survivors in the Drop-in Centre are demonstrating their readiness to detach from their suffering. For example, they are requesting lighthearted and fun-filled programs so they can enjoy themselves. This was not the case fifteen years ago when their primary focus was talking about their war experiences. Recently, I asked thirty-five Holocaust survivors in the centre if they feel they have recovered and healed from their ordeals. I also asked them to describe the factors that helped them to heal. These are some of their responses during the discussion.

Most of our members said they have healed and measure their recovery by their ability to experience pleasure and joy. Mrs H. linked her recovery to memories from her life in the ghetto where the community focused on survival and freedom. She described the ways she and her friends maintained their humanity by participating in cultural activities which brought them happiness and hope for freedom. In her words: 'In the ghetto and camps we put on plays, danced, and sang songs. We wanted to say yes to life because there will come a day when we will be free.' She continues to say 'yes to life' by living with meaning and purpose. She volunteers at the agency and speaks to individuals and groups about her past.

Some members said they did not want to give Hitler a posthumous victory by allowing him to continue to destroy their morale. Mrs V. believes that survivors had an obligation to rebuild their lives after the war. If they had not done so, they would be in the same condition as the Germans left them in. She did not want to give them that satisfaction. One member observed that, if survivors do not give themselves permission to enjoy themselves, then the Nazis are still punishing them. In Mrs A's words: 'After more than sixty years we have to enjoy ourselves. We punish ourselves if we don't. We cannot change what happened in the past. If we do not go on, then the Germans are still punishing us.'

Many attribute their personal recovery to the rebirth of the Jewish people and their own families. Mrs M. said: 'Every child born is a joy. It shows that we survived.' Mrs S. takes pride in her children, grandchildren, and great-grandchildren. Others feel good when they see Jewish youth celebrating the Jewish holidays. Mrs G. is proud that her family has four generations now. Mr D. looks forward to his grandchildren's weddings. Other survivors attribute their recovery to their solidarity with Israel, the Jewish homeland. Mr P. said: 'We have a country – we have to be happy with what we got.'

We notice another way survivors in the Drop-in Centre recover from the after-effects of their ordeals: they are aware of their needs today and are able to modulate their emotions when these are triggered by an external event that reminds them of their war experiences. The following anecdote exemplifies this observation.

* * *

After a terror attack in 2012 against Jews in Toulouse, France, some members came to the program feeling vulnerable. They were afraid that persecutions against Jews were escalating, which caused them anxiety and sleeplessness. I facilitated a discussion to give voice to their thoughts and feelings about the incident. Several members pointed out to the group that the French government denounced these acts and supported the Jewish community in its loss of a rabbi and three children. In fact, French President Nicolas Sarkozy flew to Toulouse immediately after the school shooting to support the community. He also made finding the perpetrator(s) of the attack a priority. The members recognized that these responses by the French government were different from the responses of most governments in their countries of origin during the Holocaust, some of which had collaborated with the Nazis. After our discussion the majority of members were able to internalize this information and separate the Toulouse incident from their own experiences during the Holocaust.

Some members, however, were still feeling vulnerable so I asked them what they needed from the group. One person said that reading inspirational stories and articles makes her feel better, which prompted another member to respond spontaneously by reading an inspirational poem about friendship and coping with life's challenges.

I then informed the group about a community rally that was taking place next door and asked if they wanted to attend. Most did and those who remained behind did so because they could not stand for a long time. We joined members of the Jewish community in a solidarity rally condemning the Toulouse incident and praying for the victims. When members returned to the program they were sad but also relieved to learn that Federation CJA was working with public security forces to increase patrols at local Jewish institutions. They also felt comforted by the presence of Jewish leaders from different segments of the community and government officials at the rally. We ended the morning session by singing *Am*

Israel Chai (Hebrew for: the people of Israel live). This song is an effective grounding tool and members left the program feeling less vulnerable and more secure. They also said that they felt supported by staff, volunteers, and our social-work intern. Although still saddened by the events in France, they now had a sense of community and belonging. As one man said, 'Things are different now than they were during the Holocaust. We are not alone.'

* * *

Some survivors, however, do not feel they have completely moved on. For example, Mrs R. said she wants to move on, laugh, and appreciate her family but anti-Semitism and Holocaust deniers prevent her from completely doing so. She went on to say that it is important to enjoy her life but, at the same time, not to forget. These sentiments were echoed by Mrs F., who said, 'There is a time to remember and a time to go on living and enjoy life.' Establishing a meaningful connection to their past helps these survivors give themselves permission to enjoy their lives. Some feel they have recovered by keeping the memory of their families alive and remembering to 'live each day a little bit and heal.'

A few survivors feel that they have not been able to recover. For example, Mr A. said, 'Since the war I cannot laugh in my heart. I smile at a joke but never have a good laugh.' Mrs S. was struggling with the word 'recovery' because of an encounter she had with a well-known survivor many years ago. She went to his book launch and, after his presentation, asked him why he never laughed or smiled. He responded: 'How can we laugh after what they did to us and what we lived through?' They both started to cry. Unfortunately, his comments left her feeling that she did not have the right to be happy.

If the Holocaust were the last genocide, then this book would be a memoir about services and interventions that have aided the recovery and healing of hundreds of people. Unfortunately, mass atrocities are still occurring today, in fact more so than ever. Consequently, I hope that my reflections will provide inspiration and guidance in the development of programs and services for survivors of other mass atrocities as they journey towards recovery and healing.

Appendix A
Mass Atrocity Crimes

PARTIAL LISTING OF MASS ATROCITIES COMMITTED
DURING THE PAST HUNDRED YEARS

Native Populations

For centuries, indigenous peoples around the world – also known as
Aboriginal peoples, First Nations, Native peoples, Fourth World peoples, tribal peoples, the original occupants – have faced genocide, cultural destruction, and involuntary removal from their ancestral homes
(Hitchcock & Totten, 2009). Conflicts arose as societies expanded into
new areas and indigenous peoples sought to maintain their identities,
cultural distinctiveness, lands, and resources. Beside the toll of deaths
from new diseases, they endured 'mass killings, arbitrary executions,
torture, mental and physical mistreatment, arrests and detentions without trial, forced sterilization, involuntary relocation, destruction of their
subsistence base, and taking children away from their families' (Charny,
1999:349–50). The *Encyclopedia of Genocide* (Charny, 1999) lists the atrocities (genocides according to Charny) committed against indigenous
populations in Africa, Asia, the Pacific, Latin America, the Caribbean,
South America, Central America, and North America.

1904–7: The Hereros of Southwest Africa (Herero Genocide)

The genocide of the Hereros – nomadic herdsmen in German Southwest Africa – is believed to be the first genocide of the twentieth century (Totten, Parsons, & Charny, 1995). The Hereros revolted in 1904

in response to racist tensions and the systematic expropriation of their land under German colonial rule. The German army retaliated with brutal force. Of a total population of eighty thousand Hereros, approximately sixty-five thousand were killed (Chalk & Jonassohn, 1990).

1915–23: The Armenian Genocide

The Turkish government planned and carried out the elimination of the entire Armenian population in Turkey during the First World War. The Armenian people were subjected to deportation, expropriation, abduction, torture, massacre, and starvation. Approximately one and a half million people were murdered.

1932–3: Soviet Famine

The Russians created an artificially induced famine in the Ukraine to force collectivization of agriculture and eliminate Ukrainian attempts at self-determination. This action caused the deaths of approximately three to eight million people (Totten, Parsons, & Charny, 1995).

1933–45: The Holocaust (The Jewish Genocide)

The Holocaust was a unique genocide in which the German state and its collaborators planned and carried out the systematic persecution and murder of approximately six million Jewish men, women, and children who were deemed racially inferior. They also targeted other groups for extermination, including Sinti and Roma gypsies, homosexuals, mentally and physically disabled children and adults, Polish intelligentsia and civilians, religious dissidents such as Jehovah's Witnesses, political opponents, and prisoners of war.

1965–6: Indonesia

The Indonesian government slaughtered between two hundred thousand and a half-million members of the Indonesian Communist Party (PKI) and anyone else suspected of being communist (Totten, Parsons, & Charny, 1995). This genocide also had ethnic, religious, and economic overtones (Chalk & Jonassohn, 1990), encompassing many Chinese who were viewed as potential agents of communist China.

1971: Bengalis and Others in East Pakistan

The Pakistani government killed hundreds of thousands Bengalis in Bangladesh (Frank Chalk communication, 1 April 2012). In an attempt to crush forces seeking independence from East Pakistan, the West Pakistani military regime unleashed a well- defined campaign of mass murder which targeted the Bengalis and the Hindu population in East Pakistan.

1971–9: Uganda under Idi Amin

When Idi Amin seized power in Uganda through a military coup in 1971, he created security organizations that reported directly to him. These security forces killed between one and five hundred thousand African Ugandans during his reign of terror. His rule was characterized by human-rights abuses, political repression, and ethnic persecution. In 1972 Amin ordered the expulsion of Uganda's seventy thousand Asian citizens and the expropriation of their property holdings and personal goods.

1972: Hutus and Others in Burundi

The government of Burundi, controlled by minority Tutsi military officers, tried to eliminate the entire population of educated Hutu (Chalk & Jonassohn, 1990). This 'selective genocide' was directed at the educated and semi-educated strata of Hutu society to prevent the possibility of a Hutu 'revolution,' as had happened in neighbouring Rwanda during 1959–61. By killing all potential leaders of the Hutu, these Tutsi officers hoped to guarantee their own power for another decade. The Tutsi massacred between one and two hundred thousand Hutus.

1975: East Timor

Indonesia occupied East Timor from 1975 to 1999. Indonesian rule was marked by extreme violence and brutality. The estimated number of East Timorese who died during the occupation vary between sixty thousand and two hundred thousand (available at http://www.en.wikipedia.org/wiki/East_Timor).

1975–9: Cambodia

Approximately one to three million people were executed, starved, or worked to death by Pol Pot's Khmer Rouge government (Totten, Parsons, & Charny, 1995). Among the groups persecuted were Buddhist monks and ethnic minorities including Chinese, Vietnamese, Thai, and Muslim Cham. As soon as the communist Khmer Rouge regime seized power in April 1995, they evacuated all cities and towns and forced over two million people into unpaid and exhausting agricultural work in the countryside. This new repressive regime abolished currency and money markets, newspapers, private property, and schools. Family life and freedom of movement were also restricted. Thousands of people were systematically murdered in killing fields located in the countryside.

1977–8: 'Red Terror' in Ethiopia

Marxist Colonel Mengistu Haile Mariam and members of his junta – the Dergue – overthrew Ethiopia's emperor Haile Selassie in 1974 and seized power in a bloody coup. Mengistu immediately executed by firing squad approximately sixty senior officials of the emperor's government. In the months that followed, he killed other perceived opponents, including the emperor, members of the royal family, and the head of the dominant Ethiopian Orthodox Church. In 1976 Mengistu instituted his notorious 'Red Terror,' which targeted rival leftist groups. Over a period of two years, thousands of young men and women were rounded up and executed, their bodies tossed in the streets of the capital and other cities.

1988–91: Anfal Campaign against the Kurds in Iraq

The Anfal – meaning 'spoils' in Arabic – was a systematic eight-stage Iraqi government military campaign to eliminate its Kurdish population in the north. The Anfal involved mass executions and disappearances of tens of thousands of Kurdish citizens. Government forces used nerve gas and other chemical weapons to destroy approximately two thousand villages. At least fifty thousand and possibly one hundred thousand Kurdish men, women, and children were killed. Survivors of this deadly campaign were evicted under a policy of 'Arabization' which resettled Iraqi Arabs in homes once owned by Kurds. Hundreds of thousands of villagers were forcibly displaced.

1992–5: Bosnia-Herzegovina (Muslim Genocide)

During the late 1980s and early 1990s, the Socialist Federal Republic of Yugoslavia underwent intense political and economic crisis. Amidst the collapse of communism and the rise of nationalism in Eastern Europe, its central government weakened after the death of Marshall Tito and long-suppressed tensions rose to the surface among the different ethnic groups and religions. Ethnic conflict became acute in Bosnia and Herzegovina, where a shared government reflected the ethnic composition of its population: approximately 43 per cent were Bosnian Muslims, 33 per cent Bosnian Serbs, 17 per cent Bosnian Croats, and 7 per cent other nationalities. After a referendum in March 1992, in which more than 60 per cent of those participating voted for independence, Bosnian Serbs declared a Serb republic in Bosnia and Herzegovina with the support of the neighbouring Yugoslav People's Army, based in Serbia. They immediately asserted control over more than 60 per cent of the country. Bosnian Croats declared their own republic with the backing of Croatia. The conflict escalated into a bloody fight for territories and civilians of all ethnicities became victims of horrendous crimes. More than one hundred thousand people were killed and two million forced to flee their homes. Detention centres for civilians were set up on all sides. Serb and Croat forces performed ethnic cleansing in their territories. Thousands of Bosnian women were systematically raped. The single worst atrocity occurred in the Bosnian town of Srebrenica during the summer of 1995, when Bosnian Serb commander Ratko Mladić and his forces executed more than five thousand Bosnian Muslim men and boys in an act recognized as genocide by the International Criminal Court for Yugoslavia at The Hague. The rest of the town's women and children were driven out. In May 2011 Mladić was arrested in Serbia and extradited to The Hague to stand trial on charges of genocide and war crimes. His trial began in June 2012.

1994: Rwanda (Tutsi Genocide)

In 1994 Rwanda's population numbered seven million, composed of three ethnic groups: Hutu (approximately 85 per cent); Tutsi (14 per cent); and Twa or Batwa (1 per cent). Following the assassination of President Juvénal Habyarimana in April 1994, a Hutu-led extremist government launched a plan to murder the country's entire Tutsi ethnic minority and all politically moderate Hutus. Over a period of one hundred days, Hutu militias carried out mass killings in villages and towns. Local officials and extremist-sponsored radio called on ordinary citizens to kill their neighbours. Those who refused were often murdered as well. Most estimates indicate that between five hundred thousand and one million people were murdered (Frank Chalk communication, 1 April 2012).

1998–2008: Democratic Republic of Congo

Since 1996 the Democratic Republic of Congo (formerly Zaire) has undergone two wars. The first war in 1996 began as a direct result of the 1994 genocide in Rwanda. The Second Congo War, also referred to as Africa's World War, began in 1998 and officially ended in July 2003, though violence continues to this day. It involved the armed forces of seven African countries and multiple militias. In January 2008 the International Rescue Committee reported that an estimated 5.4 million people died between 1998 and 2008; one-half were children under age five. Most of the deaths were caused by preventable and treatable illnesses, and malnutrition. Throughout the conflict, ethnic differences have played a central role in the violence perpetrated against the civilians of eastern Congo. Many civilians have been wounded, killed, forcibly displaced, or conscripted into militias. At least forty thousand women and girls have been raped. In 2008 alone at least one million people were displaced by violence (http://www.ushmm.org/genocide/take_action/atrisk/region/dr-congo/violence).

2003–Present: Darfur, Sudan

The civil war in Sudan's Darfur region began in February 2003. The roots of this conflict between Arab nomadic tribes and mainly African agricultural tribes began with tension over land, water, and grazing rights (Lippman, 2007). This tension gradually turned into a struggle for political dominance, and mass atrocities have occurred along self-ascribed racial lines. The Sudanese government in Khartoum provides financial assistance to the Janjaweed, an Arab-African militia which commits atrocities against non-Arab-African tribes in the region. Hundreds of thousands of people have been murdered and displaced. In March 2009 prosecutors at the International Criminal Court issued an arrest warrant for Sudan's president, Omar al-Bashir, on charges of war crimes and crimes against humanity, adding genocide in 2010. He is accused of implementing a plan to wipe out three tribal groups in Darfur because of their ethnicity. He remains a free man because no country through which he travels will arrest him.

2010–Present: Arab Spring

Since 2010, a wave of demonstrations and resistance against oppressive authoritarian regimes has spread across the Middle East and North Africa. Protests began in Tunisia in December 2010 when Mohamed Bouazizi set himself on fire after police confiscated his vegetable cart because he did not have a permit. Violent protests spread nationwide, toppling Tunisian President Zine El Abidine Ben and ending his more than two decades of authoritarian rule. Encouraged by these events, Egyptians from all walks of life demonstrated and called for the end to President Husseni Mubarak's regime. During his tenure, poverty and political oppression had increased under prolonged martial law, which was enforced by a large security apparatus (http://www.migs.concordia .ca/Media_Monitoring/Egypt.htm). After Mubarak stepped down on 25 January 2012, the Supreme Council of the Armed Forces (SCAF), composed of twenty army generals, ruled the country. In subsequent elections, the Muslim Brotherhood was elected into power, but in July 2013 the Brotherhood government itself was ousted by the army. Discontent spread to Yemen, Bahrain, and Libya. In Libya, an intense civil war erupted that successfully ended Muammar Gaddafi's four-decade regime with his death. The protest movement spread into Syria in January 2012 and erupted into mass protests after children were detained and tortured for allegedly scrawling graffiti on school walls calling for the 'downfall of the regime' (http://www.migs.concordia.ca/ Media_Monitoring/Syria.htm). A violent government crackdown has left thousands dead and tens of thousands detained or displaced. This situation has evolved into a full-scale civil war along ethnic lines.

Appendix B
Raphael Lemkin: A Survivor's Contribution to Society

As I searched through the literature and the Internet for information on genocide, I frequently encountered the name Raphael Lemkin. Most articles refer to him as a 'Polish-Jewish publicist' (Makino, 2001:55); a human-rights campaigner and international jurist (Stone, 2005); or a Polish-Jewish specialist in international law and historian of genocide (Schaller & Zimmerer, 2005). Few articles, however, refer to him as a Holocaust survivor. I discovered that Lemkin was a survivor when I came across an article by Steven Leonard Jacobs (2002), the international editor of Lemkin's papers. So it is fitting that I provide a description of Lemkin's life and work as an example of one survivor's contribution to society.

Raphael Lemkin was born in 1900 on the family farm in Bezwodene, a town in what was then eastern Poland. From an early age he was sensitive to the suffering of others and became interested in the concept of intentional mass murder. In this Lemkin was influenced by Polish author Henryk Sienkiewicz's book *Quo vadis*, which describes the Roman Emperor Nero's barbarity against the Christians. He began to identify 'more and more with the sufferings of the victim' (Jacobs, 2002:102) and studied the history of other attempts to destroy national, religious, and racial groups. This interest led him to study law, pursue a career as a public prosecutor in Warsaw, and write legal texts.

When Germany invaded Poland in 1939, Lemkin joined the underground resistance movement in the country's forests. After six months, he escaped to Sweden. In 1941, with the help of a colleague, he immigrated to the United States by way of Russia and Japan. Lemkin taught at Duke and Yale universities; served as an adviser to the United States government, including its War Department; and, in 1944, published his well-known book *Axis Rule in Occupied Europe*, which presented his theories on genocide.

At the end of the war, Lemkin learned that the Nazis had killed forty-nine members of his family, including his parents. Only his brother survived. Lemkin wrote the following in his unpublished autobiography: 'Soon I transformed my personal disaster into a moral striking force' (Jacobs, 2002). Learning about the murder of his family members in the Holocaust motivated him to launch a campaign for international laws defining and outlawing genocide. In his words: 'Was I not under a moral duty to repay my Mother for having stimulated in me the interest in Genocide? Was it not the best form of gratitude to make a "Genocide pact" as an epitaph on her symbolic grave and as common recognition that she and many millions of others did not die in vain? I redoubled my efforts and found temporary relief from my grief in this work' (Jacobs, 2002:103).

Lemkin honoured the memory of his family and millions of others in a variety of ways. He served as an adviser to Robert H. Jackson, the U.S. Supreme Court justice and Nuremberg trial judge. He coined, defined, and promoted his new word *genocide*, and educated the public on its meaning (Elder, 2005). He became instrumental in persuading the United Nations to adopt the Genocide Convention, which passed in 1948. Subsequently, he lobbied countries to ratify it, and in January 1951 it was adopted. This was the first international law against mass murder of a nation or of an ethnic group. He devoted the rest of his life to educating others about genocide, and also wrote his autobiography and a three-volume *History of Genocide* – both unpublished during his lifetime. He died from a heart attack in 1959.

Raphael Lemkin exemplifies the spirit of many survivors of mass atrocity who persevere, rebuild, and transform personal tragedy into accomplishment and contribution.

Glossary

Aliya Bet: A movement that transported illegal immigrants from the displaced-persons (DP) camps of Europe to Palestine.

Auschwitz: This death camp symbolizes the genocidal horrors of the Holocaust perpetrated by the German Nazi state. Auschwitz I, the main camp, was established in 1940 in the Polish city of Oswiecim. Auschwitz II, the killing centre, was built in Birkenau in 1941. Auschwitz III, also called Monowitz-Buna, was established in 1942 as a slave-labour camp.

Bris: (Yiddish). Referred to in Hebrew as *brit milah*. This circumcision ritual is performed on the eighth day of a male baby's life.

Buchenwald: Established in 1937, it was one of the first and largest concentration camps on German soil. Along with its numerous subcamps, it was an important source of forced labour.

Cheder: (Yiddish). Elementary school with emphasis on religious study.

Chevra Kadisha: (Yiddish). A volunteer organization that cares for the dead.

Chupah: (Yiddish). A canopy held up by four poles, symbolic of the bride and groom living together.

Concentration camp: A facility where inmates were imprisoned (concentrated), usually under harsh conditions. They served primarily as detention and labour centres as well as sites for the murder of targeted groups of people. Some served as transit camps for those en route to an extermination camp.

Displaced-persons (DP) camps: From 1945 to 1952 camps were set up in Germany and Austria, primarily for refugees from Eastern Europe. The majority of the inhabitants, more than two hundred thousand, were Jewish displaced persons. These facilities were administered by Allied authorities and the United Nations Relief and Rehabilitation Administration (UNRRA).

Extermination camp / death camp: Killing centre built for efficient mass murder: to kill systematically large groups of people using methods such as gas chambers and shooting. Bodies were disposed of in crematoria and mass graves. The largest killing centre was Auschwitz-Birkenau. Others were Belzec, Chelmno, Majdanek, Sobibor, and Treblinka.

Final Solution: The code name used by the German bureaucracy for destruction of the Jews. It was coined in 1942 at the Wannsee Conference where Nazi officials made plans for the annihilation of European Jewry.

Gas chambers: Special buildings with sealed chambers where people were killed by poisonous gas. Individuals were deceived into thinking they were going to take showers.

Genocide: Term that refers to crimes committed by governments with the intent to destroy, in whole or in part, a national ethnic, racial, religious, cultural, or political group.

Gestapo: Secret police force of the German Nazi state under SS control. It was responsible for investigating political crimes and activities in opposition to the government. It was notorious for its torturous methods and brutality.

Ghetto: During the Holocaust, Jews were forced into confined areas of a city or town where they were separated and isolated from the rest of the population. Thousands died from overwork as forced slave labour for German war industries, extreme overcrowding, constant hunger and starvation, substandard sanitary conditions, and diseases.

Haskarah: (Hebrew). Commemorative service.

Heim: (Yiddish). Home. Survivors use this term to refer to their pre-war European cities and towns of birth.

Holocaust (The Jewish Genocide): Between 1933 and 1945 the German state and its collaborators planned and carried out the systematic persecution and murder of approximately six million Jewish men, women, and children who were deemed racially inferior. They also targeted other groups for extermination, including Sinti and Roma gypsies; homosexuals; mentally and physically disabled adults, mainly Germans living in institutional settings; Polish intellectuals; religious dissidents such as Jehovah's Witnesses; political opponents; and prisoners of war.

Judenrat: (German). Jewish governing council appointed by the German Nazis. It was responsible for administering the affairs of the community and carrying out German orders.

Kaddish: (Yiddish). Mourner's prayer.

Kashruth: (Hebrew). Jewish dietary law.

Kibbutz (Kibbutzim pl.) (Hebrew). Collective community in Israel.

Labour camp: Concentration camp where inmates did physical labour under inhumane conditions and cruel treatment. Many died from exhaustion, starvation, and exposure. Some of these camps were subcamps of larger ones.

Landsmanschaft (Landsmanschaften pl.): (Yiddish). Organization(s) of people who originated from the same European geographic area.

Mass atrocity crimes: Term used to refer to genocide, crimes against humanity, and war crimes.

Mitsvas: (Yiddish). Good deeds.

Mohel: (Yiddish). Circumciser trained in the principles of surgery and rabbinically recognized.

Non-survivor: Anyone who does not meet the criteria of being a Holocaust survivor (see chapter 3).

Partisans: Men and women who fought in the Jewish resistance movement during the Holocaust.

Pogroms: (Russian). Violent attacks against Jews.

Rosh Hashanah: (Hebrew). Commonly known as the Jewish New Year, it is a time of introspection and reflection. One of the most important observances of this holiday is hearing the shofar, or ram's horn, in the synagogue.

Sabbath: The Jewish holy day which begins Friday night at sunset and ends on Saturday night after sunset.

Selection process: When people arrived at extermination camps, S.S. officials, such as Dr Joseph Mengele, selected who would live or die. Individuals who were unable to work, such as the very young and the very old or sick, were sent to the gas chambers.

She'erith Hapleitah: (Hebrew). Surviving remnant. This term refers to all surviving Jews in Europe, especially those who were in Germany between 1945 and 1949.

Shiva: (Yiddish). Period of mourning that lasts seven days. It is observed by parents, children, spouses, and siblings of the deceased.

Shtetl: (Yiddish). Jewish village in Eastern Europe.

Sonderkommando: Squads of inmates in the extermination camps who removed the corpses from the gas chambers and transferred them to the crematoria for disposal.

SS Schutzstaffel: (German). Elite Nazi soldiers responsible for the administration of the concentration and death camps.

Synagogue: Jewish house of worship.

Tefillin: Phylacteries or amulets encased in leather or wood boxes with straps attached to them. They contain parchment with Hebrew inscriptions. Jewish men strap one box on their head and the other on their left arm during weekday morning prayer.

Tsdakah: (Yiddish). Charity.

Yiddishkeit / Yiddishkayt: (Yiddish). A sense of Jewishness.

Yizker: (Hebrew for remembrance). Memorial prayer.

Yizker bicher: (Yiddish). Memorial books written by Holocaust survivors after
the war, which contain historical and personal accounts of Jewish life in
their pre-war cities and towns. They also contain information about their
war experiences as well as their post-war adjustment.

Yom Kippur: (Hebrew). Day of Atonement. A day set aside for fasting, depriv-
ing oneself of pleasures, and repenting for sins of the previous year.

References

Aarts, P., Op den Velde, W., Falger, P., Hovens, J., De Groen, J., & Van Duijn, H. (1996). Late onset of posttraumatic stress disorder in aging resistance veterans in the Netherlands. In P.E. Ruskin & John A. Talbott (Eds.), *Aging and posttraumatic stress disorder* (53–76).Washington: American Psychiatric Press.

Abella, I., & Troper, H. (1982). *None is too many: Canada and the Jews of Europe, 1933–1948*. Toronto: Lester & Orpen Dennys.

Action Reconciliation Service for Peace (ARSP). *Brochure*. Berlin. www.asf-ev.de

Almedom, A.M. (2005). Resilience, hardiness, sense of coherence, and post-traumatic growth: All paths leading to 'light at the end of the tunnel.' *Journal of Loss and Trauma, 10*(3), 253–65. http://dx.doi.org/10.1080/15325020590928216

American Gathering The Jewish Week. (1983, April). Ten opinions on who is a survivor, p. 14.

American Psychiatric Association (2000). *Diagnostic and statistical manual of mental disorders* (4th ed. DSM-IV-TR, text revision). Washington, DC: Author.

Antonovsky, A. (1993, Mar). The structure and properties of the sense of coherence scale. *Social Science Medicine, 36*(6), 725–33. http://dx.doi.org/10.1016/0277-9536(93)90033-Z Medline:8480217

Armour, M. (2010). Meaning making in survivorship: Application to Holocaust survivors. *Journal of Human Behavior in the Social Environment, 20*(4), 440–68. http://dx.doi.org/10.1080/10911350903274997

Article (2010, Jan). Evolution of international Holocaust day reflects changing times. Montreal: *Canadian Jewish News*.

Atwater, W.E. (1986). *Human relations*. Englewood Cliffs, N.J: Prentice Hall.

Ayalon, L. (2005). Challenges associated with the study of resilience to trauma in Holocaust survivors. *Journal of Loss and Trauma, 10*(4), 347–58. http://dx.doi.org/10.1080/15325020590956774

Ayalon, L., Perry, C., Arean, P.A., & Horowitz, M.J. (2007). Making sense of the past – perspectives on resilience among Holocaust survivors. *Journal of Loss and Trauma, 12*(3), 281–93. http://dx.doi.org/10.1080/15325020701274726

Bandura, A. (1977, Mar). Self-efficacy: Toward a unifying theory of behavioral change. *Psychological Review, 84*(2), 191–215. http://dx.doi.org/10.1037/0033-295X.84.2.191 Medline:847061

Bar-Tur, L., & Levy-Shiff, R. (1994). Holocaust review and bearing witness as a coping mechanism of an elderly Holocaust survivor. In T.L. Brink (Ed.), *Holocaust Survivors' Mental Health* (5–16). New York: The Haworth Press. http://dx.doi.org/10.1300/J018v14n03_02

Baskerville, B. (1909). *The Polish Jew: His social and economic value*. London: Chapman and Hall.

Behrman, G., & Tebb, S. (2009). The use of complementary and alternative interventions as a holistic approach with older adults. *Journal of Religion & Spirituality in Social Work, 28*(1–2), 127–40. http://dx.doi.org/10.1080/15426430802644156

Benson, H., & Proctor, J.D. (2010). *Relaxation revolution: Enhancing your personal health through the science and genetics of mind body healing*. New York: Scribner.

Berenbaum, M. (1999). The uniqueness and universality of the Holocaust. In I. Charny (Ed.), *Encyclopedia of genocide* (Vol. II, 568–9). CA: ABC-CLIO.

Bermant, C. (1974). *The walled garden: The sage of Jewish family life and tradition*. New York: Macmillan Publishing.

Brandler, S. (2000). Practice issues: Understanding aged Holocaust survivors. *Families in Society, 81*(1), 66–75.

Brodsky Cohen, B. (1991). Holocaust survivors and the crisis of aging. *Families in Society: The Journal of Contemporary Human Services, 72*(4), 226–32.

Brom, D., Durst, N., & Aghassy, G. (2002). The phenomenology of post-traumatic distress in older adult Holocaust survivors. *Journal of Clinical Geropsychology, 8*(3), 189–201. http://dx.doi.org/10.1023/A:1015944227382

Bussey, M. (2007). Transforming trauma through empowerment and resilience. In M. Bussey & J.B. Wise (Eds.), *Trauma transformed: An empowerment approach* (300–9). New York: Columbia University Press.

Byington, D. (2007). Transforming childhood physical and verbal abuse: Mind-body approaches to trauma treatment. In M. Bussey & J.B. Wise (Eds.), *Trauma transformed: An empowerment approach* (77–95). New York: Columbia University Press.

Calhoun, L.G. & Tedeschi, R.G. (Eds.). (2006). *Handbook of posttraumatic growth: Research and practice*. New Jersey: Lawrence Erlbaum.

Canadian Association of Social Workers (CASW) (2005). Guidelines for ethical practice. Retrieved 12 November 2012 from http://www.casw-acts.ca/

Carmelly, F. (1975). Guilt feelings in concentration camp survivors: Comments of a 'survivor.' *Journal of Jewish Communal Service, 52*(2), 139–44.

Cassel, L., & Suedfeld, P. (2006). Salutogenesis and autobiographical disclosure among Holocaust survivors. *Journal of Positive Psychology, 1*(4), 212–25. http://dx.doi.org/10.1080/17439760600952919

Chalk, F., Dallaire, R., Matthews, K., Barqueiro, C., & Doyle, S. (2010). *Mobilizing the will to intervene: Leadership to prevent mass atrocities.* Montreal: McGill-Queen's University Press.

Chalk, F. & Jonassohn, K. (Eds.). (1990). *The history and sociology of genocide.* Montreal Institute for Genocide Studies and Yale University Press.

Chang, H. (2008). *Autoethnography as method.* Walnut Creek, CA: Left Coast Press.

Charny, I.W. (1999). *Encyclopedia of genocide, Vols. 1 & 2.* Santa Barbara: ABC-CLIO.

Chodoff, P. (1981, Sep-Oct). Survivors of the Nazi holocaust. *Children Today, 10*(5), 2–5. Medline:7026184

Claims Conference (2001). History of the Claims Conference: A chronology 1951–2001. New York: The Conference on Jewish Material Claims Against Germany.

Claims Conference (2007–8). Annual report. New York.

Claims Conference (2010). Worldbook 2010: A guide to Claims Conference programs worldwide. New York: Claims Conference.

Cohen, H.L., Meek, K., & Lieberman, M. (2010). Memory and resilience. *Journal of Human Behavior in the Social Environment, 20*(4), 525–41. http://dx.doi.org/10.1080/10911350903275309

Cohen, J. (1977). The impact of death and dying on concentration camp survivors. *Advances in Thanology, 4*(1), 27–36.

Colerick Clipp, E., & Elder, G.H. (1996). The aging veteran of World War II. In P.E. Ruskin & John A. Talbott (Eds.), *Aging and posttraumatic stress disorder* (19–51). Washington: American Psychiatric Press.

Cook, J.M. (2002). Traumatic exposure and PTSD in older adults: Introduction to the special issue. *Journal of Clinical Geropsychology, 8*(3), 149–52. http://dx.doi.org/10.1023/A:1015997209635

Courtois, C.A., & Ford, J.D. (2009). Defining and understanding complex trauma and complex traumatic stress disorders. In C.A. Courtois & J.D. Ford (Eds.), *Treating complex traumatic stress disorders: An evidence-based guide* (13–30). New York: Guilford Press.

Courtois, C.A., Ford, J.D., & Cloitre, M. (2009). Best practices in psychotherapy for adults. In C.A. Courtois & J.D. Ford (Eds.), *Treating complex traumatic stress disorders: An evidence-based guide* (82–103). New York: Guilford Press.

Cox, E.O., & Parsons, R.J. (1994). *Empowerment-oriented social work practice with the elderly*. California: Brooks/Cole Publishing Company.

Craig, G. (2002). *The manual: Emotional freedom techniques*. Retrieved 2002 from www.emofree.com.

Danieli, Y. (1981). The aging survivor of the Holocaust: Discussion on the achievement of integration in aging survivors of the Nazi Holocaust. In D. Blau & R.J. Kahana (Eds.), *Journal of Geriatric Psychiatry, X1V(2)* (191–210). New York: International Universities Press.

Danieli, Y. (1981a, Sep-Oct). Differing adaptational styles in families of survivors of the Nazi holocaust. *Children Today, 10*(5), 6–10, 34–5. Medline:7026185

Danieli, Y. (1988). Confronting the unimaginable: Psychotherapists' reactions to the victims of the Nazi Holocaust. In J.P. Wilson, Z. Harel, & B. Kahana (Eds.), *Human adaptation to extreme stress: From the Holocaust to Vietnam* (219–38). New York, N.Y: Plenum Press.

Danieli, Y. (1994a Winter). As survivors age: Part I. *NC-PTSD Clinical Quarterly, 4*(1), 1; 3–7.

Danieli, Y. (1994b, Spring). As survivors age: Part II. *NC-PTSD Clinical Quarterly, 4*(2), 20–4.

Danieli, Y. (Ed.). (1998). *International handbook of multigenerational legacies of trauma*. New York, N.Y: Plenum. http://dx.doi.org/10.1007/978-1-4757-5567-1

Danieli, Y. (1999). Healing components: The right to reparation for victims of gross violations of human rights and humanitarian law. In M. Hayes, D. Pollefeyt, & G.J. Colijn (Eds.), *Hearing the voices: Teaching the Holocaust to future generations* (219–33). Pennsylvania: Merion Westfield International Press.

Dasberg, H. (1995). AMCHA: The national Israeli center for psychosocial support of Holocaust survivors and the second generation: Raison d'etre. In J. Lemberger (Ed.), *A global perspective on working with Holocaust survivors and the second generation* (1–9). JDC- Brookdale Institute of Gerontology and Human Development, AMCHA and JDC Israel.

David, P. (2002). *Aging survivors of the Holocaust in long term care: Unique needs, unique responses. Journal of Social Work in Long Term Care, 1(3)*. New York, N.Y: The Haworth Press.

David, P., & Pelly, S. (2003). *Caring for aging Holocaust survivors: A practice manual*. Toronto: Baycrest Centre for Geriatric Care.

Dawidowicz, L. (1975). *The war against the Jews, 1933–1945*. New York: Penguin Books.

Des Pres, T. (1976). *The survivor: An anatomy of life in the death camps*. New York: Pocket Books.

Dobroszycki, L., & Kirshenblatt-Gimlett, B. (1977). *Image before my eyes*. New York: Schocken.

Doty, R.L. (2010). Autoethnography – making human connections. *Review of International Studies, 36*(04), 1047–50. http://dx.doi.org/10.1017/S026021051000118X

Edelstein, E.L. (1981). Reactivation of concentration camp experiences as a result of hospitalization. In C.D. Speilberger, I.G. Sarason, & N.A. Milgram (Eds.), *Stress and anxiety* (401–4). New York: McGraw-Hill, Hemisphere.

Ehrlich, M.A. (2004, May-Jun). Health professionals, Jewish religion and community structure in the service of the aging holocaust survivor. *Archives of Gerontology and Geriatrics, 38*(3), 289–95. http://dx.doi.org/10.1016/j.archger.2003.12.002 Medline:15066315

Ehrlich, P. (1988). Treatment issues in the psychotherapy of Holocaust survivors. In J. Wilson, Z. Harel, & B. Kahana (Eds.), *Human adaptation to extreme stress: From the Holocaust to Vietnam* (285–303). New York: Plenum.

Eitinger, L. (1980). The concentration camp syndrome and its late sequelae. In J.E. Dimsdale (Ed.), *Survivors, victims and perpetrators* (127–62). Washington: Hemisphere.

Eitinger, L. (1981). Studies on concentration camp survivors: The Norwegian and global contexts. *Journal of Psychology and Judaism, 6*(1), 23–32.

Elder, T. (2005). What you see before your eyes: Documenting Raphael Lemkin's life by exploring his archival papers, 1900–1959. *Journal of Genocide Research, 7*(4), 469–99. http://dx.doi.org/10.1080/14623520500349910

Ellis, C. (2004). *The ethnographic I: A methodological novel about autoethnography.* Walnut Creek, CA: AltaMira Press.

Epstein, H. (1979). *Children of the Holocaust: Conversations with sons and daughters of survivors.* New York: G.P. Putnam's Sons.

Fackler, G. (2011). Music and the Holocaust. Retrieved 4 September 2011 from http://holocaustmusic.ort.org/places/camps/

Farmer, R. (2009). *Neuroscience and social work practice: The missing link.* Thousand Oaks, CA: Sage Publications.

Federber-Salz, B. (1980). *And the sun kept shining.* New York: Holocaust Library.

Feinstein, D. (2008, Jun). Energy psychology: A review of the preliminary evidence. *Psychotherapy (Chicago, Ill.), 45*(2), 199–213. http://dx.doi.org/10.1037/0033-3204.45.2.199 Medline:22122417

Feinstein, D. (2010a, Sep). Rapid treatment of PTSD: Why psychological exposure with acupoint tapping may be effective. *Psychotherapy (Chicago, Ill.), 47*(3), 385–402. http://dx.doi.org/10.1037/a0021171 Medline:22402094

Feinstein, D. (Nov/Dec 2010b). The case for energy psychology. *Psychotherapy Networker.*

Feinstein, D., Eden, D., & Craig, G. (2005). *The promise of energy psychology.* New York: Penguin Group.

Figley, C.R. (Ed.). (1995). *Compassion fatigue: Coping with secondary traumatic stress disorder in those who treat the traumatized*. New York: Brunner/Mazel.

Finger, W., & Arnold, E.M. (2002). Mind-body interventions: applications for social work practice. *Social Work in Health Care, 35*(4), 57–78. http://dx.doi .org/10.1300/J010v35n04_04 Medline:12425450

Fisher, J., & Ogden, P. (2009). Sensorimotor psychotherapy. In C.A. Courtois & J.D. Ford (Eds.), *Treating complex traumatic stress disorders: An evidence-based guide* (312–28). New York: Guilford Press.

Foa, E.B., Keane, T.M., & Friedman, M.J. (2000). *Effective treatments for PTSD. Practice guidelines from the International Society for Traumatic Stress Studies*. New York, NY: Guilford.

Fogelman, E. (1988). Therapeutic alternatives for Holocaust survivors and Second Generation. In R.L. Brahm (Ed.), *The psychological perspectives of the Holocaust and of its aftermath* (79–108). New York: Columbia University Press.

Fogelman, E. (1990). Survivor-victims of war and Holocaust. In D. Leviton (Ed.), *Horrendous death and health: Toward action* (7–45). New York: Hemisphere Publishing Corporation.

Fried, H., & Waxman, H.M. (1988, Apr). Stockholm's Cafe 84: A unique day program for Jewish survivors of concentration camps. *Gerontologist, 28*(2), 253–5. http://dx.doi.org/10.1093/geront/28.2.253 Medline:3360370

Gelbart, V., & Giberovitch, M. (Eds.) (2006). *Preserving our memories: Passing on the legacy*. Victoria, B.C: Trafford Publishing.

Geller, J.H. (2005). *Jews in post-Holocaust Germany, 1945–1953*. U.K: Cambridge University Press.

Gerdes, K.E., & Segal, E. (2011, Apr). Importance of empathy for social work practice: Integrating new science. *Social Work, 56*(2), 141–8. http://dx.doi .org/10.1093/sw/56.2.141 Medline:21553577

Giberovitch, M. (1988). The contributions of Montreal Holocaust survivor organizations to Jewish communal life. Master's thesis. McGill University, Montreal.

Giberovitch, M. (1994). The contributions of Holocaust survivors to Montreal Jewish communal life. *Canadian Ethnic Studies, 26*(1), 74–85.

Giberovitch, M. (1995). Social work practice with aging survivors. In J. Lemberger (Ed.), *A global perspective on working with Holocaust survivors and the Second Generation* (277–28). JDC-Brookdale Institute of Gerontology and Human Development, AMCHA and JDC- Israel.

Giberovitch, M. (1999). A proposal for a service network for Holocaust survivors. *Journal of Jewish Communal Service, 75*(4), 273–81.

Giberovitch, M. (2006). A Drop-in Centre for Holocaust Survivors: Inspiring, hope, meaning, and purpose. *Journal of Jewish Communal Service, 81*(3/4), 239–47.

Glicksman, W. (1966). *In the mirror of literature: The economic life of the Jews in Poland as reflected in Yiddish literature, 1914–1939*. New York: Living Books.

Grachnik, F. (1996). *Personal memoir*. Montreal.

Graziano, R. (2003). Trauma and aging. *Journal of Gerontological Social Work, 40*(4), 3–21. http://dx.doi.org/10.1300/J083v40n04_02

Greene, R.R. (2002). Holocaust survivors: A study in resilience. *Journal of Gerontological Social Work, 37*(1), 3–18. http://dx.doi.org/10.1300/J083v37n01_02

Greene, R.R. (2010). Holocaust survivors: Resilience revisited. *Journal of Human Behavior in the Social Environment, 20*(4), 411–22. http://dx.doi.org/10.1080/10911350903269963

Greene, R.R., & Graham, S.A. (2009, Jan-Mar). Role of resilience among Nazi Holocaust survivors: A strength-based paradigm for understanding survivorship. *Family & Community Health, 32*(1 Suppl), S75–S82. http://dx.doi.org/10.1097/01.FCH.0000342842.51348.83 Medline:19065097

Gross, B. (1994). Painful memories: Understanding the special needs of aging Holocaust survivors: *Discussion guide*. A project of Menorah Park Center for the Aging, Cleveland, Ohio.

Gulliford, M., Naithani, S., & Morgan, M. (2006, Oct). What is 'continuity of care'? *Journal of Health Services Research & Policy, 11*(4), 248–50. http://dx.doi.org/10.1258/135581906778476490 Medline:17018200

Gutiérrez, L.M., Parsons, R.J., & Cox, E.O. (1998). Creating opportunities for empowerment-oriented programs. In L.M. Gutierrez, R.J. Parsons, & E.O. Cox (Eds.), *Empowerment in social work practice: A sourcebook* (220–3). Pacific Grove, CA: Brooks/Cole.

Guttmann, D. (1995). Meaningful aging: Establishing a club for survivors of the Holocaust in Hungary. In J. Lemberger (Ed.), *A global perspective on working with Holocaust survivors and the Second Generation* (259–67). JDC-Brookdale Institute of Gerontology and Human Development, AMCHA and JDC-Israel.

Hamburg, D.A. (1980). Forward. In J.E. Dimsdale (Ed.), *Survivors, victims and perpetrators* (xiii–xv). Washington: Hemisphere.

Hammersley, M., & Atkinson, P. (2007). *Ethnography: Principles in practice* (3rd ed.). New York: Routledge.

Hartman, A. (1997). Working with survivors of the Holocaust/Nazi persecution. *Program handout*. Hineinu, a joint program of Council for Jewish Elderly and Jewish Family and Community Service.

Hartman-Luban, A. (1999). Reaching those who need to know: A model for training professionals and para-professionals in our communities. In P. David & J. Goldhar (Eds.), *Selected papers from A Time to Heal: Caring for the Aging Holocaust Survivor* (349–51). Toronto: Baycrest Centre for Geriatric Care.

Hass, A. (1990). *In the shadow of the Holocaust: The Second Generation*. New York: Cornel University Press.

Hassan, J. (1995). Individual counseling techniques with Holocaust survivors. In J. Lemberger (Ed.), *A global perspective on working with Holocaust survivors and the Second Generation* (185–203). JDC Brookdale Institute of Gerontology and Human Development, AMCHA and JDC-Israel.

Hassan, J. (1997). From victim to survivor: The possibility of healing in ageing survivors of the Nazi Holocaust. In L. Hunt, M. Marshall, & C. Rowlings (Eds.), *Past trauma in late life: European perspectives on therapeutic work with older people* (122–35). London: Jessica Kingsley Publishers.

Hassan, J. (2003). *A house next door to trauma: Learning from Holocaust survivors how to respond to atrocity*. London: Jessica Kingsley Publishers.

Heller, C.S. (1977). *On the edge of destruction: Jews of Poland between the two world wars*. New York: Columbia University Press.

Helmreich, W.B. (1987). Research report: Postwar adaptation of Holocaust survivors in the United States. *Holocaust and Genocide Studies*, 2(2), 307–15. http://dx.doi.org/10.1093/hgs/2.2.307

Helmreich, W.B. (1988). The impact of the Holocaust survivors on American society: A socio-cultural portrait. *Proceedings of the International Scholar's Conference: Remembering for the future: Jews and Christians during and after the Holocaust* (theme 1, 363–84). Oxford: Pergamon Press.

Helmreich, W.B. (1992). *Against all odds: Holocaust survivors and the successful lives they made in America*. New York: Simon & Shuster.

Herman, J.L. (1992). *Trauma and recovery*. New York: Basic Books.

Hirschfeld, M.J. (1977, Jul). Care of the aging holocaust survivor. *The American Journal of Nursing*, 77(7), 1187–9. Medline:587018

Hitchcock, R., & Totten, S. (2009). (Eds.), Editors' introduction. *Genocide Studies and Prevention*, 4(1), 1–7.

Hofrichter, R. (1992). Enhancing communication: triggers, words and re-sources. In R.E. Kenigsberg & C.M. Lieblish (Eds.), *The first national conference on identification, treatment and care of the aging Holocaust survivor: Selected proceedings* (58–63). The Holocaust Documentation and Education Center, Inc. & Southeast Florida Center on Aging, Florida International University.

Hollander-Goldfein, B., Isserman, N., & Goldenberg, J. (2012). *Transcending trauma: Survival, resilience, and clinical implications in survivor families*. New York: Routledge Taylor & Francis Group.

Hoppe, K.N. (1971). The aftermath of Nazi persecution reflected in recent psychiatric literature. In K. Krystal & W.G. Niederland (Eds.), *Psychic trau-matization: Aftereffects in individuals and communities* (169–204). Boston: Little, Brown.

Jacobs, S.L. (2002). Genesis of the concept of genocide according to its author from the original sources. *Human Rights Review*, 3(2), 98–103. http://dx.doi .org/10.1007/s12142-002-1008-z

Jewish General Hospital, Division of Geriatric Medicine (2011). Retrieved 17 September 2011 from http://205.237.250.153/SITES/003-09-geriatrics/ index.asp?LOCK=&M=1&C=1&DB=024_003-09-geriatrics&L=E&MINI=

Kabat-Zinn, J. (1994). *Wherever you go, there you are: Mindfulness meditation in everyday life*. New York: Hyperion.

Kahana, B., Harel, Z., & Kahana, E. (1988). Predictors of psychological well-being among survivors of the Holocaust. In J. Wilson, Z. Harel, & B. Kahana (Eds.), *Human adaptation to extreme stress: From the Holocaust to Vietnam* (171–92). New York: Plenum.

Kahana, B., Harel, Z., & Kahana, E. (2005). *Holocaust survivors and immigrants: Late life adaptations*. New York: The Plenum Series on Stress and Coping, Springer. http://dx.doi.org/10.1007/b100253

Kahana, E., Kahana, B., Harel, Z., & Rosner, T. (1988). Coping with extreme trauma. In J. Wilson, Z. Harel, & B. Kahana (Eds.), (1988). *Human adaptation to extreme stress: From the Holocaust to Vietnam*, (55–79). New York: Plenum Press.

Kaminsky, P., & Katz, R. (1994). *Flower essence repertory: A comprehensive guide to North American and English flower essences for emotional and spiritual well-being*. Nevada: The Flower Essence Society.

Kellerman, N. P. F. (2009). *Holocaust trauma: Psychological effects and treatment*. New York: iUniverse, Inc.

Kellner, R., Neidhardt, J., Krakow, B., & Pathak, D. (1992, May). Changes n chronic nightmares after one session of desensitization or rehearsal instructions. *American Journal of Psychiatry*, 149(5), 659–63. Medline:1349459

Kenigsberg, R.E., & Lieblich, C.M. (Eds.) (1992). *The first national conference on identification, treatment and care of the aging Holocaust survivor: Selected proceedings*. The Holocaust Documentation and Education Center, Inc. & Southeast Florida Center on Aging, Florida International University.

Kinsler, F. (1995). The emotional and physiologic issues of aging in North American Holocaust survivors. In J. Lemberger (Ed.), *A global perspective on working with Holocaust survivors and the Second Generation* (277–88). JDC-Brookdale Institute of Gerontology and Human Development, AMCHA and JDC- Israel.

Kisthardt, W.E. (2006). The opportunities and challenges of strengths-based, person-centered practice. In D. Saleebey (Ed.), *The strengths perspective in social work practice* (4th ed., 171–96). Boston: Pearson Education.

Klein, H., & Reinharz, W. (1972). Adaptation in the kibbutz of Holocaust
    survivors and their families. In L. Miller (Ed.), *Mental health in rapid social
    change* (302–19). Jerusalem: Academic Press.

Kobasa, S.C., Maddi, S.R., & Kahn, S. (1982, Jan). Hardiness and health: A
    prospective study. *Journal of Personality and Social Psychology*, 42(1), 168–77.
    http://dx.doi.org/10.1037/0022-3514.42.1.168 Medline:7057354

Konigseder, A., & Wetzel, J. (2001). *Waiting for hope: Jewish displaced persons in
    post-World War II Germany.* Evanston, Ill: Northwestern University Press.
    Translated from German by John A. Broadwin.

Krantiz-Sanders, L. (1984). *Twelve who survived: An oral history of the Jews of
    Lodz, Poland, 1930–1954.* New York: Irvington Publishers.

Krell, R. (1989). Alternative therapeutic approaches to Holocaust survivors.
    In P. Marcus & A. Rosenberg (Eds.), *Healing their wounds: Psychotherapy with
    Holocaust survivors and their families* (215–26). New York: Praeger.

Krell, R. (1992). Aging Holocaust survivors: Memory, nostalgia and treatment
    issues. In R.E. Kenigsberg & C.M. Lieblish (Eds.), *The first national conference
    on identification, treatment and care of the aging Holocaust survivor: Selected pro-
    ceedings* (22–31). The Holocaust Documentation and Education Center, Inc.
    & Southeast Florida Center on Aging, Florida International University.

Kren, G.M. (1989). The Holocaust survivor and psychoanalysis. In P. Marcus
    & A. Rosenberg (Eds.), *Healing their wounds: Psychotherapy with Holocaust
    survivors and their families* (3–21). New York: Praeger.

Krystal, H., & Niederland, W. (1968). Clinical observations on the survivor
    syndrome. In H. Krystal (Ed.), *Massive psychic trauma* (327–48). New York:
    International Universities Press.

Kurtz, R. (1990). *Body-centered psychotherapy: The Hakomi method.* CA: LifeRhythm.

Lapp, L.K., Abokou, C., & Ferreri, F. (2011, Mar 22). PTSD in the elderly:
    The interaction between trauma and aging. *International Psychogeriatrics/
    IPA*, 23(6), 1–11 (858-68). http://dx.doi.org/10.1017/S1041610211000366
    Medline:21418726

Laufer, R. (1988). The serial self: War trauma, identity, and adult development.
    In J.P. Wilson, Z. Harel, & B. Kahana, B. (Eds.), *Human adaptation to extreme
    stress: From the Holocaust to Vietnam* (33–53). New York: Plenum Press.

Lavsky, H. (2002). *New beginnings: Holocaust survivors in Bergen-Belsen and the
    British Zone in Germany, 1945–1950.* Detroit, MI: Wayne State University
    Press.

Leon, G.R., Butcher, J.N., Kleinman, M., Goldberg, A., & Almagor, M. (1981,
    Sep). Survivors of the holocaust and their children: Current status and
    adjustment. *Journal of Personality and Social Psychology*, 41(3), 503–16. http://
    dx.doi.org/10.1037/0022-3514.41.3.503 Medline:7288564

Lestchinsky, J. (1946). The Jews in the cities of the Republic of Poland. In *Yivo Annual of Jewish Social Science*, Vol. 1.

Lestchinsky, J. (1947). Economic aspects of Jewish community organization in independent Poland. *Jewish Social Studies, 9*(4), 334 (319–38).

Lev-Wiesel, R., & Amir, M. (2003). Posttraumatic growth among Holocaust child survivors. *Journal of Loss and Trauma, 8*(4), 229–37. http://dx.doi .org/10.1080/15325020305884

Levene, M. (2000). Why is the twentieth century the century of genocide? *Journal of World History, 11*(2), 305–36. http://dx.doi.org/10.1353/ jwh.2000.0044

Levine, P. (1997). *Waking the tiger: Healing trauma*. CA: North Atlantic Books.

Liberation of the Nazi concentration camps (1981). *Booklet: For the dead and living we must bear witness*. U.S. Holocaust Memorial Council from the International Liberators' Conference.

Lichtenberg, J., & Shapard, B. (2000). Hatred and its rewards. *Psychoanalytic Inquiry, 20*(3), 9–12.

Lifton, R.J. (1968). Observations on Hiroshima survivors. In H. Krystal (Ed.), *Massive psychic trauma* (168–89). New York: International Universities Press.

Lifton, R.J. (1988). Understanding the traumatized self. In J.P. Wilson, Z. Harel, & B. Kahana, (Eds.), *Human adaptation to extreme stress: From the Holocaust to Vietnam* (7–31). New York: Plenum Press.

Lindenfield, G. (1993). *Managing anger*. San Francisco, CA: Thorsons.

Lippman, M. (2007). Abstracts: Darfur: The politics of genocide denial syndrome. *Journal of Genocide Research, 9*(2), 179–82. http://dx.doi.org/10.1080/ 14623520701368594

Lipstein, E. (2005). *An intergenerational experience with Holocaust survivors and the grade 6 students of United Talmud Torahs-Snowdon. Manual of poetry and prose*. Montreal: United Talmud Torahs- Snowdon.

Litz, B.T., Blake, D.D., Gerardi, R.J., & Keane, T.M. (1990). Decision-making guidelines for the use of direct exposure in the treatment of post-traumatic stress disorder. *Behavior Therapist, 13*, 91–3.

Makino, V. (2001). Final solutions, crimes against mankind: On the genesis and criticism of the concept of genocide. *Journal of Genocide Research, 3*(1), 49–73. http://dx.doi.org/10.1080/14623520120037707

Mankowitz, Z. (2002). *Life between memory and hope: The survivors of the Holocaust in occupied Germany*. U.K: Cambridge University Press. http:// dx.doi.org/10.1017/CBO9780511497100

Marcus, E.L., & Menczel, J. (2007, Nov). Higher prevalence of osteoporosis among female Holocaust survivors. *Osteoporos International, 18*(11), 1501–6. http://dx.doi.org/10.1007/s00198-007-0389-x Medline:17492392

Marcus, J. (1983). *Social and political history of the Jews in Poland, 1919–1939*. New York: Mouton Publishers. http://dx.doi.org/10.1515/9783110838688

Marcus, J.R. & Peck, A.L. (Eds.). (1982). *Among the survivors of the Holocaust – 1945: The Landsberg DP camps letters of Major Irving Heymont, United States Army (Monograph No. 10)*. Cincinnati: American Jewish Archives.

Matussek, P. (1975). *Internment in concentration camps and its consequences*. New York: Springer-Verlag. http://dx.doi.org/10.1007/978-3-642-66075-7

McInnis-Dittrich, K. (2009). *Social work with older adults* (3rd ed.). Boston: Pearson Education.

McPherson, B.D. (1983). *Aging as a social process*. Toronto: Butterworth & Co. Ltd.

Meichenbaum, D. (1994). *A clinical handbook/practical therapist manual: For assessing and treating adults with post-traumatic stress disorder (PTSD)*. Waterloo: Institute Press.

Melendez, P., Maramaldi, P., & Naleppa, M.J. (2008). Late adulthood. In E.D. Hutchison (Ed.), *Dimensions of human behaviour: The changing life course* (3rd ed., 386–413). Thousand Oaks, CA: Sage Publications.

Meltzer, M. (1976). *World of our fathers: The Jews of Eastern Europe*. New York: Dell.

Mendelsohn, E. (1983). *The Jews of East and Central Europe between the world wars*. Bloomington: Indiana University Press.

Mollica, R. (2006). *Healing invisible wounds*. Orlando, FL: Harcourt.

Naparstek, B. (2004). *Invisible heroes: Survivors of trauma and how they heal*. New York: Bantam Books.

Nelson-Becker, H., Chapin, R., & Fast, B. (2006). The strengths model with older adults. In D. Saleebey (Ed.), *The strengths perspective in social work practice* (4th ed., 148–69). Boston: Pearson Education.

Never Again (Summer 2009). *A newsletter for and by Holocaust survivors*, 8(4). Drop-in Centre for Holocaust Survivors, Cummings Jewish Centre for Seniors.

Never Again (Fall, 2010). *A newsletter for and by Holocaust survivors*, 10(1). Drop-in Centre for Holocaust Survivors, Cummings Jewish Centre for Seniors.

Never Again (Summer/Fall 2012). *A newsletter for and by Holocaust survivors*, 11(1). Drop-in Centre for Holocaust Survivors, Cummings Jewish Centre for Seniors.

Ochberg, F.M. (1993). Posttraumatic therapy. In J.P. Wilson & B. Raphael (Eds.), *International handbook of traumatic stress syndromes* (773–83). New York: Plenum Press. http://dx.doi.org/10.1007/978-1-4615-2820-3_65

Ordre professionnel des travailleurs sociaux et des thérapeutes conjugaux et familiaux du Québec [l'OTSTCFQ]. Retrieved 12 November 2012 from http://www2.publicationsduquebec.gouv.qc.ca/dynamicSearch/telecharge.php?type=3&file=/C_26/C26R286_A.HTM

Pearsall, P. (1996). *The pleasure prescription*. CA: Hunter House.

Pennebaker, J. (1990). *Opening up: The healing power of confiding in others*. New York: William Morrow and Company.

Porter, J.N. (1981). Is there a survivor's syndrome? Psychological and socio-political implications. *Journal of Psychology and Judaism, 6*(1), 33–52.

Rabinowitz, D. (1979). *About the Holocaust: What we know and how we know it*. New York: Institute of Human Relations Press of the American Jewish Committee.

Rankin, P. (2006/2007). Exploring and describing the strength/empowerment perspective in social work. *IUC Journal of Social Work: Theory and Practice.* Retrieved 12 October 2011 from http://www.bemidjistate.edu/academics/publications/social_work_journal/issue14/articles/rankin.htm.

Rosenberg, L. (1957). *Russian and Polish Jews in Canada. Golden Jubilee Souvenir Book 1907–1957*. Montreal: Russian Polish Hebrew Sick Benefit Association.

Rosenbloom, M. (1983). Implications of the Holocaust for social work. *Social Casework, 64*(4), 205–12.

Rosenbloom, M. (1985). The Holocaust survivor in late life. *Journal of Gerontological Social Work, 8*(3–4), 181–91. http://dx.doi.org/10.1300/J083V08N03_12

Rosenfarb, C. (1985). *The tree of life*. Melbourne: Scribe Publications.

Rothschild, B. (2000). *The body remembers: The psychophysiology of trauma and trauma treatment*. New York: W.W. Norton & Company.

Rothschild, B. (2003). *The body remembers: Casebook unifying methods and models in the treatment of trauma and PTSD*. New York: W.W. Norton & Company.

Rothschild, B. (2006). *Help for the Helper: The psychophysiology of compassion fatigue and vicarious trauma*. New York: W.W. Norton & Company.

Russell, A. (1980). Late effects: Influence on the children of the concentration camp survivor. In J.E. Dimsdale (Ed.), *Survivors, victims and perpetrators* (175–204). Washington: Hemisphere.

Saakvitne, K.W., & Pearlman, L.A. (1996). *Transforming the pain*. New York: Norton & Company.

Safford, F. (1995). Aging stressors for Holocaust survivors and their families. *Journal of Gerontological Social Work, 24*(1–2), 131–53. http://dx.doi.org/10.1300/J083V24N01_10

Saleebey, D. (1996, May). The strengths perspective in social work practice: Extensions and cautions. *Social Work, 41*(3), 296–305. Medline:8936085

Saleebey, D. (2006). Introduction: Power in the people. In D. Saleebey (Ed.), *The strengths perspective in social work practice* (4th ed., 1–24). Boston: Pearson Education.

Schaller, D.J., & Zimmerer, J. (2005). From the guest editors: Raphael Lemkin: 'The founder of the United Nations Genocide Convention' as a historian of mass violence. *Journal of Genocide Research, 7*(4), 447–52. http://dx.doi. org/10.1080/14623520500349860

Scott Boeckh, J. (May 1995). Conflict management. *Program handout.* Federation CJA.

Scott-Jones, J. (2010). Introductions. In J. Scott-Jones & S. Watt (Eds.), *Ethnography in social science practice* (3–12). New York: Routledge.

Seligman, M.E.P. (2002). *Authentic happiness.* New York: Free Press.

Shahar, C. & Tobman, H. (June 2004). *2001 Census analysis series: The Jewish community of Montreal (part III)* The Jewish Elderly. Federation CJA Montreal.

Shapiro, F. (2001). *Eye movement desensitization and reprocessing* (2nd ed.). New York: Guilford Press.

Shelton, D.L. (Ed.). (2004). *Encyclopedia of genocide and wars against humanity.* USA: Macmillan Reference.

Sherwood, R.J., Shimel, H., Stolz, P., & Sherwood, D. (2004). The aging veteran. *Journal of Gerontological Social Work, 40*(4), 73–86. http://dx.doi .org/10.1300/J083v40n04_06

Shmotkin, D., Shrira, A., Goldberg, S., & Palgi, Y. (2011). Resilience and vulnerability among aging Holocaust survivors and their families: An intergenerational overview. *Journal of Intergenerational Relationships, 9*(1), 7–21. http://dx.doi.org/10.1080/15350770.2011.544202

Shour, A. (1990). The aging Holocaust survivor in the institution. *Journal of Aging and Judaism, 4*(3), 141–60.

Shrira, A., Palgi, Y., Ben-Ezra, M., & Shmotkin, D. (2010, Jun). Do Holocaust survivors show increased vulnerability or resilience to post-Holocaust cumulative adversity? *Journal of Traumatic Stress, 23*(3), 367–75. Medline: 20564370

Shrira, A., Palgi, Y., Ben-Ezra, M., & Shmotkin, D. (2011). Functioning and mortality of Holocaust survivors: Physical resilience and psychosocial vulnerabilities. *Journal of Loss and Trauma, 16*(1), 67–83. http://dx.doi.org/ 10.1080/15325024.2010.519297

Shulman, L. (2009). *The skills of helping individuals, families, groups, and communities* (6th ed.). Belmont, CA: Brooks/Cole.

Siegel, D.J. (2006). An interpersonal neurobiology approach to psychotherapy. *Psychiatric Annals, 36*(4), 248–56.

Sigal, J.J. (1998, Aug). Long-term effects of the Holocaust: Empirical evidence for resilience in the first, second, and third generation. *Psychoanalytic Review, 85*(4), 579–85. Medline:9870243

Sigal, J.J., & Weinfeld, M. (1989). *Trauma and rebirth: Intergenerational effects of the Holocaust.* New York: Praeger.

Sindler, A.J., Wellman, N.S., & Stier, O.B. (2004, Jul-Aug). Holocaust survivors report long-term effects on attitudes toward food. *Journal of Nutrition*

Education and Behavior, 36(4), 189–96. http://dx.doi.org/10.1016/S1499-4046(06)60233-9 Medline:15544727

Srebrnik, H. (1982). Two solitudes: Immigrant-native divisions in Jewish Montreal. *The Eye: Friends of Pioneering Israel, 8*(6), 4; 13–14.

Stamm, B.H. (Ed.). (1995). *Secondary traumatic stress: Self-care issues for clinicians, researchers, and educators. Lutherville.* MD: Sidran Press.

Stone, D. (2005). Raphael Lemkin on the Holocaust. *Journal of Genocide Research, 7*(4), 539–50. http://dx.doi.org/10.1080/14623520500349985

Suedfeld, P., Soriano, E., McMurtry, D.L., Paterson, H., Weiszbeck, T.L., & Krell, R. (2005). Erikson's 'components of a healthy personality' among Holocaust survivors immediately and 40 years after the war. *International Journal of Aging & Human Development, 60*(3), 229–48. http://dx.doi.org/10.2190/U6PU-72XA-7190-9KCT Medline:15934215

Sykes Wylie, M. (Sep/Oct 2004). Mindsight. *Psychotherapy Networker, 28*(5). Washington, DC.

Sykes Wylie, M. (March/April 2010). The long shadow of trauma. *Psychotherapy Networker, 34*(2). Washington, DC.

Szatmari, A. (1968). Forensic psychiatry of schizophrenia in survivors: General discussion. In H. Krystal (Ed.), *Massive psychic trauma* (131–3). New York: International Universities Press.

Terry, J. (1984). The damaging effects of the'"survivor syndrome.' In S.A. Luel & P. Marcus (Eds.), *Psychoanalytic reflections on the Holocaust: Selected essays* (135–48). New York: Ktav Publishing House.

The Jewish Week (September 2010). More on the Claims Conference: A half truth is a whole lie.

Torczyner, J., & Brotman, S. (1994). *Diversity and continuity: The demographic challenges facing Montreal Jewry.* McGill Consortium for Ethnicity and Strategic Social Planning, Council of Jewish Federations–Canada, Federation CJA, Statistics Canada.

Toseland, R.W., & Rivas, R.F. (2009). *An introduction to group work practice* (6th ed.). Boston: Pearson Education.

Totten, S., Parsons, W., & Charny, I. (Eds.). (1995). *Genocide in the twentieth century.* New York: Garland Publishing.

Trappler, B., Cohen, C.I., & Tulloo, R. (2007, Jan). Impact of early lifetime trauma in later life: Depression among Holocaust survivors 60 years after the liberation of Auschwitz. *American Journal Geriatric Psychiatry, 15*(1), 79–83. http://dx.doi.org/10.1097/01.JGP.0000229768.21406.a7 Medline:17035355

Trepman, P. (1957). On being reborn. In *Belsen.* Israel: Irgun Sheerit Hapleita Me'Haezor Habriti.

United States Holocaust Memorial Museum. (2012). 'The Holocaust.' Holocaust
    Encyclopedia. http://www.ushmm.org/wlc/en/?Moduleid=0005143.
    Accessed on 18 March 2012.

van der Kolk, B.A. (1996a). The body keeps score: Approaches to the psy-
    chobiology of posttraumatic stress disorder. In B.A. van der Kolk, A.C.
    McFarlane, & L. Weisaeth (Eds.), *Traumatic stress: The effects of overwhelming
    experience on mind, body, and society* (214–41). New York: Guilford Press.

van der Kolk, B.A. (1996b). Trauma and memory. In B.A. van der Kolk, A.C.
    McFarlane, & L. Weisaeth (Eds.), *Traumatic stress: The effects of overwhelming
    experience on mind, body, and society* (279–302). New York: Guilford Press.

van der Kolk, B.A. (2006). Clinical implications of neuroscience research in
    PTSD. *Annals New York Academy of Sciences*, 1–17. Retrieved 17 September
    2011 from http://www.traumacenter.org/products/pdf_files/NYASF.pdf.
    http://dx.doi.org/10.1196/annals.1364.022

Walsh, K. (2012). *Grief and loss: Theories and skills for the helping professions*
    (2nd ed.). New Jersey: Pearson Education, Inc.

Wardi, D. (1992). *Memorial candles: Children of the Holocaust*. New York, N.Y:
    Tavistock / Routledge.

Weinfeld, M., Sigal, J.J., & Eaton, W.W. (1981). Long-term effects of the
    Holocaust on selected social attitudes and behaviours of survivors:
    A cautionary note. *Social Forces*, *60*, 1–19.

White, S. (2001). Auto-ethnography as reflexive inquiry: The research act as
    self-surveillance. In I. Shaw & N. Gould (Eds.), *Qualitative research in social
    work* (100–15). Thousand Oaks, CA: Sage. http://dx.doi.org/10.4135/
    9781849209694.n7

Wiesel, E. (1982). 'The Holocaust patient.' *Address to staff* at the Cedars-Sinai
    Medical Center, Los Angeles.

Williams, T. (1988). Diagnosis and treatment of survivor guilt. In J.P. Wilson,
    Z. Harel, & B. Kahana (Eds.), *Human adaptation to extreme stress: From the
    Holocaust to Vietnam* (319–36). New York: Plenum Press.

Wilson, J.P., & Tang, C. (Eds.) (2007). *Cross-Cultural Assessment of Psychological
    Trauma and PTSD*. Retrieved 22 September 2011 from http://www.springer
    .com/psychology/community+psychology/book/978-0-387-70989-5.
    http://dx.doi.org/10.1007/978-0-387-70990-1

Witztum, E., & Malkinson, R. (2009). Examining traumatic grief and loss
    among Holocaust survivors. *Journal of Loss and Trauma*, *14*(2), 129–43.
    http://dx.doi.org/10.1080/15325020902724511

Wolcott, H.F. (2008). *Ethnography: A way of seeing* (2nd ed.). Lanham, MD:
    AltaMira Press.

Worwood, V.A. (1995). *The fragrant pharmacy: A complete guide to aromatherapy and essential oils*. New York: Bantam Books.

Wyman, D.S. (1984). *The abandonment of the Jews: America and the Holocaust 1941–1945*. New York: Pantheon Books.

Yad Vashem: The Shoah Victim's Names Recovery Project. Retrieved 31 March 2012 from http:www1.yadvashem.org/yv/en/remembrance/names/feedback.asp.

Yehuda, R. (2002, 10 Jan). Post-traumatic stress disorder. *The New England Journal of Medicine, 346*(2), 108–14. http://dx.doi.org/10.1056/NEJMra012941 Medline:11784878

Yehuda, R., Elkin, A., Binder-Brynes, K., Kahana, B., Southwick, S.M., Schmeidler, J., & Giller, E.L., Jr. (1996, Jul). Dissociation in aging Holocaust survivors. *The American Journal of Psychiatry, 153*(7), 935–40. Medline:8659617

Yehuda, R. & Giller, E.L. (Fall 1994). Comments on the lack of integration between the Holocaust and PTSD literature. *PTSD Research Quarterly, 5*(4). Vermont: The National Center for Post-Traumatic Stress Disorder.

Yehuda, R., Kahana, B., Southwick, S.M., & Giller, E.L., Jr. (1994, Oct). Depressive features in Holocaust survivors with post-traumatic stress disorder. *Journal of Traumatic Stress, 7*(4), 699–704. http://dx.doi.org/10.1002/jts.2490070414 Medline:7820358

Yehuda, R., McFarlane, A.C., & Shalev, A.Y. (1998, 15 Dec). Predicting the development of posttraumatic stress disorder from the acute response to a traumatic event. *Biological Psychiatry, 44*(12), 1305–13. http://dx.doi.org/10.1016/S0006-3223(98)00276-5 Medline:9861473

Zborowski, M., & Herzog, E. (1962). *Life is with people: The culture of the shtetl*. New York: Schocken.

Zilberfein, F., & Eskin, V. (1992). Helping Holocaust survivors with the impact of illness and hospitalization: Social worker role. *Journal of Social Work in Health Care, 18*(1), 59–70. http://dx.doi.org/10.1300/J010v18n01_04

Zimmerer, J. (2006). From the editors: Genocidal terrorism? A plea for conceptual clarity. *Journal of Genocide and Research, 8*(4), 379–81.

Index

McPherson, B.D., 52, 115
Meichenbaum, D., 272
Melendez, P., et al., 106, 224
Meltzer, M., 21
Mendelsohn, E., 20, 24
Mengele, Joseph, 32, 33
Minorities Treaty, 24
Mladić, Ratko, 301
Mollica, R., 56–7, 61
Montreal: creating a specialized
    program for survivors in, 141–57;
    economic resources of Montreal
    Jewish elderly, 90; Holocaust sur-
    vivors' contribution to the Jewish
    community in, 7, 50, 54–6, 95; ice
    storm in, 216; Jewish community
    in, 3, 10, 18, 20, 46, 58, 133, 186,
    262; *landsmanschaften* in, 92, 176–7;
    neo-Nazism in, 55–6, 172–4, 261–2;
    in the post-war period, 40, 41,
    132, 262. *See also names of Montreal
    agencies and institutions*
Montreal Holocaust Memorial
    Centre (MHMC), 94, 142, 143, 183,
    189, 202–5, 214
Mubarak, Husseni, 303
muselmen (walking dead), 80
music in the ghettos and camps,
    242–3

Naparstek, B., 235, 237
Native peoples, 297
Natural Health Consultants (NHC)
    Institute, 227
Nazism: Nazi Germany, 28–33,
    45–6, 47, 48, 172, 261, 262, 287,
    294, 304–5; neo-, 55–6, 169, 261–2,
    295–6. *See also* Holocaust
Neidik, Abbey Jack, 203
Nelson-Becker, H., et al., 128

Netherlands, 18, 48
Niederland, W.G., 43–4
Norway, 18, 48

Ochberg, F.M., 131
outreach, 103, 132–5, 145–6, 183

Pakistan, 299
Palestine, 25, 35, 36, 38, 46
Pearsall, P., 275
peer-to-peer support, 137–8, 188
Pennebaker, J., 81
Persian Gulf War, 88, 167, 223–4, 227
Piłsudski, Jósef, 22
Poland: *halupniks* (home workers),
    22; life of Polish Jews before the
    Holocaust, 19–28; life of Polish
    Jews during the Holocaust, 28–33,
    45–6; life of Polish Jews in the
    post-war period, 33–44; Łódź,
    18–19; Łódź before the Holocaust,
    20–8; Łódź Ghetto, 6, 19, 31, 32–3,
    74, 103, 112, 142, 170, 218; Łódź in
    the post-war period, 36; March of
    the Living, 93, 197–8; Nazi con-
    quest of, 30, 31, 304; Polish survi-
    vors, 9, 18–44, 45–6, 97, 104, 129,
    133–4, 197–8, 304–5; Polonization,
    26; *shtetl* life, 19–20, 23; Warsaw
    Ghetto, 103, 133–4, 220
Porter, J.N., 58
Post-Traumatic Stress Disorder
    (PTSD). *See under* trauma
professional interactions with
    survivors: changing negative self-
    perceptions of survivors, 124–5,
    218–20; changing staff perceptions
    of survivors, 161–3; common
    themes and responses, 214–26;
    communicating empathy, 82–4,